Personal Computing for Business

Personal Computing for Business

Personal Computing for Business

Jane Knight BA, MSc

Senior Lecturer
Computing and Information Systems
London Guildhall University

PITMAN PUBLISHING
128 Long Acre, London WC2E 9AN

A Division of Longman Group Limited

First published in Great Britain 1995

© J Knight 1995

British Library Cataloguing in Publication Data
A CIP catalogue record for this book can be obtained fom the British Library.

ISBN 0 273 61271 9

10 9 8 7 6 5 4 3 2

Printed and bound in Great Britain by Bell and Bain, Glasgow

The Publishers' policy is to use paper manufactured from sustainable forests.

Contents

Preface

This is not a book about using PCs - this is a book about using PCs *effectively*.

PCs are commonly referred to as "personal productivity tools" - but like any tool they can be used effectively or they can be misused. In the latter case this is normally due to the fact that the user does not have the necessary *theoretical* underpinning to carry out the task. For instance, word processing software is frequently used by those who have no formal knowledge of document design, and spreadsheet software by those who have no understanding of basic mathematical and financial analysis. PC users of this type are at best ineffectual, at the worst dangerous especially since current software puts a lot of power into their hands. What is worse, however, is that many users do not realise they fall into this category. Many believe that being a PC user means no more than using the most basic features of a particular software package to "get by" or that technical expertise is the only necessary pre-requisite.

This book attempts to address this situation by providing, in Part One, the fundamental theoretical principles of how to approach common business tasks. It describes the essential features of PC software that can be used to carry these out and also identifies further features that can help to improve productivity. It illustrates this through the generous use of examples and exercises rather than lengthy technical explanations. In Part Two a series of graded exercises permit the user to put theory into practice, and since the chapters in Part Two mirror the structure of those in Part One, this allows for a similar progression of concepts and ideas.

What is important to realise about the material in Part Two, however, is that it provides *generic* guidance, i.e. it is not applied to specific software packages. This serves a number of purposes: it makes the book relevant to all users of PC software and it also helps to provide high-level software skills which can be transferred from one package to another - something which experienced users, remarkably, find quite difficult. This is mainly due to the fact they are "locked into" the mechanics of the software itself and do not understand the concepts behind its use.

To this end, users are encouraged to find out for themselves how the software works. After over 10 years of experience of teaching students how to use software packages I have found, and academic research supports this viewpoint, that students learn to use software more effectively if they are *not* given step-by-step instructions for completing tasks, e.g. press X key, then press Y key, etc., since this makes them heavily reliant on their learning materials, but rather if they are given guidance on what is to be learned in a structured way, i.e. "guided learning". Such "guidance" is provided in Part Two and is gradually reduced as each chapter progresses and the user becomes more competent.

Since it is also important for users to realise that business tasks and software concepts do not occur in isolation, e.g. as uniquely "word processing" or "spreadsheet" issues, they are encouraged to relate their study of one area of PC use to others. Consequently, there are a large number of cross-references[*] in this book, for which I make no apology.

Learning to use a PC effectively is not just about learning to use the software appropriately but is also about remaining effective in one's work and protected from possible problems that might occur. Part Three therefore provides essential reference material in this respect which should not be disregarded.

As an introduction to the subject of personal computing this book covers a vast range of material. It is not intended to be an in-depth study of the full potential of PC use: it merely lays the foundations, provides examples and exercises that are easy to emulate and a taste of what is possible. It also aims to be a spring-board from which the user can move on to further exploration and study, for instance in the specialist areas of software use that require far more expert knowledge than can be provided here. Appendix 1 offers selected references for further reading and this should therefore provide a suitable starting point.

Finally, I should like to take this opportunity to thank a number of my colleagues, friends and family, in particular Jenny Collyer, Philip Hart, Ian Hollender, Alan Hudson, Philip Jones, Cassie and Peter Kinslow, for their advice, support and encouragement in the preparation of this book, and for their help in testing the materials.

Jane Knight
September 1994

---

[*] Such references as **3** or **4-7** refer to sections within that chapter. A reference such as **5:10** refers to section 10 in chapter 5.

Part one
Theoretical principles

1

Information searching and retrieval

1. Introduction

In order to carry out many business tasks it is first necessary to collect information on a particular subject. The key to this activity is knowing what information is available in a particular field of work and where to find it. This chapter therefore aims to provide an introduction to the wide range of information sources available (4) although it concentrates on computer-based sources of information and the ways in which PCs can be used to search for information (5-7) as well as the services provided by on-line information networks both commercial and non-commercial (8-13). It also offers advice on capturing information from these sources (14-16) as well as how users might collect their own data (17). It concludes by indicating how PCs might be used to assist in the analysis and presentation of the information that has been collected (18).

However, the chapter begins by looking at the meaning of the term *information* and in particular, the term *business information*.

2. What is "information"?

The Concise Oxford English Dictionary defines *information* as "informing, telling; thing told, knowledge, (desired) item of knowledge, news". However, there is no one standard definition of information: many people have attempted to define it but each provides a different perspective according to their background. Hence it is possible to obtain different definitions from a telecommunications engineer, a philosopher and a sociologist.

Commonly, the two terms *data* and *information* are used synonomously, although it has to be said that this is not an accurate use of the two terms. Firstly, it should be pointed out that the word data is in fact a plural noun, the singular noun being *datum*, i.e. data item, although it is frequently used as a collective noun and this is how it will be is used throughout this book.

Data is generally defined as being "numbers representing events or facts". So for example, basic data in an organisation might include the number of hours worked by each employee, the pay rate, the overtime rate and so on. *Information*, on the other hand, is generally accepted to be "processed data" that has been interpreted by a human user. So the data items mentioned above might only become meaningful information for a user like a finance director once they have been processed into total monthly pay figures and presented in such a way that they can be interpreted as such. It is important to understand this distinction between data and information since businesses are often said to be "data rich, information poor".

Businesses require a vast range of information so the term *business information* covers an enormous range of topic areas: information on companies, markets, economic trends, financial indicators, and so on.   Access to this type of information is vital for any business if they want to remain competitive in their market.

Within an organisation information is used primarily by managers to make decisions, plan for the future, and to control business activities. However, to be of any value, the information needs to have the following characteristics, that is it must be:

- *accurate*: only accurate information has any validity. However the level of accuracy will depend on the circumstances: in some cases it will have to be highly accurate (e.g. to the nearest penny), in others a lower level of accuracy will be acceptable (e.g. to the nearest £1,000);

- *complete*: that is all the information must be provided.   If any information is missing and the user is not aware of it, any decisions based upon it will be unsound;

- *up-to-date*: the time at which information becomes out of date will depend on the circumstances. In some areas information a couple of years old is still up-to-date but in others information over a few hours old will be out of date, e.g. stock prices;

- *timely*: the information should arrive in time for it to be used. Information that arrives after it is needed is worthless. This means there may have to be a trade-off between the completeness of the information and the timing;

- *relevant*: only relevant information should be provided. Irrelevant information is a distraction and a waste of time;

- *cost-effective*: information should not cost too much to generate or collect. The more accurate and up-to-date the information, the more expensive it is likely to be. The "cost" of the information must be weighed against the possible benefits to be gained from it.

If information has these qualities it will also help to address the problem of *information overload*.   In its general sense this refers to a user who is overwhelmed with information, which nowadays is quite common since the amount of information available is growing at an exponential rate.

Generally, the material that is collected on any given subject will be no more than data. It will therefore need to be processed, i.e. analysed and re-presented, to ensure that it is usable information.

3.   Information searching

When tackling an information gathering task, the first point to determine is what information is required and then where that information can be found. Information searching within a business context generally falls into three main categories:

- searching for facts or statistics;
- searching for information on companies and markets;
- searching for substantial information on a specific topic;

There are a vast number of sources that can be used for specific business information requests and the following diagram shows the main sources that could be used for the three types of information searches identified above.

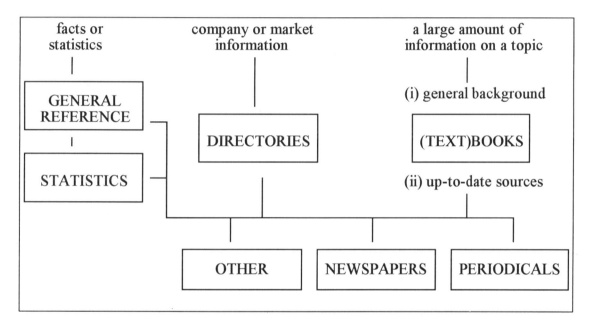

Although section **4** briefly describes these main sources of information and the formats in which they are available, i.e. paper-based or computer-based, it is also important to know where this information can be located:

Libraries are obviously the main stores of paper-based information and they also provide access points for many computer-based sources of information. Admission to libraries is usually free and librarians are always pleased to give guidance on the most suitable source of information for a particular request.

Many in-company libraries, often termed *business information units*, have large stores of company- or industry-specific information as well as access to relevant computer-based sources. These are usually staffed by professional information scientists who specialise in particular types of information.

Information brokers, on the other hand, are private, specialist, information gatherers who charge a fee for their services.

4. Sources of information

The main sources of information are briefly described below together with the formats in which they appear:

General reference material

The works in this category are useful for finding hard facts or to begin any research on a subject as they will help to define the terms of the subject. Examples of the major reference works include:

- *Dictionaries*, e.g. English dictionaries like *Collins*, *Oxford* or *Chambers*, or dictionaries of terminology like *Chambers Science and Technology Dictionary*;
- *Encyclopaedias*, e.g. general encyclopaedias like *Encyclopaedia Britannica* or subject encyclopaedias like *McGraw-Hill Encyclopaedia of Science and Technology*;
- *Biographical dictionaries*, e.g. *Who's Who, Statesman's Year Book*;
- *Atlases, gazetteers and maps*, e.g. *Times Atlas of the World, Ordnance Survey*;
- *Almanacs*, e.g. *Whitaker's Almanac*.

The traditional, printed reference works are normally available in the General Reference section of a library, however many of these works are now published in computer-based formats, e.g. on CD-ROM (see **6**) and appear in the reference sections of some of the main on-line services (see **8-12**).

Government statistics

The Central Statistical Office produces a number of statistical publications. These are detailed in their *Guide to Official Statistics*, which indicates whether statistics have been compiled on a particular subject and where they are published. The main paper-based CSO publications include:

- *Monthly Digest of Statistics*, which consists of monthly data on a wide range of data collected by government departments;
- *Annual Abstract of Statistics*, which provides annual figures for most of the data published in *Monthly Digest*;
- *Social Trends*, which provides key social and demographic data in charts and tables.

The annual publications are probably to be found in the General Reference section of a library whilst the monthly publications should be available in the Periodicals section.

The CSO *Databank*, on the other hand, is a collection of macro-economic time-series, organised into Data Sets, e.g. the Main Economic Series and Financial Statistics This data is available on tape, disk and on-line.

Market research statistics and reports

There are a large number of market research organisations that provide both market and trade statistics.   One example is *Romtec* an organisation that specialises in producing market research reports for the computing industry, another is *Infocheck* which produces a range of industry-specific reports.

Directories

There are a large number of directories that are extremely useful for finding a wide range of company, financial, product and market information.   The following are just a few examples:

- *Croner's A-Z of business information*;
- *Kelly's Business Directory*;
- *Key British Enterprises*;
- *Kompass Register of British Industry and Commerce*;
- *Stock Exchange Official Yearbook*;
- *The Times 1,000*;
- *Trade and professional directories*, e.g. *Directory of British Associations;*
- *Publishers guides*, e.g. *Willings Press Guide*;
- *Handbooks* and *Yearbooks*, e.g. The *Municipal Year Book, Computer Users Yearbook.*

Printed directories can normally be found in the General Reference section of a library. However, due to the need for constant updating of the material held in them, many of the major directories are more commonly available in the form of on-line databases (see **7**) or on **CD-ROM** (see **6**).

Books and textbooks

Books (or monographs) and textbooks provide a general understanding of a topic area, useful background material as well as specialist information. However, books go out of date very quickly since it can take up to two years to get into print. Hence they will not provide up-to-the-minute information. *Whitakers Books in Print - on microfiche* lists the current availability of published books. This is also available on-line (see **7**) and in a CD-ROM version (see **6**).

Periodicals

Periodicals are defined as publications which are issued more than once a year, and this is the place to find up-to-date information in any subject area. Periodicals can be classified as:

- *learned journals* which re published by academic and professional societies: e.g. in the Information Technology field this includes the publications of the IEE (Institution of Electrical Engineers), and *Computer Journal,* the journal of the British Computer Society;

- *professional journals* which are intended for non-academic, practising professionals, e.g. *Computer Bulletin* produced by the British Computer Society;
- *trade journals* e.g. *Computer Weekly* (a newspaper for professionals in IT); and
- *popular magazines* intended for the public at large, e.g. *Byte, PC Magazine.*

To discover the journals that are available in a particular field, the directory *Current British Journals: a bibliographic guide* is a useful place to start.

In addition to the periodicals themselves there are journal *abstracts* and *indexes.* *Abstracts* provide summaries of the original articles in the periodicals together with details of the author and the publication in which they first appeared. *Indexes* are similar, except that they only provide details of the title, author, publication and date. It should be noted, however, that with the advent of computer-based or "electronic" journals and abstracts (see **6** and **7**), many no longer appear in paper-based form.

Newspapers

Newspaper articles are a useful source of up-to-date information on topics of interest, especially in the business area. The following should prove relevant reference material:

- Quality *national newspapers*, e.g. *Times, Telegraph, Independent, Guardian*;
- *Financial press*, e.g. *Financial Times, Wall Street Journal*;
- *Trade press.*

In a similar way to journals, *indexes* are produced for the major national newspapers, e.g. the *Monthly* and *Annual Index to the FT.* Although back-copies of newspapers are normally retained in the periodicals sections of libraries, newspaper articles can be found in on-line and CD-ROM versions (see **6** and **7**).

Other sources

There are many other sources of business information, collectively known as "grey literature" and this includes the following types of material. In their printed version they may be kept in special "business" or "commercial" collections in libraries, although they may also be available in other computer-based formats:

- *Patents*;
- *Conference proceedings*;
- *Company reports;*
- *Catalogues;*
- *Product literature;*
- *Official publications.*

5. On-line library catalogues

In a modern library details of the book and other stock is held on-line, i.e. on computer. This is known as an OPAC (on-line public access catalogue) and allows a library user to search quickly for books by author, by title or by subject area.

Although it would appear that a subject search could be done by simply going to the appropriate section of the library and perusing the shelves for suitable material, this may not locate all possible sources since a lot of material is cross-disciplinary and is therefore shelved elsewhere. To carry out a subject search on an OPAC and thereby locate all suitable references, the user is required to enter one or more *keywords* which summarise the topic area.

6.   CD-ROMs

As CD-ROMs are able to hold a large amount of information, e.g. the equivalent of over 250,000 A4 pages of text, this makes them a highly suitable medium for distributing large reference works which would otherwise need to appear in a number of printed volumes.   The following is a summary of the main types of information available on CD-ROM:

- full text of newspapers and news services: normally the final editions of the papers without the weather, classified advertisements or appointments pages, e.g. *The Times and Sunday Times* (4 disks per year); *The Independent* (issued quarterly), *Northern Echo* (updated three times a year);
- full text and abstracts of periodicals: e.g. *Computer-Select* (the full-text of 28 computer magazines and abstracts from 100 other periodicals);
- full text of legislation: e.g. *Justis* (the European legal database) and *OSH-UK* (health and safety legislation);
- full text of market research reports, e.g. *ICC Keynotes*;
- full text of company annual reports, e.g. *UK Corporations CD* (UK company annual reports and financial statements);
- a wide range of reference material, many of which appear in multimedia format (i.e. in addition to text they hold graphics, animation, video sequences, and sound): dictionaries e.g. *Oxford Reference Shelf;* encyclopaedias, e.g. Microsoft's *Encarta;* atlases, e.g. *Countries of the World;* and literature works, e.g. Shakespeare's Complete Works;
- specialist material, e.g. the *PAF (Postcode Address File,* which gives every postcode and address in Great Britain) and is therefore useful for direct marketing.

There are significant advantages in searching for information held on a CD-ROM rather than in its paper-based equivalent: generally, it is much easier and faster. However, searching of the text will depend very much upon how it was entered in the first place by the distributor.   If it was typed in, then every word is "searchable"; if it was scanned in from the original paper-based document, search facilities will be limited.

Lists of commercially available CD-ROM titles appear in directories like *CD ROMs in Print,* and *The CD-ROM Directory* (both available in printed and CD-ROM form). These directories also contain details of how often the CD-ROMs are updated, the subscription price, whether they can be purchased or leased, together with the CD-ROM drives that support each product.

For more technical details about CD-ROMs see **15:10**.

7. On-line databases

As has been mentioned above, much valuable information is held in *on-line databases*. In summarising the information to be found on them, these databases are categorised by type:

Full text databases: These hold the complete articles from paper-based documents, such as:
- *newspaper articles* and a wide range of press and current affairs articles, e.g. *Guardian, Times* and *Financial Times*;
- *periodicals,* e.g. journal articles on science, technology and patent information, conference proceedings and research papers - so-called "electronic journals";
- legal specialist databases, like *Justis*, the legal database, which holds information on European Union law, and full text of directives and treaties.

Abstracting databases: The material in these databases is either the computer-based version of paper-based abstracts or uniquely produced in this format, e.g.
- *ABI Inform*, which contains abstracts of 800 business and management journals, including *Harvard Business Review* and *Accountancy*;
- *Predicast* series, e.g. *PROMT (Predicast's Overview of Markets and Technology)*, which is a comprehensive summary of all international developments.

Bibliographic databases: These hold the reference details of books, journals and reports, and can be compared to printed indexes, e.g.
- *Books in Print*, bibliographic references to all UK books in print;
- *MSI (Marketing Surveys Index)*;
- *UKOP (UK Official Publications)*
- *INSPEC* (the major bibliographic database covering information technology);

Business databases: These provide the same type of information as found in printed company directories, e.g.
- *ICC* and *Jordans,* which hold information on all companies registered with Companies House as well as other financial data;
- the *Dun and Bradstreet* database that holds information on company credit ratings;
- *FAME (Financial Analysis Made Easy)* which holds company reports and financial ratios of major UK companies.

Statistical databases: These hold time-series of data, e.g. *Datastream,* which holds details of companies, financial markets and economic indicators.

The main question for someone searching for information is how to access these databases. In order to answer this, it is first necessary to explain the structure of the on-line business. A *database* is created from a collection of information (the *source*) either by the originator of the source or by a third party. This database is then mounted on a large computer known as a *host*. Hosts are therefore vast depositories of information and it is via a host that a particular database is accessed.

Examples of hosts include:

Host name	Databases held
Blaise-Line	(the British Library host) holds 20 databases of books, journals, official publications, etc. from all subject areas
Datastar	holds 250 databases on science, engineering and business
Dialog	holds 400 databases on e.g. science, business, technology and economics
FT Profile	holds full-text databases of news and current affairs as well as financial data, trade information, market research and other data
Kompass	includes information from printed Kompass Directories, Kellys, etc.,
NEXIS	holds business and company news, financial information, legislation and political information, etc.
ORBIT	includes databases on business, health and safety, patents and trademarks

The *On-line Manual (1993)* provides a useful guide to sources of information, their equivalent on-line databases and the hosts on which they are based. Databases can either be held exclusively on one host or appear on a number of hosts. To demonstrate this, the 1993 edition of the *On-line Manual* lists the following databases and hosts for *The Times* newspaper:

Database	Host
AUTOMOTIVE NEWS	DATASTAR, PFDS ONLINE
BMA PRESS CUTTINGS	DATASTAR
EUROPE LIBRARY	NEXIS
FOSCAN	LEATHERHEAD FOODLINE
GENERAL NEWS LIBRARY	NEXIS
HSE-LINE HEALTH AND SAFETY	DATASTAR, ESA, ORBIT
INFOMAT INTERNATIONAL BUSINESS	DATASTAR, DIALOG, MAID, PFDS ONLINE
MAID NEWSLINE	MAID
MANAGEMENT AND MARKETING ABSTRACTS	DATASTAR, PFDS ONLINE
MCCARTHY COMPANY/INDUSTRY PRESS NS/COMME	FT PROFILE
PIRA	DATASTAR, ORBIT, PFDS ONLINE
PREDICASTS PROMT	BRS, DATASTAR, DIALOG, FT PROFILE, MAID
TEXTLINE	DATASTAR, DIALOG, FT PROFILE, MAID
TIMES & SUN TIMES	DIALOG, FT PROFILE
WORLD LIBRARY	NEXIS

To access a host the user requires a computer connected to a dedicated telephone line, a modem, some communications software, a printer and a subscription to the host. When accessing the host, in addition to the telephone call, a connect time is payable as well as print and other charges (which are usually dependent on the database used).

Searching of on-line databases (commonly referred to as *on-line searching*) is in principle carried out in much the same way as searching of an OPAC (i.e. through the use of keywords). However, in reality it is often much more complex than this as the host provides the search language and there is little standardisation of search commands. Although training is available for subscribers to these hosts, it means that often a trained information specialist is required to carry out a search for a user to ensure that costly on-line time is not wasted. However, some communications software can help with setting up the search off-line (i.e. before connecting to the host) so that valuable on-line time is not wasted.   Academic libraries often offer on-line searching as a free service although other public libraries may make a charge.   Libraries normally encourage enquirers to be present when on-line databases are being searched to help with developing and refining a search.

Most large libraries have on-line facilities and they   generally hold a list of the databases that can be accessed in the library, although they may charge for an on-line search.   Business information units will need to consider the expense before investing in subscriptions to relevant on-line databases.   However, this cost may be considered necessary to provide the organisation with the up-to-date information it requires.

8.   On-line services

There are a number of other commercial as well as non-commercial on-line services which provide a range of facilities to both corporate and individual members.   These facilities can normally be categorised as:

Electronic mail services: Electronic mail (or e-mail) is the facility to send messages to another user's electronic mailbox rather than through the normal postal system.   This means that users can send and receive information at a fraction of the time and cost. The use of electronic mail has had a great impact on the business community.

Bulletin board systems (or BBS): Computer bulletin boards are the electronic equivalent of paper-based message or information boards.   Here messages can be left to be read by any user, and this is a means by which users with common interests can communicate with one another.

Conferences: Conferences are "on-line clubs" of subscribers with common interests, allowing them   to communicate with one another. A "sysop" (system operator) controls each conference.

Gateways: Gateways provide access to other on-line services and networks.

Commercial on-line services include CompuServe and CIX, non-commercial information networks include JANET and the Internet, and these are described briefly below.

9.   CompuServe

This is a US-based, international, commercial on-line service, with about 2 million users world-wide.   Users of this service are both corporate and individual users. The main services it provides include:

- a wide range of special interest *forums* (i.e. conferences), e.g. sports forums, games forums, computer support forms for both hardware and software; computer magazines forums; financial forums and professional forums;
- access to 2,000 *business and financial* databases, e.g. *ICC,   Jordans, Dun and Bradstreet*;

- a *news service*, e.g. access to *Reuters* and *Associated Press* wires as well as news agencies from around the world; access to full text databases, e.g. *Financial Times, Times, Economist*; access to *sports news* and *weather reports*;
- a *reference library*, e.g. access to the 21 volume on-line *Grolier's Academic American Encyclopaedia*, and *Healthnet* a medical reference.
- *email* facilities with access to other networks, e.g. to an Internet address, although an additional charge is made for telex and fax facilities;
- access to down-loadable *shareware software*.

Membership includes a copy of CIM (CompuServe Information Manager) software (either DOSCIM or WinCIM) as well as printed documentation and free first month's usage credit. There is a monthly charge for the "basic" service, but "extended" services are charged as they are used, and an additional further charge is payable for "premium" services. Access is via a local telephone call in the UK.

10. CIX (Compulink Information Exchange)

This is one of the largest (although probably the cheapest) UK-based on-line services, with about 13,000 members. The cost of membership includes a registration fee, a minimum monthly bill and on-line charges. A copy of a Windows-based interface is also supplied to subscribers. It offers the following services:

- *conferences*, which are either "open" to anyone and include those that provide technical PC support; "closed", which means a user can only join with the permission of a *moderator*, or "confidential", in which case the conference name does not appear on any lists;
- *bulletin boards;*
- *e-mail* service with access to most global networks, e.g. Internet and JANET.

11. JANET (Joint Academic Network)

This is a "network" that links together computers sited at UK academic and research institutions. Users will normally be students, academics or researchers. A demand for the ability to transmit images, video and audio has led to the upgrading of the system to *SuperJANET,* which provides high-capacity communications between major sites.

12. Internet

This is the world's largest computer network as 30 million computers are connected to it world-wide. It is also known as the "Information SuperHighway". Users are primarily individuals but businesses have begun to realise that a world (or "virtual library") of information is available to them by being connected to the "Net". Access to the Internet is possible through one of the commercial on-line services, via a commercial "access provider" (e.g. *Demon, Cityscape* and *Delphi)* or through JANET. Once connected, a user can:

- gain access to large *computer databases* around the world, e.g. the Library of Congress or Harvard University and the information stored on them, which can range from satellite weather maps, to software programs, to business and financial

> data, to US policy documents, and if desired, down-load them onto their own computer.

- read the many news services, known as *USENET news* (the USENET being the equivalent of a large BBS) or sign-up to world-wide *newsgroups*;
- send *e-mail* messages.

Although, more and more paper-based guides to the Internet are being published, there are a number of *navigator tools* on the Internet itself to help users "surf the Internet", as it is called, and find useful and relevant information.

- *Archie:* The user types in a keyword and Archie searches titles of information around the world and returns the network addresses of files that match.
- *Gopher:* The user works through a series of menus to locate useful information and can also set up "bookmarks" to go back to information passed by.
- *WAIS (Wide Area Information Servers):* The user types in keywords to be used to search the contents of files around the world.
- *WWW (World Wide Web):* Here documents across the world are linked together. *Mosaic*, a graphical browser program, produced by the National Center for Supercomputing Applications (NCSA), has revolutionised the way these documents can be viewed by the user and how these links can be followed to search for information. The WWW is probably the best place to start a search on the Internet. (To obtain a free copy of Mosaic for Windows, log in to the NCSA server: `ftp.ncsa.uiuc.edu` with the username `anonymous` and your email address as the password. The software will be found in the `/Mosaic` directory.)

13. On-line conversation

One of the significant features of on-line services is to facilitate communication between users. However, a normal and important part of face-to-face communication, the smiles, frowns, winks, etc., that make up the so-called "body language", is not possible with electronic conversation. However, there is a way of representing this essential aspect of conversation by the use of "emoticons" or "smileys". These are created by typing combinations of colons, hyphens and brackets: turn your head sideways to the left to read them. Examples of the basic smileys are shown below:

`:-)` Smile	`:-(` Frown	`;-)` Wink

A further step is to create a personal emoticon to describe the user, for example:

`:-{)` User has a moustache	`8-)` User wears (sun)glasses
`@:-)` User wears a turban	`:-Q` User smokes

These are just a fraction of the emoticons in use. If a reader is interested in finding out more, lists of emoticons are available in a number of paper-based publications and in text files on most on-line conferences and on the Internet. One final point about electronic conversation: messages should not be typed in CAPITAL LETTERS as this is the equivalent of shouting!

Exercise 1

Use the most appropriate, available and up-to-date source of information to find the answers to the following questions:

(a) What happened on 23 March 1765?

(b) Who said: "Happiness is no laughing matter"?

(c) How much was a 1951 pound worth in 1992?

(d) Which British standard is the specification for folded continuous stationery for impact printers?

(e) On which database and host would you find the North Sea Monitor?

(f) What is the largest industrial company in Europe and when was it established?

(g) In which language is the CD-ROM Town Pages produced?

(h) Who is the publisher of *PC Magazine*, and how often is it published?

(i) What was John Major's personal majority in his Huntingdon constituency in the general election in 1992?

---

14. Retrieving information

Having searched for and located useful information, the user will want to capture that information for future use. There are a number of ways of doing this but there are also a number of issues that need to be considered.

Photocopying paper-based sources: This might seem the most obvious way of obtaining a copy of a relevant paper-based document. However, photocopying should be undertaken with care as the *Copyright, Designs and Patents Act (1988)* applies. The following are some basic points that should be borne in mind:

- a user can make one copy of the material for their own research and private use but not make another copy for another person;
- a user may only copy one article in a single issue of a periodical or set of conference proceedings, or an extract from a book amounting to 5% of the whole, or a complete chapter;

Printing on-line sources: This might seem a sensible way of obtaining a copy of computer-based material for later reference, however, the user should take care as there may be print charges. It should also be remembered that data in on-line databases is also protected by copyright.

Downloading on-line sources: This might be appropriate if data is to be processed further, for example in a spreadsheet or word processor. However, it should be noted that downloaded files are generally unformatted and each line ends with an [Enter] character. This can cause problems if the text is to be read by word processing software.

Making notes: This is by far the most obvious method to use where it is impossible to photocopy a large number of pages or too costly to download computer-based material. However, a methodical, organised system of note-taking is essential so that when the notes are referred to at a later date they are still understandable. Section **15** discusses the important skill of making notes.

Recording sources of information

Whichever method is used for capturing information, it is important that an accurate note of the source of any material is also recorded. This is so the document can be retrieved at a later date if required and so that the ideas or words of the original author can be acknowledged if they are subsequently cited. The following bibliographic details should therefore be recorded:

Book	Author. Date (i.e. year). Title. Publisher
Journal article	Author. Date (i.e. year,month). Title. Journal (or standard abbreviation). Volume. Pages.
Article in a collection	Author. Date (i.e. year,month). Title. Names of Editor(s). Collection. Publisher.
Magazine article	Author. Date (i.e. year,month,day). Title. Magazine. Pages
Newspaper article	Author. Date (i.e. year,month,day). Title. Newspaper. Pages

15. Making notes

Note-taking is a skill which comes through practice. It is not a matter of re-writing verbatim the original words of the source material but assessing what is relevant and summarising or paraphrasing the main points. If notes are made correctly at this stage it will save a lot of time later when they are being used to prepare a report or other document. The following are some simple points to keep in mind when making notes:

- Skim through the material before making any notes to establish the essential and relevant parts of the material and determine if it is necessary to summarise the whole argument or each part of the argument.

- Develop a system of abbreviations for words, e.g. "shd" for "should", but do not abbreviate sentences so much they cannot be deciphered when they are read back.

- Start a new idea on a new line but keep the same order of ideas as the original.

- Do not add ideas or opinions that are not included in the material. At this stage the notes should only represent the original writer's ideas.

- Only use the original writer's own words when it is not possible to paraphrase the words more effectively, and then enclose them in quotation marks so that they can be easily recognised later as the author's original words.

Exercise 2

You are writing a report on the effect of future technologies on business. A book called "IT strategy for business", edited by Joe Peppard and published by Pitman in 1993, includes a chapter (11) written by Ciaran Redmond called "Future technologies and their business impact" that provides you with relevant material. Section 11.6 reproduced on page 17 discusses virtual reality.

(a) Make brief notes that are relevant to your report;
(b) Record the source of the information.

Virtual reality

A term you are going to hear a lot of in the next five years is VR or virtual reality. Virtual reality is an extension of robotics into the world of computers and it has major implications for all. VR is already well out of the laboratories but its current use is niche oriented and expensive. Virtual reality is defined as the simulation of real world events and responses in a computer generated environment. If you have ever seen the Holo-deck in *Startrek - The Next Generation* you will see where the simulation is heading. VR grew out of NASA's programme to develop remote robotic devices that could allow a human to interact with an environment that would stimulate a real world situation in the future.

While they are not VR devices, aircraft simulators are along the same lines as VR devices. The training a pilot gets in a simulator is intended to provide him with a realistic approximation of the real experience he will have in flight. The crucial difference is that a VR equivalent of a training simulator would have no real parts, they would all be computer simulations. You may have seen examples of current VR interfaces in the popular press. They consist of VR gloves and wraparound headsets, in the main, and while practical for use in specialised environments they are not practical, yet, for use in normal office environments.

VR devices work in a manner akin to the 1950s 3-D glasses you received on entry to see a 3-D film, they seem to take you into a three dimensional environment. An application of today's technology is where the participant dons a headset and gloves for a walkround of a virtual building. As you progress through this 3-D building you can open doors, just as you would real doors, but your hand actions are transferred into the computer simulated landscape and as you reach for the door your hand "appears" in the computer scene and opens the door. You can look around the scene by turning your head and look up and down also. It is easy to envisage the major impact such devices will have on architects and engineers. They will be able to take clients on full walkthroughs of buildings not yet built, change designs as they "stand" in the building and generally get client approval without the expensive errors and reworks that are necessary during the physical construction stage of the building.

Reality is hard enough

The impact of VR will be very strong on design environments of all descriptions. That is not to say that it will not strongly affect other business activities. Reality is harsh and virtual reality will be virtually harsh. As this technology permeates the office environment, it is conceivable that simulations of all descriptions will become as everyday events as we today simulate business decisions and effects by using spreadsheets. The concept of planning merchandise presentation on supermarket shelves by a virtual reality simulation is not far off. Jaron Lanier coined the term "Virtual Reality" in the early 1980s. As chief scientist of VPL Research he is a pragmatist about the impact of VR on business and social environments. Concerns about the use and abuse are real, but he dismisses many of the concerns in the 10-20 year time frame because he firmly believes that *there is absolutely no chance whatsoever of virtual reality becoming so good or so cheap that it will be confused with reality.*

VR will give us a new 3-D spreadsheet type tool. If we forget that spreadsheets are only simulations and have no validity in the real world (they are, at best, only approximations), then VR will have serious impact and not all of it will be for the best. If we remember that simulations allow us to speculate about possible future events, and use them to determine the optimum actions we should take, then we will find that they further revolutionise how we do business and we will in twenty years time look back and ask how did we ever manage without it.

Some useful source material may appear in tables or charts as is the case with government statistical material and it may not be felt appropriate to reproduce the information in the same way.   In fact presenting a large number of charts is not advisable in any document, instead the data should be analysed and interpreted to present points that support or contradict the argument.

Since tables and charts are used to communicate information quickly to the reader, it is necessary to look carefully at them to work out the message they are trying to convey. When analysing charts and graphs, keep in mind the following points:

- Look for trends, marked changes, or patterns occurring, but do not use emotive language to describe them. Be clear, unambiguous and specific.

- Be objective and do not add opinions or try to find reasons at this stage: these can always be included later after due consideration of the data.

Exercise 3
In order to create an effective marketing campaign for sports goods, you have been asked to write a report on leisure pursuits in the United Kingdom. The table below taken from the 1992 edition of CSO's *Social Trends* provides you with relevant data. (Note: the symbol .. means data not available.)

(a) Summarise the main trends in the chart;
(b) Record the source of the information.

Spectator attendance[1] at selected sporting events

Thousands

	1971/72	1981/82	1990/91
Football League (England and Wales)	28,700	20,006	18,828
Greyhound racing	8,800	6,100	5,121
Horse racing	4,200	3,700	4,698
Scottish Football League	4,521	2,961	3,377
Rugby Football Union (England)	799	750[6]	1,250
Motor sports[2]	..	1,300	2,275
Rugby Football League[3]	1,170	1,226	1,539
Test and County cricket	984	994	..
English basketball	2	85	140
Motorcycle sports[4]	250	250	250
Scottish basketball[5]	9	14	9

---

1   Estimated
2   Car and kart racing only, not including rallying
3   League matches only
4   Excluding speedway
5   National league and cup matches only
6   1982 season

16. Own data collection

It may well be that data is not available on a particular topic so that it is necessary to collect one's own data. In fact, carrying out original research is the only way to collect data for some projects. Although there are a number of different ways this can be done, the best way will depend on what type of data is to be collected, the resources that are available as well as the time span in which the research has to be carried out.

An understanding of the different research methods is extremely important, and the small amount of space available here cannot do justice to this subject, hence only a few major points are made.

It is essential that any collection of data must be carefully planned to ensure that the results are valid and this includes determining the size of the sample and how the data is collected. This is often done through the use of interviews or questionnaires:

Interviews

If people's opinions are being sought then interviews are an appropriate means of collecting this data. However, they are really only useful for a small sample of people. There are two main types of interview: structured and unstructured.

Structured interviews are based around a formal set of questions whereas unstructured interviews are based around only a few questions thus giving subjects more freedom to express ideas. Unstructured interviews therefore provide "open-ended" data which may be more difficult to analyse.

Questionnaires

Questionnaires are a useful method of collecting data from a large sample of people and especially so if the people are geographically dispersed or time does not permit each one to be interviewed. Questionnaires should be planned and designed carefully as it must be clear what information is being requested. Questionnaires can collect:

- *numerical data*, e.g. How many PCs are there in your organisation?
- *fact*, e.g. What word processing software do you use?
- *opinion*, e.g. Do you enjoy using the word processing software?

Although questions collecting numerical data and fact will obtain clear responses, questions on opinion are usually very open-ended. If this is intentional, enough space should be left for respondents to write their answers.

However, if questions are structured then clearer data can be elicited. The following types of questions might be suitable and can be used for collecting both numerical data and fact.

- *Yes/No questions*, e.g.
  Do you use PCs in your organisation?   Yes/No   Circle the answer that applies.

- *Tick boxes,* e.g.
  How many PCs are there in your organisation? Tick one box only.

0	☐
1-10	☐
11-99	☐
100+	☐

- *Check boxes*, e.g.
  What type of software do you use? Tick one or more boxes.

Word processing	☐
Spreadsheet	☐
Presentation graphics	☐
Databases	☐
Other	☐

- *Rating scales,* e.g.
  What do you think of the usability of the software?

Very difficult				*Very easy*
1	2	3	4	5

  (Note: when using rating scales it is essential that there are clear anchoring points so that the respondent knows what the numbers mean.)

In addition, the following points should be noted about questionnaires:

- Questions should not ask for more than one piece of data.
- Questions should not include jargon or difficult terminology.
- Questions should be clear and unambiguous.
- Questions should not be biased or "leading" in any way.
- Questions should be presented in a logical order.
- There should be clear and adequate instructions (both general and specific) on how to complete the questionnaire and for their return;
- Questions asking for personal details of respondents should be uncontroversial. Age, for instance, is a sensitive subject and needs to be handled with care.

It is important that a representative sample of people are approached and the response rate considered. The response rate for questionnaires is notoriously low and it is important to realise that the validity of data collected from less than   50% of the sample is dubious.

Exercise 4

You work for a small marketing and PR company and have been asked to prepare a report for senior managers on computer-based sources of information. In particular you have been asked to identify the availability and usability of relevant on-line databases.

(a) What published information would you want to collect?

(b) What other information might you wish to collect on this subject, and how might you approach this task?

17. Analysing and presenting information

Once relevant material has been collected it will need to be processed in some way to produce useful information. This is where PC software can help as they can provide useful tools for analysing and presenting information. The following describes the most effective ways in which PC software tools can be used.

Producing written documents: Once the facts have been collected they may need to be presented in the form of a written document such as a report, brochure or letter. Whatever the type of document, effective presentation of the material is necessary. Chapters 2 looks at the theoretical principles of producing written documents, and Chapter 8 at the necessary word processing software skills to put theory into practice to create effective documents.

Analysing numerical data: Numerical, financial and statistical data that has been collected may require further analysis. Chapter 3 looks at the different ways in which this may be achieved, and Chapter 9 at the spreadsheet software skills required to carry out such numerical analysis.

Charting and graphing data: Numerical and statistical data, once analysed, may be more appropriately presented in the form of charts and graphs. Chapter 4 looks at the design of business graphics, and Chapter 10 at the graphing and charting software skills that are required to put this into practice.

Producing a business presentation: Information may need to be conveyed to others by means of a formal business presentation. Chapter 5 looks at the principles of giving business presentations, and Chapter 11 gives practice in developing presentations using PC software.

Designing a database: Having collected both textual and numerical data it may be necessary to store this information in an organised fashion so that further manipulation and analysis can take place at a later date. Chapter 6 looks at the theory of data management and database design, and Chapter 12 provides the database software skills that are essential to put theory into practice.

2

Document production

1. Introduction

The most common information handling activity in business is the production of written documents. Managers, administrative and clerical staff all have to prepare a variety of business documents including memos, letters and reports, as part of their daily work.

However, document production is not confined solely to the commercial world: professional people like lawyers and accountants prepare specialist financial and legal documents; writers and journalists compose magazine and newspaper articles; academics and students produce research papers, essays and dissertations; and officials of clubs and societies write letters and prepare newsletters. Hence this chapter is relevant for anyone who needs to produce written documents of any kind.

2. Word processing software

The typewriter has traditionally been used to produce documents but it has now been replaced by the computer and word processing software as the main productivity tool for this type of work. Word processing software has many advantages over the typewriter, the main one being that the user can type in the text as with a typewriter, but then edit it, revise it, restructure it and improve its presentation as many times as desired before printing it out. The essential difference is then that the text is typed in only *once* so this is very time-saving. There is also no need for the use of unsightly correction fluid.

Word processing software can also assist in reducing the amount of paper produced, although it has to be said that because it is all too easy to print a copy of a document, it often means more paper is produced rather than less!

Word processing software also offers many other features that support the production of a document. These include those that can improve its presentation as well as those that save further time. Additionally, some word processing software is very sophisticated and can assist in the production of "publication quality" documents that could once only be produced by specialist desktop publishing (DTP) software.

3.   Creating a document

It is important to remember, however, that the use of a word processing package will not in itself produce a piece of perfect prose or an attractive document. In fact quite the contrary: if the software is used without any theoretical underpinning the resultant documentation can be a disaster, e.g. it might look unattractive due to the use of too many presentation features because the user has no design skills. The purpose of this chapter therefore is to provide the theory of good document design together with a guide as to how word processing software can assist and support this.

This chapter will look, firstly, at the essential elements of producing all types of documents (**4-10**) and then at the specific requirements of producing correspondence (**11-15**) and displayed documents (**16-22**), concluding with a discussion of some further productivity aids useful for the production of all documentation (**23-24**).

4.   Planning a document

Every document needs to be planned and there are a number of aspects that need to be fully considered before work is even begun. These include:

- the purpose of the document (i.e. its aims and objectives or terms of reference) as well as what is to be achieved; and
- who the readers of the document are to be (e.g. managers, colleagues or clients) and the extent of their knowledge of the subject matter of the document.

These two factors will determine not only what material is to be included but also the presentation of the document in terms of its structure, appearance, length and readability. For example, sales literature intended for customers will look and read very differently from a report intended for management decision making.

5.   Drafting a document

Any document can be built up gradually using word processing software - it does not have to be typed all in one go, and this supports the way most people work, i.e. by making notes and then refining those notes into a finished document. When collecting information on a subject (see Chapter 1) writers may prefer to make hand-written notes on paper first before typing them up. Others may find it is easier to compose directly at the computer. Whichever method is adopted, these draft notes can then be amended (e.g. corrections made, parts deleted, extra opinions and ideas added, or text reworded) and re-structured (e.g. blocks of text moved). Word processing software can support this editing process in the following ways:

- Extra characters, words, sentences and paragraphs can be inserted into the document and the existing text simply moves along to make room.
- Unwanted material can be deleted and the rest of the text joins up so that there is no evidence that anything has been removed.
- Blocks of text can be moved from one position to another, e.g. a paragraph from the beginning can easily be moved to the end of a document, or a sentence can be copied to other places in the document.

It is important to remember that it is unlikely that an acceptable first draft will be produced immediately: the document will need to go through a number of drafts as it is refined and hence these basic word processing features will be invaluable in this process.

6.   Written presentation of a document

The importance of good written presentation skills cannot be over-emphasised in the creation of any document. Written presentation skills involve correct spelling, punctuation, grammar, style and the readability of the material. Simple guidance is given below on common mistakes made in this area and how on-line software tools can help to exclude them from documents.

Spelling

Some people have particular problems with spelling whilst many others make typing mistakes (known as typographic errors or typos, for short).   Proof-reading the document is the only way of eliminating such errors, but it is very difficult to spot one's own mistakes, especially on the screen.   However, most word processing software packages come with an on-line *spell checker*, which can help to identify spelling mistakes.

This is essentially an on-line dictionary that the software uses as it checks a word or words of the document.   It can be used either to check the whole document once completed or the spelling of individual words as they are typed.

A spell checker may also be able to spot double words, i.e. words that have been typed in twice, and typographical errors that involve double capitals, e.g. "MOnday". A user should note, however, that spell checkers do not provide definitions for words, although computer-based dictionaries can be bought separately, e.g. the Oxford English Dictionary on CD-ROM.

There are a number of other limitations of using a spell checker. Firstly, it will not be able to identify a word that has been misspelled in one context but is right in another, e.g. "there" and "their". Secondly, the size of the dictionary may mean that it is unable to locate complex words - the dictionaries of word processing packages vary from between 2,000 words for a minor package to 180,000 words for a major software package. Additions can usually be made to the dictionary, especially commonly used proper names (i.e. of people, companies and places) or special terms. Foreign dictionaries as well as specialised dictionaries, e.g. medical or legal, can also be purchased separately. It is also important to have the British rather than the American version of the spell checker, otherwise words like "colour" and "organise" will be flagged up as being incorrect. In the latter case this is due to the fact that in American English they are spelt with a "z".

Spell checkers are becoming more and more sophisticated: software is already available that corrects common typing mistakes as they are made, e.g. "teh" would automatically be changed to "the".

Punctuation

A number of the most common uses of the main punctuation marks are described below together with some of the frequently made errors:

The use of the *apostrophe* is often misunderstood. Its main use is to show the possessive and it is written as -*'s* after singular nouns and -*s'* after plural nouns. It is also used to replace missing letters in contractions (e.g. *it's* instead of *it is*). However, it should not be used to form the plural of words, acronyms or dates, (e.g. it is *businesses* not *business's, PCs* not *PC's* and *the 1990s* not *the 1990's*).

A *full stop* is only used at the end of a sentence, i.e. one that includes a finite verb. "Thanking you in anticipation", a phrase commonly found at the end of letters, is not a sentence, since "thanking" is not a finite verb, and therefore should end with a comma. However, full stops should not be used at the end of headings (even if there is a finite verb).

The use of *brackets* and *quotation marks (*also known as *inverted commas*) can cause problems too, especially with respect to where the full stop should be placed, i.e. inside or outside the bracket or quotation marks. (If the whole of the sentence is inside the bracket or quotation marks - as in this sentence - then the full stop is placed inside.) If the sentence begins outside the bracket or quotation marks then the full stop is placed outside (as in this sentence). Full stops are also commonly used after abbreviations.

Colons and *semi-colons* can cause difficulties too. The most frequent use of the colon (:) is before a list of items, and of the semi-colon (;) to separate a list of phrases or clauses.

On-line support for punctuation problems is available in the form of a *grammar checker*. Although not all word processing packages have one as a standard feature, they can be bought as an extra piece of software. However, the main function of a grammar checker (also referred to as a *style checker)* is to check for grammar and style.

Grammar

Frequent grammatical errors include *split infinitives, subject-verb agreements* and *double negatives*. These terms probably mean nothing to many people as English grammar is not taught as a formal subject in schools nowadays. However, inadvertent grammatical mistakes can sometimes lead to misunderstandings, and might also give the impression of incompetence or even a lack of intelligence, therefore a basic understanding of sentence structure is useful.

Grammar checkers can help to spot odd or incorrect sentence construction. One type of sentence structure they commonly flag up is the *passive*, as in the phrase "it was decided". This is because passive sentences are considered to be more difficult to read. However, if such a sentence construction is desired then this rule, like any of the other rules, can be turned off.

Style

It is difficult to define what is meant by good style, but the way in which vocabulary is used and the tone that is adopted are important considerations. However, there are distinct business and academic styles of writing so the writer should become familiar with accepted practice for the relevant type of document that is being produced. As a general rule, the use of the first person (i.e. *I* or *we*) should be avoided, although in some internal business reports it may be appropriate and for external reports the use of *we* is often acceptable nowadays.

There are a number of expressions to avoid when attempting to achieve good style. These include the use of slang; colloquialisms (e.g. contractions like *isn't* and *doesn't*); clichés; jargon; Americanisms; and acronyms. A style checker will spot many of these and may even identify politically incorrect, e.g. sexist, terms and expressions.

If it is difficult for the writer to think of alternatives for inappropriate or over-used words, an on-line *thesaurus* can help by offering synonyms (i.e. words with similar meanings) and indeed antonyms (i.e. words with the opposite meaning). However, the size of the thesaurus will determine how much choice is provided, as these can range from 10,000 words to 1.5 million words.

Exercise 1

Do you need to make use of a spell or grammar checker? In the following 10 sentences there are a total of 10 grammatical and spelling errors, although not all sentences contain an error. Can you spot them? Once you have attempted this exercise, type the sentences into your word processing software and put your on-line spell- and grammar-checkers through their paces to see how many errors they are able to detect.

(a) He lived seperately from his wife.
(b) She told him to practice the piece twice a day.
(c) There acommodation was very basic.
(d) The girls embarrasment was obvious.
(e) By doing this you will be able to continuously improve your performance.
(f) What did you do that for?
(g) I should of asked his permission.
(h) This new law will effect all of us.
(i) Its a pity he decided to carry on.
(j) I spoke to the man who's son had won the award.

Readability

This concerns how easily a document can be understood by an average adult, and is determined by the choice of vocabulary and the level of explanations, although it is primarily influenced by the length of sentences, the number of long words, the number of sentences in a paragraph and the number of passive sentences.

There are a number of ways of analysing the readability of a piece of text, e.g. Rudolph Flesch's Reading Ease and Grade Level, and Gunning's Fog Index. Flesch's Reading Ease and Grade Level indexes are based on the average number of words per sentence and the average number of syllables per 100 words whilst Gunning's Fog Index is based on the length of sentences and the number of words per sentence with more than 3 syllables.

A piece of text scoring less than 50 on Flesch's Reading Ease index would be considered difficult whilst one that scored more than 70 would be considered easy. With the Fog Index, however, a document scoring less than 10 would be considered easy whilst a score greater than 13 would signify a difficult passage.

Grammar checkers often provide readability statistics and it is a good idea to check the reading level of a document, as material that is too easy to read might insult a reader, and material that is too difficult might similarly cause offence.

If a readability analysis cannot be performed automatically by the software, then it is quite simple to work out the reading level of a document manually using Gunning's Fog Index on a sample passage of approximately 100 words, by:

(a) working out the average number of words in a sentence (i.e. by dividing the number of words by the number of sentences); and
(b) counting the number of words with 3 or more syllables; and
(c) adding the results of (a) and (b) and then multiplying them by 0.4. The resultant figure is the Fog Index.

Exercise 2
(a) Work out the reading level of the following sample passages taken from two different daily newspapers. If you have an on-line grammar checker that provides readability statistics use that. If not, use the manual method to work out the Fog Index of the following two paragraphs

Passage A
British Rail is to abandon the notorious cast-iron conditions of carriage that have absolved it of any liability for late and cancelled trains since nationalisation in 1948. BR's revised conditions of carriage, which will be published in December, are expected to acknowledge liability in certain strictly defined circumstances, and provide passengers with a guide to the type and levels of compensation available. Liability will be restricted to direct loss, enabling passengers to claim compensation for the cost of rail journeys subject to delays or cancellations. It will not cover consequential loss, where passengers suffer further because of late or cancelled services.

Passage B
Women are more likely to fall in love at first sight a new report says. Nearly one in four has fallen head over heels instantly - compared to one in five men. But half the women found their passion cooled, according to a survey by romance publishers Mills and Boon. Men stayed in love longer, with 60 per cent sticking with their partner. Researchers found three in four people formed a permanent relationship with the one who bowled them over - even if initially the feeling was not mutual. But 42 per cent of women ended up with partners they disliked at first compared to 28 per cent of men.

(b) On the basis of the readability analysis, make a reasoned guess in which newspapers (or types of newspapers) the two passages might have appeared.

7. Visual presentation of a document

The visual impact that a document makes is extremely important as it can influence the attitude of the reader. It is very difficult to read a mass of closely typed text, so the more attractive the layout the greater the likelihood it will be read and understood.

Example 1
The following example demonstrates poor presentation of a piece of text.

```
Presentation of a document
This is an example of a poorly presented piece of work in which no
design skills have been applied.The text is densely typed,there are
no spaces between the headings and the paragraphs, and the text has
not been separated into paragraphs.No space has been left after the
punctuation marks,so there is no breathing space between sentences
either.There is no interest in the passage and therefore it appears
very boring to read.What do you think about the fact that it is
presented with a ragged right-hand margin?Does the appearance of this
piece of text suggest that no care or interest has been taken with
its preparation-i.e.it was more a drudge,something that had to be
endured,rather than an interesting and inspired piece of work.So much
is given away about the writer's feelings and attitudes to the work
by its presentation.It is very revealing.Don't fall into the trap of
presenting an unattractive piece of work thinking that the content is
all that is important.Yes,the content is very important,but if the
document looks unappealing it may well not even be read.A busy
manager may simply throw it into the wastepaper basket-he or she will
not even have the energy to read through it.You are therefore not
doing yourself a favour.If you were trying to win a contract or get
something done, you will have failed miserably-simply because the
document looked unenticing and difficult to read.
```

There are simple techniques for enhancing the look of a document, which can easily be implemented using the most basic of word processing features. These will be extremely effective so long as they are used *consistently*. Variety is not the spice of life - it only confuses the reader, and there is also no need to use sophisticated DTP-style features unless they are appropriate for the type of document.

White space

The easiest way of ensuring that the document looks attractive and easy to read is to make sure there is enough *blank* or *white space* after headings, between paragraphs, and between sentences. White space is almost as important as the text itself, and it can help to improve the visual presentation dramatically.

The paragraphs themselves should be reasonably short, each covering only one theme. The white space provides a breathing space and indicates to the reader that they are about to encounter a new point.

Typeface

The choice of *typeface* is also important. There are two basic types of typeface: *serif* - which has small lines that finish off the main strokes (e.g. Times and Times New Roman typefaces); and *sans serif* - which only has the main strokes (e.g. Helvetica or Arial). Although there is an enormous number of possible typefaces a package will only offer a selection of these, although others may be obtained separately. The choice of typeface is a matter of personal preference although long pieces of text that use a serif typeface are easier to read.

The size of the typeface is also important. This is measured in *points* and there are 72 points to the inch. It is recommended that the main text should not be smaller than 10 point although 12 point is to be preferred. Anything smaller becomes too difficult to read if it is used for a long time, although it can be effective if used sparingly. Larger point sizes can be used for headings and in fact sans serif typefaces look better in large sizes. Three different sizes of typeface is the maximum number that should be used in a document.

Generally, it is quite adequate to use one typeface throughout a document but if a user wants a little more variety, two typefaces are often effective. Style rules suggest that if this is the case then headings should use a sans-serif typeface and the main text a serif typeface. Two different sans serif or serif typefaces do not normally work well together.

The *style* of the type can also be changed, e.g. text can be CAPITALISED, underlined, **emboldened**, or *italicised*, and if consistent modifications are made to the type they can assist the reader of the document in a number of ways:

- They can be used in headings and sub-headings to help the reader understand the structure of the document. (In this book chapter headings and sub-headings are emboldened, and sub-sub-headings are italicised.)
- They can also be used to highlight key words. (In this book key words are italicised.)

Note: The term *font* is generally used synonymously with the term *typeface* although it more correctly refers to a set of characters with a specific typeface, size and style, e.g. 10 point italic Times New Roman is a font.

Alignment and layout

The *alignment* of paragraphs in the document also needs to be considered. Paragraphs are usually described as being either *justified* or *unjustified*. Paragraphs in this book are justified. This means that all the lines at the right-hand side of the page end at the same point which creates a flush right-hand margin. It gives a professional appearance to any document and is achieved by the printer automatically inserting extra space between the characters or words. Unjustified text has a ragged right-hand margin, i.e. each line ends at a different place. The choice of whether to use justified or unjustified text for paragraphs will depend upon a number of factors, although headings should never be justified.

Firstly, the font that is being used will influence the decision, and particularly whether the printer can adequately insert the extra spaces without the text becoming very difficult to read. Secondly, whether a professional impression is required. In some organisations justified text may be expected in reports but frowned upon in correspondence, because the organisation wants to portray a more personal image.

Hyphenating words at the end of lines can help to improve the look of text by reducing the raggedness of unjustified text and by reducing the number of extra spaces inserted into the lines of justified text. Manual hyphenation is difficult as the writer must obey strict rules where to split words, e.g. between double letters, as in rag-ged. Word processing software can hyphenate automatically if required, although this feature needs to be used carefully as it can sometimes produce strange splits in words and too many hyphens in a document may not look aesthetically pleasing.

Two further types of alignment exist: *centred* text, which is used primarily for headings in reports and for displayed material, and *right-justified* text, which has become quite popular for company letterheads and for presenting titles on title pages.

There are also a number of different paragraph *layouts*. These include *indented, blocked* and *hanging* paragraphs. Every line of a *blocked* paragraph starts at the left-margin (as do the paragraphs in this book), whilst *indented* paragraphs start a few spaces in from the left margin.   Paragraphs can also be *indented* from both margins, e.g. when quotations are used. The first line of a *hanging* paragraph also starts at the left-margin but subsequent lines are indented a few spaces. The choice of paragraph style is a personal matter, although the use of blocked paragraphs is considered more modern.

When most documents are printed they normally use single *line spacing*. However, in some documents, e.g. legal documents, it may be necessary to use double- or 1.5-line spacing. This is also very useful for producing drafts as there is room to insert hand-written amendments. The line-spacing can easily be changed to single before a final printout is taken.

A useful word processing feature is the ability to set up *paragraph styles*. These can be defined in terms of the font, the paragraph alignment and layout. (For example, this particular paragraph could be defined as using justified alignment and 12 point Times New Roman font with no indents.) Styles can be stored separately and applied to paragraphs as required. Making any changes to the stored paragraph style will alter all of the paragraphs created using that style. It is therefore a powerful formatting facility, time-saving and ensures a consistent format across the document.

Page layout

Finally, the impression of the page as a whole must be considered. No odd lines of text should appear at the end of one page or at the beginning of the next page. These are known as *widows and orphans* and sophisticated word processing software normally ensures that they do not occur.

Word processing software differs in how the formatting features described above are displayed on the screen. With some software the user is able to gain a better impression of the way the page will look when printed than with others. However, with most word processing software, there is a WYSIWYG (What You See Is What You Get) *Print Preview* facility that lets the writer see the look of the printed page. Often the preview facility will display two pages at one time, or even multiple pages, which is useful to check on the look of each page of the document as well as the consistency of the document as a whole.

Example 2
The example below shows how the passage in Example 1 above (with minor textual alterations) could be transformed by the use of very basic features, i.e. the use of white space, a change of typeface and size (to Times Roman 12 point), minimal type modifications (e.g. bold and underlined), and use of justified and blocked paragraphs.

Presentation of a document

This is an example of a piece of work which is well presented although only basic design skills have been applied to it. The text is no longer densely typed, there are spaces between the headings and the paragraphs, and the text itself has been separated into paragraphs. Space has been left between the punctuation marks, so there is now breathing space between sentences too.

The passage appears more interesting to read. The fact that it is now presented with justified paragraphs also gives it a more professional appearance and there seems to have been more care taken with its preparation. So much is given away about the writer's feelings and attitudes to the work by its presentation. It is very revealing.

You should therefore pay due attention to the presentation of any piece of work. The content is important, but if the work looks appealing it is more likely to be read. A busy manager is less likely to throw it into the wastepaper basket!

Tables

Documents often need to include tables, charts or graphs, particularly if numerical, financial or statistical data is being presented. *Tables* are a means of presenting columns of data and they can easily be set up using word processing software. However, the following points should be kept in mind to assist with the interpretation of the data:

- The table should have an explanatory title;
- The figures in the table should be arranged in rows rather than columns;
- Columns of figures that need to be compared should be placed close together;
- Columns and rows should be clearly labelled;
- All units of measurements should be provided, e.g. £m;
- Any notes required to explain the data in the table should be provided (possibly as a footnote).

The Central Statistical Office (CSO) creates tables that conform to these guidelines. An example taken from a CSO publication is shown in Chapter 1 Exercise 3 and this table can be used as a model.

Word processing software can also insert leader dots, dashes or lines to link the columns of data if it is felt this makes the data in the table easier to read. Some software provides a *table facility* which automates the production of a table, and there is often an associated *maths* function which allows simple mathematical operations to be carried out, e.g. adding numbers in rows and columns, although some of today's word processing software packages provide almost spreadsheet-like functionality.

However, if more complex or extended analysis needs to be carried out on the numerical data then it is probably more appropriate that spreadsheet software is used to analyse and present the data (see Chapter 3). The work produced in the spreadsheet can then be included on a separate sheet or copied into the word processed document. In a similar way *graphs* and *charts* created in other software (see Chapter 4) can either be printed independently or copied into a word processed document.

8. Attributing sources in a document

It is very important, especially in academic material, that any words or ideas that are used in a document that originate elsewhere are attributed to the original author. It has already been stated in **1:16** that it is necessary to keep a record of the source of the material that has been collected. These bibliographic details are now used as the document is prepared.

There are a number of ways of citing published material, but the two most commonly used in this country are the *British* and the *Harvard* methods. This section will describe the *Harvard* method, using the notes made in Chapter 1 Exercise 2.

If the original words are to be cited this could be done by indenting the citation (from the left and right margin) and then attributing it afterwards, using the author's surname and date of publication, as shown below.

"Reality is harsh and virtual reality will be virtually harsh." (Redmond, 1993)

It is also possible to introduce the citation with the author's surname and date of publication in brackets, e.g. *Redmond (1993) defines virtual reality as "the simulation of real world events and responses in a computer generated environment".*

If the ideas rather than the words are to be used, they still need to be attributed, by showing the author's name and the date of publication. However, in this case quotation marks are not used as the original words have been re-phrased and it is simply the ideas that are being expressed. For example, *Redmond (1993) believes that the impact that virtual reality will have will not always be for the best.*

Note: if there is more than one author, then all authors are named e.g. *(Adams, Brown and Clark, 1995)* although subsequently it is acceptable to shorten this to e.g. *(Adams et al, 1995).*

Full reference details must be provided in a list of References at the end of the document so that anybody who wants to find the article or book that is cited can do so. Using the *Harvard* method, references are provided in alphabetical order by author's surname followed by the date.

The following formats should be used when creating the References section. The position of each item on the line, the punctuation marks used as well as the formatting features shown below are all essential requirements and should be followed implicitly. Unjustified text and hanging paragraphs are best for long references.

Book	Surname, first name. (year) *Title*, Publisher.
Journal article	Surname, first name. (year,month) "Title", *Journal*, **Vol No**, pp 00-99.
Article in a collection	Surname, first name. (year,month) "Article title" in Editors surname(s) and first name(s). (Ed(s)) *Collection*. Publisher.
Magazine article	Surname, first name. (year,month,day) "Title", *Magazine*, pp 00-99.
Newspaper article	Surname, first name. (year,month,day) "Title", *Newspaper*, pp 00-99.

If reference is made to more than one book or article by an author with the same publication date, letters should be placed after each date, e.g. (Jones,1994a) (Jones,1994b).

Example 3
The main article cited in this section would appear in the References as:
Redmond, Ciaran. (1993) "Future technologies and their business impact" in
  Peppard, Joe. (Ed) *IT strategy for business*. Pitman.

If, on the other hand, the *British* method of citation is used, this requires the use of *footnotes* or *endnotes*. Major word processing packages have the facility to mark these in the text, and print them either at the bottom of the page (hence *footnotes)* or at the end of a chapter or at the end of the whole document (*endnotes*).

9. Structuring a document

All documents need to be structured. At a very simple level a document should consist of three main elements: an *introduction* which sets the scene and outlines the aims and objectives or purpose of the document; the *main body* of the document in which the facts and any analysis of the facts are presented; and a *conclusion* or *summary*, which may include *recommendations*.

This basic structure is appropriate for most short reports and other documents like academic essays, although longer or more complex documents may require a much more defined structure. The *formal report* structure is frequently offered as a model but it is not appropriate for all types of report.

It is recommended, therefore, that writers understand the exact format and structure that is required of their documents. This might involve following a *house style* (i.e. organisational rules on layout and presentation) or, in the case of specialist documents, a very explicit structure. For longer documents, e.g. major reports and academic dissertations, the following structure may be required:

A first part that consists of one or more of the following items:
- a *title page* showing at least the title of the document, the author's name, and the date of submission;
- an *acknowledgements* page thanking those who helped in the preparation of the document;
- a *table of contents* giving a list of the various parts of the document together with page numbers;
- a *summary* or *abstract* summarising primarily the conclusions of the document.

A middle or main part that consists of:
- an *introduction*, outlining the aims and objectives of the work, the scope of the document, and the methodology (i.e. method of working) that was used, together with an indication of the structure of the rest of the document;
- the *main body* providing the information and any analysis of the information;
- the *conclusions and/or recommendations* of the document (closely linked to the aims and objectives).

A final part that consists of one or more of the following items:
- a list of *references* or a *bibliography* (see **8**);
- *appendices,* i.e. material that is referred to in the body of the document but that does not easily fit into the main part of the work e.g. technical specifications, statistics, etc;
- an alphabetical *index.*

It is important that the structure of the document is implemented in some way so that readers can locate their position in the document. The following are suggestions how this might be done:

- by the use of simple text headings, sub-headings and sub-sub-headings (e.g. words and phrases that briefly summarise the contents of the sections that follow);
- by the use of a hierarchical numbering system, e.g. 1, 1.1, 1.1.1. (This is useful for formal reports, but it is important to ensure that not more than three levels of the hierarchy are developed);
- by the use of Arabic numbering (1,2,3) for headings, letters (a,b,c) for sub-headings, and roman numerals (i,ii,iii) for sub-sub-headings.

Whichever method is used, or even if a hybrid method is developed, it is essential that it is used consistently throughout the document otherwise it will only confuse the reader. (This book uses a combination of the first and third methods described above.)

10. Productivity aids for extended documents

Many word processing packages have an *outliner* facility, which allows the writer to create a system of headings and sub-headings that show the structure of a document and which can be built upon and reorganised as the structure of the document develops. They can also assist in automating the *numbering* of sections and sub-sections or by *bulleting* points (i.e. •) as in this book.

Other word processing features that can be usefully employed for long documents include a *page numbering* facility that can insert page numbers automatically onto each page. The position of the numbers on the page can be set up to match the general look of the document, i.e. at the top or bottom or left-aligned, right-aligned or centred.

Headers and *footers* can also be produced. These are one or more lines of text that appear on the top or bottom of every page. They only need to be typed in once and are printed automatically on each page. The most common footer is the page number, which is usually the default footer for any word processed document, but they can also incorporate other items of text. The software may allow the user to set up different headers and footers for the first page of a document and for odd and even pages, as well as select the position of the header and footer. (In this book there are no footers, the first page of every chapter does not have a header, but even pages show the page number and the section name (left-aligned), and odd pages show the chapter number, chapter name and page number (right-aligned).) Headers or footers can also be set up to show the page numbers in other formats, e.g. "Page 1 of 5" or "Page: 1"

Consistency of documents, e.g. in-house reports, can be ensured by the use of document *templates*. These can be conceived of as "patterns" which define the layout of a page or document. A template might contain text, a set of paragraph *styles*, as well as other features like margins and page length. Very long documents, i.e. those over 20 pages, can more effectively be set up as a series of short documents, which can then be connected together. Applying a template to each of the documents will ensure consistency across the document as a whole.

All long documents should have a *table of contents* which should show up to three levels of the structure (as well as provide a list of appendices). The page numbers should, ideally, be situated close to the text to which they refer or else joined to it by leader dots. (In this book the table of contents shows three levels of the structure: the part number and name, the chapter number and name (closely followed by the starting page number) together with the main topics discussed in each chapter.)

Certain long documents, especially books, also require the inclusion of an *index*. The entries in an index might be the main topics covered in the document or any special terms used. A simple index shows one level of entries, whilst a more complex index includes multiple levels of entries (such as the one in this book). In a simple index the text is usually separated from the page number(s) by a comma and a space (e.g. 6, 21). It can show page ranges (e.g. 21-24) or refer to text rather than page numbers (e.g. "See xyz"). Indexes and tables of contents can automatically be compiled by word processing software from one or more files.

Some documents have to be written to a certain word length and most software has the facility to carry out a *word count*. Others are able to maintain additional *statistical information* about the document, e.g. the total editing time of the document.

Finally, documents sometimes need to be reviewed by others who are not the writers. This is often possible on-screen and *annotations* can be inserted into them in a separate section so that they do not interfere with the original text. The annotations can then be printed out at a later stage with or without the text to which they refer.

Exercise 3

You work for a market research company where short reports are frequently produced on a wide range of subjects. However, the presentation, structure and style of these reports differs greatly from author to author. You have, therefore, been asked to design a house style to ensure consistency across the reports.

(a) How might you go about this?

(b) What type of style rules would you specify?

(c) How might you put this house style into operation?

---

11. Correspondence

There are a number of different forms of correspondence: personal and business, internal and external, formal and informal. The next few sections are primarily concerned with the production of business correspondence, i.e. letters, memos and faxes, and in particular the structure and layout of these documents.

One essential point to make at the outset is that the overall impression of all correspondence is extremely important, especially if it is to be the first contact with a company as it must convey the right impression. Consequently, many organisations adopt a house style for their external (and sometimes even their internal) correspondence. If one is in place it should be followed closely as it is there for a purpose, namely to ensure consistency and to project a company image.

12. Correspondence: letters and envelopes

This section looks at the structure and layout of business letters and envelopes.

Letters

There are a number of elements to a business letter. All letters, normally, have a *letterhead* that shows the company's name and address, telephone number, fax number and possibly a company logo. As letter-headed stationery is often pre-printed it is essential to take account of the depth of the letterhead when preparing a letter in a word processed document.

The *date* is the first piece of information to be recorded on the letter, and this can usually be extracted automatically from the computer system itself. However, it should show the British format, i.e. day-month-year (as in 20 January 1995) and not the American format, i.e. month-day-year (as in January 20, 1995). The date should not be abbreviated, as in 20-01-95 or 20 Jan 1995, and it is now considered unfashionable to write 1st, 2nd, 3rd, 4th, etc. (as in 20th January 1995).

Letters often include *references,* which can help writers keep track of their correspondence. However, the next main item in the letter is the *inside address.* This shows the name of the recipient, their position in the company, and the company's name and address, although sometimes it is necessary to write directly to the company rather than to a named individual. When typing addresses, the town or city of the address should be in capital letters with the postcode written underneath the county.

Commonly used names and addresses can be maintained by the word processing software in a *glossary* (together with commonly used paragraphs).

The *salutation* follows next. This is the formal opening of the letter, and there are a number of conventions in the use of the salutation and the *complimentary close* (i.e. the way the letter is ended).

- If a letter is addressed to a company, then it should begin *Dear Sirs* and end with *Yours faithfully*

- If the letter is addressed to a named individual who is not known by the writer or a more formal approach is required, then it should begin *Dear Sir* or *Dear Madam* and end with *Yours faithfully*

- If the letter is addressed to a named individual who is known by the writer or a less formal approach is required, then it should begin *Dear Mr Adams* or *Dear Mrs Brown* (but not Dear Mr Peter Adams nor Dear Mrs Jane Brown) and end with *Yours sincerely*

- If the letter is addressed to an individual who is well known to the writer then it can be addressed personally e.g. *Dear Peter* or *Dear Jane* (but not Dear Peter Adams nor Dear Jane Brown) and this is usually followed by either *Kind regards* or *Best wishes.*

An optional *subject heading* describes the content of the letter to follow, and the *body of the letter* is divided into short paragraphs. Finally, the relevant *complimentary close* is used as detailed above and adequate space (normally 5 line spaces) is allowed for the writer's signature. This is followed by the *writer's name* and usually their *position in the company.* If there are *enclosures* in a letter, this is usually denoted by the abbreviation *Enc* or *Encs* at the end of the letter.

There are a number of layout styles for business letters. The two most commonly found are the *fully-blocked* and the *semi-blocked* styles. The *fully-blocked* style is by far the simplest as everything is typed in at the left hand margin. With the *semi-blocked* style, some elements are blocked and others are centred. Although this layout is now somewhat old-fashioned, it is still in use today. The paragraphing in the body of both layout styles can be either justified or unjustified according to taste. However, *open punctuation* is commonly used in fully-blocked letters nowadays, which means that all punctuation marks are omitted except for grammatical punctuation in the body of the letter.

One important aspect of the presentation of the letter is that it should appear balanced on the page. Although there are minimum spacing requirements between each element of the letter, as shown in Example 4 below, these can be increased in a consistent fashion to ensure that a one-page letter is not printed all at the top of the paper. When producing letters of more than one page, a writer should not allow only the complimentary close and writer's name to appear on the final page. In multi-page letters, pages can be *numbered*, although the number itself is not normally displayed on the first page of the letter.

Example 4
This is a model of a fully-blocked business letter with open punctuation and justified paragraphs.

Company Letterhead

20 January 1995

Office Designs Ltd
96 High Street
NEWBURY
Berks
BA29 3XZ

Dear Sirs

New office design

We are currently reviewing the design and layout of our offices as we have recently appointed a number of new staff.

We would therefore be grateful if you would send us a copy of your recent brochure together with a list of your consultancy charges.

Yours faithfully

Angus Robertson
Office Manager

If a house style is in place it will determine not only the layout of the letter but also whether open punctuation is accepted practice and whether justified or unjustified paragraphs are to be used together with the spacing between the items. The use of *templates* or *style sheets* (already described in **10**) is particularly useful for this purpose. If the company does not have a template for its house style, there are usually a number of pre-defined templates available in the software, although of course they can be designed by the company itself.

Envelopes

The layout of envelopes normally follows the layout and punctuation of the accompanying letter, e.g. fully-blocked and using open punctuation. Addresses are usually placed in the middle of the envelope.

Example 5
This is a model of the layout of a fully-blocked envelope using open punctuation.

Office Designs Ltd
96 High Street
NEWBURY
Berks
BA29 3XZ

With some word processing software *envelopes* and *labels* can automatically be prepared, although the printer must be able to support their production. It is common practice in the United States (and indeed in continental Europe) to include a return address. Since most word processing packages emanate from the States, the provision for the inclusion of a return address is usually available. However, whereas in Europe the return address is normally written on the back of the envelope, in the US it appears on the top left hand corner of the envelope, so this is where it is normally printed by the word processing software.

Exercise 4
Draft a letter and an envelope, using the fully-blocked style and open punctuation, to be sent to Mrs Mary Brown of Stoneways Ltd, a regular customer, thanking her for her recent order (A3456) for business stationery and informing her that her order will be despatched within the week. The company address is 59 Hampshire Road, Torquay, Devon TQ9 6ZY.

13. Correspondence: memos

A memorandum (or memo for short) is the standard means of internal business correspondence. Although it is mainly intended to communicate short items of information, its format is often used to present internal reports. There are four main elements to a memo. *To:* followed by the name of the recipient; *From:* followed by the name of the writer; *Date:* followed by the date of writing; and finally the *Subject:* of the memo. The main body of the memo nowadays is generally fully-blocked.

Example 6
Two simple models of memo formats are shown below.

MEMORANDUM

To:	John Morris	From:	Jennifer Adams
	Sales Manager		Personnel Officer
Subject:	New appointments	Date:	27 June 1995

Further to our recent telephone discussion ...

```
MEMORANDUM

To:      John Morris, Sales Manager
From:    Jennifer Adams, Personnel Officer
Date:    27 June 1995
_____


New appointments


Further to our recent telephone discussion ...
```

14. Correspondence: faxes

The term *fax* (short for facsimile) is used to describe any document sent by a fax machine. It is a form of external communication that is becoming more common with the widespread use of fax machines. Documents that are faxed to companies are sometimes just short messages but can also be copies of letters or other documents that are also sent by post. When documents are sent by fax they are usually headed by a cover sheet that includes:

- the recipient's name, company and fax number;
- the sender's name, company and fax number; and
- the number of pages being faxed.

Example 7
An example of a fax cover sheet is given below. Note that the names and fax numbers are neatly aligned below one another

```
                    FAX COVER SHEET

        To:                  Petter Jensen,  Nordic Sun Ltd,
                             0181-567-6789
        From:                Chris Peter, Harrisons Travel,
                             0171-234-3456
        Date:                30 May 1995
        No. of pages (incl this one):  2
        _____


        Message
```

Many writers prepare their fax messages using their word processing software, print them and then send them out using a separate fax machine. However, others have fax facilities installed in their PCs that allow writers to send out their faxes directly. In this case the fax software will very often set up a cover sheet automatically, if desired.

15. Correspondence: mail merging

With word processing software it is very easy to create a *standard* or *form letter*, i.e. one that contains the main text and leaves space to enter individual details, and then merge this with a file of names and addresses, so that each letter is personalised. This is known as *mail merge* and is an extremely useful feature for all businesses, e.g. for mailshots, etc., as it gives the impression that each letter has been individually prepared.

Example 8

(a) A form letter might be set up to invite job applicants to interview as shown below. Note, that in this particular case, the data to be merged is marked with *, although the way this is achieved in any particular software package will vary.

Company Letterhead

1 December 1995

title *firstname* *surname*
street
LONDON
postcode

Dear *title* *surname*

<u>Trainee manager</u>

Thank you for your application for the above post. I should now like to invite you to interview on *date* *year* at *time*.

Please confirm that you will be able to attend at this time either in writing or by telephoning this office.

I look forward to meeting you on *date*.

Yours sincerely

John Adams
<u>Human Resources Manager</u>

(b) This letter could then be merged with a data file of interviewees' names and addresses, in the format:

title, firstname, surname, street, postcode, date, year, time.

One of which might be as below:

Miss, Tracey, Green, 25 Willesden Road, NW6 7TY, Friday 17 December, 1995, 12.30 pm.

(c)   The resultant letter would appear as below:

Company Letterhead

1 December 1995

Miss Tracey Green
25 Willesden Road
LONDON
NW6 7TY

Dear Miss Green

Trainee manager

Thank you for your application for the above post. I should now like to invite you to interview on Friday 17 December 1995 at 12.30 pm.

Please confirm that you will be able to attend at this time either in writing or by telephoning this office.

I look forward to meeting you on 17 December.

Yours sincerely

John Adams
Human Resources Manager

Exercise 5
Prepare a form letter to be used by a company writing to its regular customers advising them of a new product. Show where the merged data would appear.

There are other forms of mail merging. For instance, a standard letter can be merged:

- with data input directly from the keyboard; or
- with selected names from a file, when this is known as a conditional merge; or
- with a file of names and addresses created using database software (see Chapter 6) or with a list of names and addresses held in a spreadsheet worksheet (see Chapter 3).

16. Displayed documents

The following sections look at features that provide a greater level of visual presentation than has been previously described. Although a number of documents like reports and some forms of correspondence may be able to take advantage of these features, they will be more effectively employed in documents of "publication-quality", like adverts, flyers, forms, brochures and newsletters.

Until recently many of these features were only possible in desk top publishing (DTP) software, but they are now commonly available in the major word processing packages. However DTP packages are still necessary where complex page layout and typographic control are required.

When using any of these advanced presentation features, however, it is important to consider the overall design of the document. Although some people are visually competent and have a good sense of design, others will need to pay special care and attention to this aspect as it is all too easy to incorporate too many special effects into a document. Individually these features are extremely impressive and effective, but if too many are used together they will only fight for attention, and this will mean that not only will the design of the document be unappealing but also the message will be obscured. Inexperienced designers cannot go far wrong if they keep in mind two basic concepts: simplicity and clarity. Hence when a document of this kind is being planned and drafted, both its content and its visual presentation must be considered. These two aspects cannot be separated.

17. Displayed document: special text effects

Some special text effects can be achieved very easily in word processing software. These include <u>double underlining</u>, SMALL CAPITALS, the use of superscript, e.g. $E=mc^2$, subscript, e.g. H_2O, and the use of colour (but only, of course, if it can be supported by the printer).

The *extended character set* will also allow the user to type characters not on the standard keyboard, e.g. foreign characters for use in words like arrivé, reçu, hôpital, Schlüß, and for other characters, like the trade mark symbol ™, the copyright symbol ©, fractions like ¼, the degree symbol, as in °C, and other characters, e.g. §.

Other special text effects, not so widely available in the software, include *shadowing* and *outlining*, and printing text in special ways, e.g. in a circle, semi-circle, angled or vertically. A variety of less well known typefaces may also be available, although additional typefaces can be purchased separately in *font packs* (or *TrueType font packs,* as Windows fonts tend to be), if required.

Example 9
The following are examples of three special effects using less well known typefaces.

18. Displayed documents: graphics

Most word processing packages can support the inclusion of graphics of one sort or another. This might simply be unusual and interesting characters maintained in a set of *symbols* (also known as *dingbats*) within the software or from libraries available from third-parties. Examples of symbols include ✈ ✓ ◷ ✳.   Some packages also include *drawing tools*, which allow the user to draw simple free-hand drawings using lines, boxes, circles, arcs.   More sophisticated drawing packages should be used, however, for the design of more complex images and also to manipulate photographic images.

Example 10
This drawing of an envelope was created using word processing drawing tools.

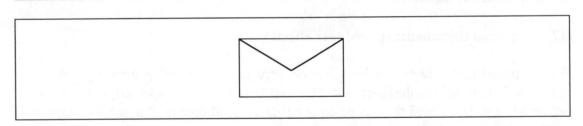

Libraries of *clipart images* are also commonly available in major word processing packages. Once inserted into a document these graphics can then be scaled (i.e. increased or decreased in size), rotated or mirrored, if desired.   Some software packages can also draw background graphics (known as *watermarks*) on the page.

Example 11
The image below was copied from a clipart library within a word processing package.

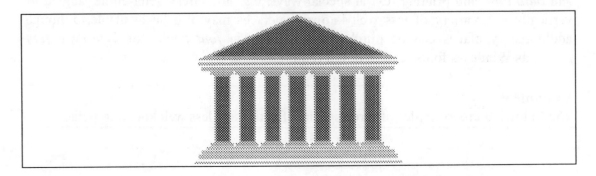

Lines (of different thicknesses) and *boxes* (sometimes known as *borders*) can be placed around headings, paragraphs and graphics (e.g. as used in the Examples and Exercises in this book), and boxes can also be shadowed.

Example 12
This is an example of a shadowed box with a double line border.

---

19. Displayed documents: simple display

Many of the features described above will be useful in the display of simple documents like *adverts, posters, flyers, menus, announcements, invitations* or even *title pages* of reports. Each line of such a document should be short, sharp and snappy and should be considered for its importance and hence for the most effective means of its presentation. Lines should not compete for prominence, so it should be quite clear which are the more important lines and which secondary. The overall look of the page must be balanced, and in its simplest terms this might mean *centring* the design *vertically* on the page.

Title pages and large adverts are normally printed on A4, whilst flyers, menus, announcements and invitations normally fit on A5. As A5 is half of A4 this means that two can be set up on one A4 page.

Exercise 6
Design a menu to be displayed at a Company's Christmas Dinner to be held at the Grand Hotel on Friday 22 December 1995.

---

20. Displayed documents: forms

Organisations use *forms* for many different purposes, e.g. order forms, invoices and questionnaires. (See **1:17** for a discussion of questionnaires.) Forms should be brief and functional, i.e. they should provide enough space and enough instructions for them to be completed quickly and easily.

Word processing software can be used to design forms, e.g. if boxes are placed around tables created with the *table* facility. Boxes can then be *shaded*, if required, although it should be noted that shading can affect the legibility of text. Shading is normally specified as a percentage of grey shading usually from 5% to 90%. 10%-20% is an acceptable level of shading and still allows the text to be readable.

Example 13
This is a section of an order form used for the entry of the product details.

Product No	Product Name	Quantity	Price	Total
		Total price		

Some word processing software provides extra facilities like check boxes for the design of on-screen forms. However, if the user needs to produce many different types of forms, a dedicated *forms designer* package may be more suitable. It should be noted however that forms being designed for use with database or spreadsheet applications should be created using the appropriate software so that they fully match the on-screen forms (see Chapters 3 and 6).

Exercise 7
Draft the design of a form to be used as an application form for a car parking permit for the company car park.

---

21. Displayed documents: brochures

Parallel (or *table*) columns are useful for the design of certain displayed documents as this allows blocks of text to appear side by side. The material in each column, whether text or graphics, can then be formatted or aligned independently.

Example 14
This example demonstrates three independent parallel columns.

Column 1	Column 2	Column 3
This is an unjustified paragraph within a column	centred text	
	This paragraph has been justified within this column.	This is right-justified text
This is another unjustified paragraph within a column.	This column has been shaded.	

Parallel columns can be put to good use in the production of brochures, either 4-page or 6-page. A 4-page brochure can be produced by folding A4 paper once, either horizontally or vertically and might be used for a programme or news sheet.

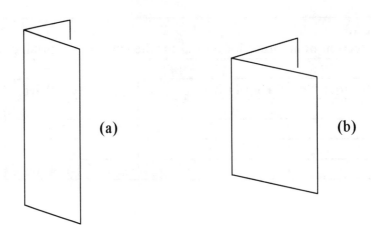

(a)   (b)

To produce such a 4-page brochure requires two 2 parallel columns on 2 pieces of A4, either in portrait mode for (a) or in landscape mode for (b). However, it is important to realise which column represents which page of the brochure.

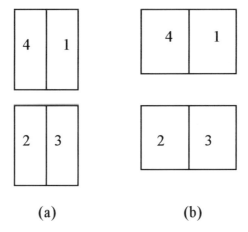

(a)   (b)

A 6-page brochure can be produced by folding A4 paper twice vertically. This type of brochure is very popular in business for advertising purposes, and specially pre-printed, two-sided paper can be purchased to support the production of top quality brochures.

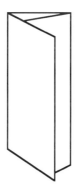

To create a 6-page brochure, three parallel columns are set up on 2 pages of A4 in landscape mode. Again it is important to realise which column represents which page of the brochure.

page 1	Inside page 2	page 3

Inside flap	Back cover	Front cover

Exercise 8
Design the layout of a 6-page brochure to be used as advertising literature for a conference. This should include information on the conference programme as well as a tear-off section for registration.

---

22. Displayed documents: newsletters

Newspaper columns are useful for the production of newsletters and magazines, as they allow the text from the bottom of one column to flow to the beginning of the next column. The designer should choose the number of columns to be used (probably 2 or 3) and control the width of the columns by adjusting the *gutter*, i.e. the space between the columns. Columns should not be too wide, especially if the font size is small as this means there will be too many words per line in a column: 10-12 words is about the maximum. If the gutter is too small or too wide the text will be hard to read. The use of a *vertical line* is effective to separate columns of text, especially if the text is unjustified, as is the use of a *horizontal line* to mark the top and bottom of the page or to separate items on the page.

Example 15
The text in these four columns is justified, and the default size gutter has been used.

With newspaper columns text flows from the bottom of one column to the next. However, if there are a number of narrow columns only a few words will fit on each line. Therefore it would probably be necessary to hyphenate the text to aid readability.

Example 16
The text in these three columns is separated by a a narrower gutter.

With newspaper columns text flows from the bottom of one column to the next. However, if there are a number of narrow columns only a few words will fit on each line. Therefore it is probably necessary to reduce the space between columns to aid the readability of the text.

Example 17
The text in these two columns is justified, the default size gutter has been used but a vertical line has been added between the columns.

With newspaper columns text flows from the bottom of one column to the next. However, if there are a number of narrow columns only a few words will fit on each line. Therefore it may be necessary to hyphenate the text, use unjustified paragraphs, or add a vertical line to aid readability.

Although columns do not necessarily have to start or even end at the same line on the page, the bottoms of the columns should either be very different or exactly the same since the bottoms of columns that are only fractionally out (e.g. by ½ a line) look very unprofessional. It is generally possible to control the spacing between the lines of the text known as *leading* (pronounced "ledding") to remedy any problems.

A document like a newsletter should be well planned so that it is not a jumble of disorganised features. Although a balanced page is essential, a symmetrical page gives a static appearance. Each page (and in long documents, each two-page spread) should be sketched out to show the number and width of columns, the size of the text and graphics (as shown here).

Within the columns, not only text but also graphics (and this includes photos) and white space can be used to good effect, and the text can be made to flow around the graphics. It is also possible to have graphics (or text) positioned between two columns in which case the text flows around the graphics.

The size of the typeface can be used to emphasise text, e.g. 10-12 point for the body, 12-14 for sub-headings, 24 point for headlines and 36 point for the *masthead* (or *banner*).

With some recent versions of word processing software even more sophisticated text formatting is now possible, for instance, *kerning* (which involves controlling the spacing between letters, particularly in mastheads), the use of *large initial capitals* (also called *drop capitals*) as shown at the beginning of the next paragraph, and *micro-adjustable line-spacing*.

Designing a newsletter or in-house magazine requires design skills, style and ideas. This section has only provided an introduction to this type of work. If writers consistently produce material of this nature then they can do no better than to look in magazines, newspapers and other publicity material for typefaces that work well together and for effective and striking layouts.

Exercise 9
Design the layout (not the text) of the front page of an in-house magazine, to include the following items:
(a) an open letter from the new Managing Director on the future of the company (together with a photograph);
(b) a write-up of a Charity football match (including a photo of the winning team); and
(c) an advert for a holiday competition, full details of which appear inside the magazine.

23. Further productivity aids

Although this chapter has detailed many word processing features that can help to support the work of a writer, a few more general features are mentioned here.

Often tasks need to be automated so that work can be completed more efficiently and quickly. *Macros* are useful for this. These are commands written by the user using a macro language. Macro languages vary in sophistication from package to package: some are only able to record and automate a series of keystrokes whilst others include a very powerful programming language. An example of a macro might be to place the writer's home or business address automatically at the top of a letter.

There are also a number of features that can help with the management of files, like copying, renaming and deleting files, as well as the ability to search files for words or phrases. These file management features may to some extent replace the need for the user to revert to the operating system to carry out these tasks.

If documents need to be *protected* this can be done in a number of ways. They can be made *read-only* (which ensures that no inadvertent changes are made) or *password protected* (so that others cannot either read or change a document without the relevant password); or *locked for annotation* (which allows a reviewer to make comments but not edit the text itself).

Some word processing software that is termed *group-enabled* can support group working, i.e. a team working environment where a number of users work on the same document at the same time. Future versions of word processing software will continue to improve support for group working.

24. Multimedia documents

Some word processing software can support the creation of *multimedia* documents. These are documents that include not only text and graphics, but also sound, video and animation. With the necessary hardware installed, sound messages can be stored in a document, and played back when activated, as too can video clips and animated annotations. One possible example of a multimedia document might be a letter that not only includes the text of the message but also contains an embedded video clip of the writer speaking to the recipient of the letter.

25. Further work with word processing software

The basic foundations for the use of word processing software as an effective productivity tool have been laid in this chapter. But this tool is only as powerful as the user's skill and experience in document design, so it is therefore very much up to each user to experiment and gain experience in using the word processing software and in this way develop their own style.

3

Numerical data analysis

1. Introduction

Many common information handling tasks involve the manipulation of numerical data. These tasks can range from carrying out simple mathematical calculations to complex statistical and financial analysis of data.

Numerical analysis is extremely important in business and is not only undertaken by financial specialists and accountants but also by general managers for decision-making and planning. It is also used in research and academic life to carry out statistical analysis of research data.

2. Spreadsheet software

Many tasks involving mathematical calculations can be performed with the use of a calculator although there are a number of limitations associated with their use. For instance, the work may involve a substantial amount of "number-crunching", and the fact that calculators can only deal with values and do not assist with the labelling of data means that they are no help in presenting the data understandably or attractively.

However, there are a number of powerful software tools that can assist with numerical data analysis and these include spreadsheet software for personal computers. They not only provide the means for carrying out a range of mathematical, financial and statistical analysis but can also support the creation of graphs and charts as well as having some database and text processing capabilities.

Although spreadsheets do offer a vast amount of functionality, an average user will be able to make effective use of spreadsheet software by employing only a small amount of the available features - provided that they have the necessary basic mathematical skills. More ambitious use of the software for complex statistical and financial applications will, however, require far more specialist knowledge.

This chapter begins by explaining basic spreadsheet terminology and use (3-10). It then looks at numerical data modelling (11) and further work with spreadsheets (12-19), and concludes with a discussion of specialist spreadsheet use (20).

3. Spreadsheet terminology

Spreadsheeting is not confined solely to the electronic world: in fact the first spreadsheet program was developed from the paper tool used by accountants and finance specialists. A *spreadsheet* is the term used to describe a piece of paper ruled up with columns (labelled A, B, C etc.) and rows (numbered 1, 2, 3 etc.) where each intersection of a column and row is known as a *cell* and has a unique address (e.g. A1, B2, K4).

	A	B	C	D	E	F	G	H	I	J	K
1											
2											
3											
4											

Spreadsheets vary in size but a major spreadsheet program has about 256 columns and 16,384 rows, totalling over 4 million cells, although a user will probably only need to use a small proportion of these to create a working spreadsheet.

Each cell can contain one piece of data:

- a *value*;
- a *label*;
- a *formula;* or
- a *function*.

Values are numbers, dates and times to which mathematical calculations can be applied.

Labels are usually pieces of text, e.g. the word "Product". However they might be a mixture of alphabetic and numeric characters as in "Product 123" or even be a numeric label like "123". In this latter case if entered as a label it will only be considered as a piece of text and cannot be used in any mathematical calculations.

Formulae and *functions* are more complex so are discussed in detail in sections **4** and **5** below.

4. Formulae

Formulae are instructions to carry out mathematical calculations. Therefore if any calculations, however simple, need to be carried out, formulae should be used. (Calculations should never be carried out mentally or with the use of a calculator.)

A formula displays the results of the calculation in the cell rather than the formula itself. If any changes are made to the dependent cells of the formula, the formula is automatically re-calculated and the cell displays the new result.

Example 1
(a) In the worksheet below, a formula is used in C1 to add up the values in A1 and B1, i.e. =A1+B1. With the current values of 20 and 30 displayed in A1 and B1, the result displayed in C1 is 50.

	A	B	C
1	20	30	50

(b) However, if the value in A1 is changed, e.g. to 10, the value displayed in C1 now becomes 40.

	A	B	C
1	10	30	40

When using formulae the following should be noted:

- Formulae make use of the basic mathematical operators: addition; subtraction; multiplication; and division, which in spreadsheets (as on some calculators) are expressed as + - * and /

- The normal order of operators applies in most spreadsheets, i.e. in the following order: Brackets; Of; Division; Multiplication; Addition; Subtraction. (This order can easily be remembered using the mnemonic BODMAS.) Hence 1+2*3 equals 7 not 9.

- Brackets are used to force operations to be completed first so that, for example, (1+2)*3 does equal 9. When used appropriately, brackets can help to clarify formulae.

Exercise 1
Using the spreadsheet below what would be the result displayed in E1 if the cell contained the following formulae:
(a) =A1/B1*C1+D1   10
(b) =C1+D1*A1/B1   14
(c) =A1/B1*(C1+D1)   16
(d) =A1/(B1*C1)+D1   7

	A	B	C	D	E
1	10	5	2	6	

Constant values can also be used in formulae, e.g. =B2+100 but *variable* values should be placed in a cell. For example, if a formula is to work out the VAT of a product, then the VAT rate should be placed in a cell and the cell address should be used in the formula rather than value itself.

As a general rule, formulae should be kept as simple as possible. In fact, it is more useful to store intermediate results in separate cells rather than create very long complex formulae.

5.   Functions

Functions are "in-built" formulae.   There are over 200 functions in the major spreadsheet packages covering both common and complex mathematical, statistical and financial operations, although in reality an average user will only need to use a small sub-set of these. Functions have a *name* and usually an *argument* in brackets.

The most common function is the SUM function which adds up a row or column of numbers and replaces the need for a formula that uses a long string of cell addresses like =A1+A2+A3+A4+A5.

The argument of the SUM function like many functions is a *range* of cells, i.e a rectangular block of cells. A range is always specified by giving its beginning cell address and end cell address. Hence a range might be A1 to A5 or A1 to E1 or A1 to E5. Ranges can also be *non-contiguous* (i.e. non-adjacent), e.g. A1 to E1 and A3 to E3. It is possible and indeed very useful to give names to ranges as this makes it easier to refer to them. It is also possible to use one function in the argument of another function and this is known as a *nested function*.

It should be noted that although the same types of functions appear in all spreadsheet packages, function names may differ slightly. During the course of this chapter a number of functions will be described and examples of nested functions will be demonstrated.

6.   Setting up a worksheet

Having covered the fundamentals of spreadsheets it is now time to consider setting up a working spreadsheet for a particular task. This is often referred to as a *worksheet* and is a useful term that will be adopted here as it helps to differentiate between the spreadsheet program as a whole and a spreadsheet designed for a particular task.

Example 2
(a) A worksheet is to be set up to keep a record of shares held, and is to show the names of the company shares, the number held, the price paid (in pence) per share and the value of each share holding (in £), together with the total shareholding.

There are two basic steps to designing a worksheet:

- Arrange the values in well-defined rows and columns together with explanatory labels. (Note: normally, values of time are displayed horizontally.)
- Devise the formulae or functions for the calculations.

(b) The details of the shareholding are as follows: 250 Amstrad shares @ 35p; 75 Wimpey shares @ 186p; 125 Sirdar shares @ 101p and 250 Kleeneze shares @ 20p. Hence, column A is used to list the names of the company shares, column B to show the number of shares held and column C for the price per share:

	A	B	C
1	Name	Number	Price
2	Amstrad	250	35
3	Wimpey	75	186
4	Sirdar	125	101
5	Kleeneze	250	20
6	Total		

(c) Column D is then used to hold the value of each company shareholding, and formulae are entered in D2 to D5 to work out the value of each company's shares (in £), that is by instructing the spreadsheet to multiply the number of shares by the price and then divide by 100 to display the result in £ rather than pence, i.e for D2 this is **=(B2*C2)/100**

(c) The SUM function is then used in D6 to add together all the values from D2 to D5 to work out the total shareholding.

	A	B	C	D
1	Name	Number	Price	Value
2	Amstrad	250	35	=(B2*C2)/100
3	Wimpey	75	186	=(B3*C3)/100
4	Sirdar	125	101	=(B4*C4)/100
5	Kleeneze	250	20	=(B5*C5)/100
6	Total			=SUM(D2:D5)

Although the formulae are entered in the cells as shown above, on the screen the worksheet will be displayed as below:

	A	B	C	D
1	Name	Number	Price	Value
2	Amstrad	250	35	87.5
3	Wimpey	75	186	139.5
4	Sirdar	125	101	126.25
5	Kleeneze	250	20	50
6	Total			403.25

7.   Developing a worksheet

Once the initial data has been entered, much of the development work of a worksheet may seem repetitious. However, the spreadsheet user does not need to type the same data or formulae more than once but rather can *copy* (or *replicate*) these into further cells. This facility should be exploited to the full in order to cut down development time and to ensure that needless typing errors are not made. Data and formulae can be copied in the ways described below:

Copying data

If a piece of data (either a label or value) in a cell is to be repeated across a row or down a column, it only needs to be typed in once and then copied into the subsequent cells. Some spreadsheet software even has an "intelligent" facility which allows a *series* of data to be created in the same way: the user only needs to type in the first piece of data in the series, e.g. "January", and then copy it across the row to create the months of the year automatically.

Copying formulae

The same copying procedure can be used with formulae although it requires more care. In the worksheet developed in Example 2, the formulae in D2, D3, D4 and D5 were worked out individually. Although this was good practice on paper it is unnecessary work when using a spreadsheet program since it is possible to copy a formula from one cell into subsequent cells to generate formulae relative to the new cells. Hence it is only necessary to enter the formula in D2 and then copy it down to the other cells, D3, D4 and D5. The formula is adjusted automatically for each row.

When copying formulae, however, it is important to understand the difference between *relative*, *absolute* and *mixed* addressing. *Relative addressing* is, as described above, where cell addresses are automatically adjusted during the copying process to make them relative to the new rows or columns. *Absolute addressing*, on the other hand, is where certain cell addresses must not be adjusted during the copying process. In order to fix a cell address so that it is not adjusted, the $ sign is normally placed before each part of the cell address.

Example 3
If the same number of shares were held for each company, e.g. 250, then the worksheet might have been set up to look like the one below, with the number of shares held in B2. The formula in D2 now needs to be **($B$2*C2)/100** so that when it is copied down to D3, D4 and D5 reference is always made to cell B2 for the number of shares.

	A	B	C	D
1	Name	Number	Price	Value
2	Amstrad	250	35	=($B$2*C2)/100
3	Wimpey		186	=($B$2*C3)/100
4	Sirdar		101	=($B$2*C4)/100
5	Kleeneze		20	=($B$2*C5)/100
6	Total			=SUM(D2:D5)

Mixed addressing, as its name suggests, is a mixture of both relative and absolute addressing. This might be used, for example, when a column address is absolute but a row is relative, in which case the $ would only appear before the column letter, e.g. $B2, or where a row address is absolute and a column address is relative, e.g. B$2.

8.   Improving the presentation of a worksheet

Having entered the data and formulae into the worksheet the user will need to improve its presentation to aid understanding of the data.

Numeric values should be presented in the most appropriate way and there are a number of ways of formatting numeric values. For example, the value 1001.253 could be formatted to be displayed as an *integer* (i.e. to the nearest whole number), e.g 1001 or 1,001; or with a *specified number of decimal places*, e.g. 1001.2; or as *currency*, e.g. £1,001.25; or as a *percentage*, e.g. 1001%.

It should be noted, however, that when formatting a value, the original value is still retained in the cell and it is this value that is used in future calculations. This can sometimes cause anomalies in the results, and one way of addressing this problem is described later in **12**.

All *column* or *row headings* should be clear and show any units of measurement where appropriate. Column headings, in particular should be attractively and suitably aligned over data, i.e. formatted to appear left, right or centred. Some software packages permit more than one line of text to appear in a cell, and others the use of vertical labels.

All *columns* should be *wide* enough to hold the labels and values in the cells of the column. Some software has a "best fit" facility which can adjust the column width to exactly the right size.

There should be a relevant *heading* to the worksheet, which summarises the contents of the worksheet and all important data (e.g. totals) should be *emphasised* or *separated* from the rest of the data.

With spreadsheet programs further improvements to the presentation of the worksheet can be made through the print facility, e.g.:

- The column and row *borders* (i.e. the A, B, Cs and 1, 2, 3s) can be removed, although in most cases this is done by default.

- *Headers* and *footers* can be used. These are one or more lines of information that appear at the top or bottom of each page and can include the page number and the date (both of which can be extracted from the system). This feature is obviously most useful when setting up a worksheet that is printed on more than one page. However, some spreadsheet programs automatically set up a header using the file name and the page number, and it may be more appropriate to remove this and have no header or footer on a one-page worksheet.

- *Page set up* features can be altered, e.g. the size of the margins or the page length can be specified to suit the layout of the worksheet.

Example 4

The worksheet in Example 2 has been improved in the following ways:

(a) A worksheet heading appears in A1 and column headings are shown in A3/A4, B3/B4, C3/C4 and D3/ D4.

(b) The headings in columns B, C and D have been right-aligned to match the alignment of the values in the columns

(c) The values in column D have been formatted to show two decimal places.

(d) Lines have been added (in rows 2, 5, 10 and 12) to separate the data.

(Although the borders have been retained here for ease of reference, when the worksheet is printed they would be removed.)

	A	B	C	D
1	Share portfolio			
2	--------------------	----------	--------------	--------------
3	Name	Number	Price	Value
4	of company	held	in p	in £
5	--------------------	----------	--------------	--------------
6	Amstrad	250	35	87.50
7	Wimpey	75	186	139.50
8	Sirdar	125	101	126.25
9	Kleeneze	250	20	50.00
10	------------------	----------	--------------	--------------
11	Total			403.25
12	------------------	----------	--------------	--------------

9. Further presentation features

If a worksheet is only to be used by the original designer, the basic presentation features described in **8** above are quite adequate. However, if it is to be presented to others, e.g. as an on-screen file for management use or to be included in a report, then it is essential that the worksheet is presented as effectively and attractively as possible.

Although there are further ways in which the presentation of a worksheet can be improved these are mainly supported by Windows-based spreadsheet packages.

The *typeface*, *size* and *style* can be changed, perhaps to match an accompanying document. The guidance provided in the section on *Typeface* in **2:7** is therefore relevant here and should be consulted. (It should be noted, however, that making changes to the typeface may mean that column widths and row heights will need to be adjusted.)

Zero values can be "blanked" if they are considered distracting and the *gridlines* (i.e. the lines marking the cells) can be removed if it is felt this aids the presentation of the data.

Boxes or *lines* (of different thickness) can be drawn around cells to highlight data. In fact, in most Windows-based software these boxes and lines are much more effective than the lines created within cells.

Cells can be *shaded* using different shading patterns to emphasise specific pieces of data. The level of shading is usually defined as a percentage of grey shading, i.e. from 5% to 90%: 10-20% is an acceptable level of shading that still allows the data in the cells to be readable.

Colour can be used in worksheets for on-screen display and indeed a small amount of colour can be very effective, although too many bright colours should be avoided. If the worksheet is to be printed, then, of course, colour can only be used if the printer can support it.

It should be noted, however, that as with the design of any written document, too many different enhancements should not be included in one worksheet, otherwise they will compete with one another for attention and the result will be confusion. Previewing the worksheet using the *print preview* facility is a valuable way of checking its presentation before it is printed.

Example 5

The worksheet in Example 4 has been further improved:

(a) The Times Roman font has been used throughout although the size varies: the heading is in 14 point, the column headings and total are in 12 point and the data itself is in 10 point.

(b) Bold and italic fonts have been used for emphasis.

(c) The gridlines have been removed, and the separating lines have been replaced by boxes to highlight the data.

(d) The cells in the total row have been shaded.

Share Portfolio

Name of company	Number held	Price in p	Value in £
Amstrad	250	35	87.50
Wimpey	75	186	139.50
Sirdar	125	101	126.25
Kleeneze	250	20	50.00
Total			**£403.25**

Some software offers a set of presentation *styles* for the designer to select. This obviates the need for formatting of columns, rows or cells on an individual basis and may be useful for a new user. However, undoubtedly more experienced users will wish to fine-tune the presentation of the worksheet to their own requirements.

10. Extending a worksheet

Once a basic worksheet has been set up it is very easy to extend it to carry out further analysis work. This might mean *inserting, deleting, replacing, copying* or *moving* data in cells, rows and columns. It should be noted that if this is done, then all the formulae in the worksheet are adjusted accordingly.

Extending the analysis of data using an electronic spreadsheet is far easier than on paper since this would otherwise mean re-designing the layout and re-calculating the formulae.

Example 6
The worksheet in Example 5 is to be extended to show the number of shares held today, today's share price and the value of today's share holding, together with an indication of the increase/decrease in the value of the shareholding.
(a) All the data from B2 to D8 can be copied into cell E2 to G8, i.e. the shaded area of the worksheet below.
(b) Formulae can then be added in column H to work out the increase or decrease in the value of the shareholding.

	A	B	C	D	E	F	G	H
1	Share Portfolio				Today			
2	Name	Number	Price	Value	Number	Price	Value	Increase or
3	of company	held	in p	in £	held	in p	in £	decrease
4	Amstrad	250	35	=(B4*C4)/100	250	35	=(E4*F4)/100	=G4-D4
5	Wimpey	75	186	=(B5*C5)/100	75	186	=(E5*F5)/100	=G5-D5
6	Sirdar	125	101	=(B6*C6)/100	125	101	=(E6*F6)/100	=G6-D6
7	Kleeneze	250	20	=(B7*C7)/100	250	20	=(E7*F7)/100	=G7-D7
8	Total			=SUM(D4:D7)			=SUM(G4:G7)	=G8-D8

(c) The current prices of the shares can then be overtyped in column F so that the worksheet now looks as below.

Share Portfolio				Today			
Name	*Number*	*Price*	*Value*	*Number*	*Price*	*Value*	*Increase or*
of company	*held*	*in p*	*in £*	*held*	*in p*	*in £*	*decrease*
Amstrad	250	35	87.50	250	37	92.50	5.00
Wimpey	75	186	139.50	75	176	132.00	-7.50
Sirdar	125	101	126.25	125	120	150.00	23.75
Kleeneze	250	20	50.00	250	25	62.50	12.50
Total			£403.25			£437.00	£33.75

Exercise 2

The data below (taken from the August 1994 edition of the CSO's *Monthly Digest of Statistics*) shows the number of employees in employment (in thousands) during the last quarter of 1992 and the last quarter of 1993:

> 1992 Q4: Agriculture 244; Production 4,653; Construction 849; Service Industries 15,264; and Total 21,010
>
> 1993 Q4: Agriculture 239; Production 4,583; Construction 781; Service Industries 15,422; and Total 21,024

(a) Design, on paper, a worksheet to calculate the percentage increase or decrease in each industry over the year. Show the labels, values and formulae for the calculations but do not work out the mathematics.

(b) What improvements could be made to the presentation of this worksheet if it is to be included in a report on employment patterns.

(c) How could the worksheet be extended to include and to analyse the figures for the last quarter of 1994?

11. Numerical data modelling

As has been demonstrated above spreadsheets can be used to work out solutions to a variety of ad hoc problems. However, they can also help to analyse a particular problem or situation, by allowing the user to represent it as a series of figures and then try out different solutions in order to make decisions. This is known as *numeric data modelling*.

A *model* is a description of an object or a particular situation or state of affairs. It can be physical, e.g. a model boat or airplane; textual, e.g. a narrative account of a situation; graphical, e.g. a map or chart; or numeric as a table of figures in a spreadsheet.

A spreadsheet can be used to build both *static* and *dynamic* models. A *static* model is one that does not include time as a variable, i.e. it describes a particular state of affairs at one particular position in time, e.g. the balance sheet below shows liabilities and assets on 31 March 1995.

XYZ Co Ltd				
Balance Sheet as at 31/3/95				
Liabilities	*£*	*Assets*		*£*
Capital	30,000	Shop		17,000
Bank loan	8,000	Shop fittings		9,500
Creditors	3,500	Van		4,500
		Stock		5,700
		Debtors		2,300
		Cash		2,500
	£41,500			**£41,500**

A *dynamic* model, on the other hand, represents behaviour over time and therefore describes a changing situation. Dynamic business models of this type include sales forecasts or cash flow statements (like the one below).

XYZ Co Ltd						
Cash flow: Jan-June 1994	*Jan*	*Feb*	*Mar*	*Apr*	*May*	*June*
	£	£	£	£	£	£
Cash in bank	300	400	550	750	1,000	1,300
INCOME						
Sales	750	800	850	900	950	1,000
Total income	1,050	1,200	1,400	1,650	1,950	2,300
OUTGOINGS						
Labour	250	250	250	250	250	250
Rent	350	350	350	350	350	350
Materials	50	50	50	50	50	50
Total outgoings	650	650	650	650	650	650
Cash to bank	400	550	750	1,000	1,300	1,650

When a particular problem or situation is to be modelled designers have to think very carefully and logically about it in order to reduce it to a table of figures. However, there is a drawback in that once designers begin to work solely with figures it is very easy for them to lose any intuition they might have which would be of value in solving the problem.

Designing a model

There are a number of basic principles and techniques in data modelling. Firstly, the problem should be fully understood before work is begun on the design of the model. If work is started too quickly, early attempts will probably have to be abandoned as the problem becomes clearer. However, it should be said that some re-design work is probably inevitable with complex modelling.

The problem should then be tacked logically, step-by-step. With some models it may be a good idea to set up a paper model first to work out the logic of the model before setting it up on a PC. The data, both *given* and to be *calculated*, should then be identified and appropriate labels used. However, in order to think about the logic of the model, actual numeric values should not be used at this stage.

The formulae for the data to be calculated should then be devised. If they are very complex they should be broken down into smaller formulae to hold intermediate results. The model at this stage, if set up on a PC, will now only display a series of zero values due to the results of formulae with no data in the model.

In order to illustrate the design of a model a problem situation is described and a simple model designed.

Example 7

(a) Seaside Gift Shops Ltd own a group of four shops in Hastings, Brighton, Eastbourne and Bournemouth which are trading well and producing a clear profit each month. The company would like to open a new shop in Folkestone (initial start-up cost £25,000). If the existing shops maintain a steady 5% increase in profit each month when will the company be able to afford to open the new shop? A paper-based worksheet could be set up as below, which indicates both the logic of the model and how the formulae should be copied across the rows and down the columns.

	A	B	C	D	E	F	G	H
1	Seaside Gift Shops							
2								
3	Shops	Jan	Feb	Mar	Apr	May	Jun	Jul
4								
5	Hastings		=B5*1.05	→	→	→	→	→
6	Brighton		↓	→	→	→	→	→
7	Eastbourne		↓	→	→	→	→	→
8	Bournemouth		↓	→	→	→	→	→
9								
10	Profit at end of month	=SUM(B5:B8)	→	→	→	→	→	→
11	Cumulative profit	=B10	=C10+B11	→	→	→	→	→

Testing the model

Once the model has been designed it needs to be thoroughly tested to check for errors in the logic before it is used with real data. This is an essential stage in data modelling especially if the model is to be used for critical decision-making purposes since it must be based on accurate logic. Testing can take place in a number of ways:

- A printout of the formulae can be produced to allow the designer to examine each formula one by one;
- Dummy data like 10, 100 or 1000 can be entered into the worksheet to test the results of formulae: complex or real data should not be used at this stage as it will be very difficult, if not impossible, to see if the model is working properly;
- Someone other than the designer could work through the model to check it, as it is not easy to spot one's own errors.

Using the model

Once the model has been tested, real data can be used so that the model can be used to help make decisions or to plan for the future. The presentation of the model may then need to be improved in order to highlight the significant features arising from the results.

(b) Once the profit for the four shops for January is entered into the worksheet it can be seen that Seaside Gift Shops Ltd would be able to afford to open their new shop in June. G11 is therefore shaded to highlight this fact.

	A	B	C	D	E	F	G	H
1	**Seaside Gift Shops**							
2								
3	Shops	Jan	Feb	Mar	Apr	May	Jun	Jul
4								
5	*Hastings*	1,550	1,628	1,709	1,794	1,884	1,978	2,077
6	*Brighton*	850	893	937	984	1,033	1,085	1,139
7	*Eastbourne*	1,050	1,103	1,158	1,216	1,277	1,340	1,407
8	*Bournemouth*	900	945	992	1,042	1,094	1,149	1,206
9								
10	Profit at end of month	4,350	4,568	4,796	5,036	5,287	5,552	5,829
11	**Cumulative profit**	**4,350**	**8,918**	**13,713**	**18,749**	**24,036**	**29,588**	**35,418**

What-if analysis

In order to come to a final decision, however, the user might wish to interrogate the model in order to build alternative scenarios. This is known as *what-if analysis* and means that the user can ask the model to show the effects of *x* or *y*. If paper-based tools were used, this would involve a considerable amount of erasing of data and recalculation of formulae. With spreadsheets, however, only small changes need to be made to the data or the formulae and the spreadsheet automatically carries out the recalculation.

(c) Would the company be able to afford to open the new shop any sooner if the Hastings shop were able to sustain a 10% increase in profits from February? An answer to this what-if requires the formula in C5 to be changed to =B5*1.1 and this copied across the row. The model, below, shows that although this would increase the cumulative profit, in fact it makes no difference to the month in which the business could afford to open the new shop.

	A	B	C	D	E	F	G	H
1	**Seaside Gift Shops**							
2								
3	Shops	Jan	Feb	Mar	Apr	May	Jun	Jul
4								
5	*Hastings*	1,550	1,705	1,876	2,063	2,269	2,496	2,746
6	*Brighton*	850	893	937	984	1,033	1,085	1,139
7	*Eastbourne*	1,050	1,103	1,158	1,216	1,276	1,340	1,407
8	*Bournemouth*	900	945	992	1,042	1,094	1,149	1,206
9								
10	Profit at end of month	4,350	4,645	4,963	5,304	5,673	6,070	6,498
11	**Cumulative profit**	**4,350**	**8,995**	**13,958**	**19,262**	**24,935**	**31,005**	**37,503**

Sophisticated spreadsheet software programs further support numeric data modelling and what-if analysis by the use of *what-if tables* and the provision of sample models, e.g. for break-even analysis or budgeting. They also allow different values to be saved as *scenarios* to try out different effects.

Additionally, some software is also able to support *goal-seeking analysis*, where the goal or target to be achieved is specified and the spreadsheet program itself continuously adjusts the values in specified cells until the goal is met. Goal-seeking analysis can be controlled by time (e.g. number of seconds) or by precision and once again, sample models are often available, e.g. to find the most profitable product mix or for optimum staff scheduling.

Spreadsheets are therefore an extremely useful tool to support management decision-making and planning. However, it must be realised that it is not the spreadsheet software itself that makes the decision but spreadsheet users who make effective use of the software to design models to help them come to a decision. If used incorrectly or inappropriately, a user could quite easily produce results which could lead to some very wrong decisions.

Exercise 3

(a) You have just set up a small company to produce a new executive toy and want to model the activities of the business over the next year in order to work out projected income.

You have already calculated the manufacturing cost per unit, and estimated the number of sales for the first quarter and that a 10% increase in sales from the second quarter onwards is likely. You also intend to sell the product at a mark-up of 20%. From these figures you therefore intend to calculate estimated total sales (in £) per month as well as total costs (in £) of sales and hence find the gross profit per month. However, in addition you would like to calculate over the whole year total units sold, total sales, total costs and total profit.

Using the worksheet below, fill in the necessary formulae and indicate what copying should take place.

	A	B	C	D	E	F
1	**EXECUTOYS: PROJECTED INCOME**					
2						
3	*Cost per unit:*			*Selling price per unit:*		
4						
5		**Qtr 1**	**Qtr 2**	**Qtr 3**	**Qtr 4**	**Total**
6	Units sold					
7						
8	Total sales					
9	Total costs					
10	**PROFIT**					

(b) What changes would you need to make to the worksheet to answer the following "what-if's.?
- what if the cost per unit is decreased or increased?
- what if sales increase by 20% from the second quarter?
- what if the selling price per unit is marked up by 30%?

12. Further spreadsheet functions

The models designed in Example 7 and Exercise 3 have only used very basic formulae, yet they are very functional. Hence it is not the complexity of the formulae and functions that is of importance but the essential skill of developing a model by converting a situation into a table of figures. However, there are a number of further functions that might be of use when designing models and these are described below:

Rounding function

The ROUND function is an important function as it can be used to address the problems of arithmetic errors which often occur when numerical data is formatted. These types of errors should be avoided else the integrity of the worksheet will be in doubt. The argument of the function is the value or cell address to be rounded and the number of decimal places to be used, i.e. **=ROUND(value,number of decimal places)**

Example 8
The following worksheet demonstrates the problem (in rows 1 and 2) and the solution (in row 3) by showing how the values in column C would appear if they were the result of multiplying the values in columns A and B.

	A	B	C	Notes
1	1001.253	4	4005.012	unformatted display in A1
2	1001	4	4005	A2 and C2 formatted to display integers
3	1001	4	4004	=ROUND(1001.253,0) function used in A3

Logical functions

The most useful logical function is the IF function. This tests a condition and carries out one action if the test is true and another if the test is false. The argument of the function is in three parts: the test; the action to be taken if true; and the action to be taken if false, i.e. **=IF(test,action if true,action if false)** The test itself requires the use of one of the following operators:

= equal to	< less than	> greater than
<> not equal to	<= less than or equal to	>= greater than or equal to

---

Example 9
(a) In the worksheet below, the IF function is used (in B1) to test whether the value in A1 is 0: if it is true, a zero value is placed in B1; if it is false, the value in A1 is multiplied by 5.

	A	B
1		=IF(A1=0,0,A1*5)

(b) The two worksheets below demonstrate how the data would be displayed.

	A	B
1	0	0

	A	B
1	5	25

(c) Alternatively, the IF function in B1 could be used to print a message, e.g. "No data entered" if the value in A1 is 0. The worksheets below show, firstly the function, and secondly how the data would be displayed.

	A	B
1		=IF(A1=0,"No data entered",A1*5)

	A	B
1	0	No data entered

If the IF function needs to carry out two or more tests, this may be possible either through the use of a nested IF function or by use of the logical functions AND, OR and NOT. The arguments of these functions are one or more tests, e.g. **=AND(test1,test2)** and **=NOT(test)**. The AND function returns the value true if *all* the tests are true, the OR function returns the value true if *one* of the tests is true, and the NOT function returns true if the test is false and false if the test is true.

Example 10
The IF function might be used in a number of ways to test whether a value in a cell falls within a particular range, e.g. between 5 and 10.
(a) This example shows how the logical expression AND might be used to test the value in A1 and to multiply the value by 5 if it falls within the range. If it fails the test it prints the message "Data out of range".

	A	B
1		=IF(AND(A1>=5,A1<=10), A1*5,"Data out of range")

(b) This example shows how a nested-IF function might be used to test firstly whether the value in A1 is less than 5, and if it is true prints the message "Data too low", if it is false it then tests the value to see if it is more than 10. If this is true it prints the message "Data too high", otherwise it multiplies the value by 5.

	A	B
1	4	=IF(A1<5, "Data too low",IF(A1>10,"Data too high",A1*5))

Date and time functions

Dates and times can often be entered into cells in the format in which they are to be displayed, although some software requires them to be entered using the DATE and TIME functions, i.e. **=DATE(year,month,day)** and **=TIME(hours,minutes,seconds)** The current date and time can be extracted from the system using special functions, e.g. **=TODAY( )** and **=NOW( )** and is updated each time the worksheet is retrieved.

Dates are stored in the spreadsheet as numeric values (usually the number of days since 1 January 1900) and these values can be used in calculations. Hence elapsed time can be worked out for time sheets or invoice dates, e.g. **=TODAY( )+30**

Lookup functions

Lookup functions allow a data item to be looked up in a table of data held elsewhere in the worksheet in order to retrieve a further data item from the table. A lookup table is a particularly useful way of holding data together that needs to be frequently updated.

There are two main types of lookup function: the horizontal lookup function HLOOKUP which looks up data held in columns and the vertical lookup function VLOOKUP which looks up data held in rows. The argument of both of these functions is the data to be looked up - a value or a cell address, the range of cells where the lookup table is kept, the column in which the data to be retrieved is kept, e.g. **=VLOOKUP(data, range,column)**

Example 11
A lookup function might be used to search a lookup table (in A11:C13) for a customer number entered in B1 in order to return their name and address in B2 and B3.

	A	B	C
1	Customer No:		
2	Customer Name:	=VLOOKUP(B1,A11:C13,1)	
3	Customer Address:	=VLOOKUP(B1,A11:C13,2)	
4..9			
10	Customer No	Customer Name	Customer Address
11	101	Mr John Adams	25 High Street
12	102	Mrs Alison Brown	34 King Road
13	103	Miss Mary Grey	56 Station Road

Hence, if the Customer No: 101 is entered into B1, the worksheet would show:

	A	B
1	Customer No:	101
2	Customer Name:	Mr John Adams
3	Customer Address:	25 High Street

13. Worksheet protection

If worksheets are to be used by users other than the designer of the worksheet, it is important that data and formulae held within them are protected as they may be inadvertently corrupted or erased. There are usually a number of ways of doing this and the most appropriate type of protection should be applied to a worksheet when required.

- *Hiding data*: columns of data can be hidden so that the cells are not displayed;
- *Cell protection* or *cell locking*: the contents of cells, although displayed, cannot be edited;
- *Password protected*: the file itself can only be opened with the relevant password. This is a powerful feature and with some software if the password is lost or forgotten the file cannot be re-opened.
- *Write-reserved* or *read-only file*: the file itself can only be read and not written to.

14. Templates

If a worksheet is to be used on more than one occasion then productivity can be increased by the creation of *templates*. This term is used to refer to a "pattern" for a particular style of worksheet, i.e. a re-usable worksheet which has built-in labels and formulae developed for specific applications.

These worksheets do not usually contain any data, it is the user, who may not necessarily be the model designer, who enters the data when required. Although pre-designed templates are often available in the software for a variety of different applications, it is a simple process for users to build their own.

Templates can be designed for many different applications, e.g. for on-line use or to produce a printed output. An example of a template is shown below. It is very functional and demonstrates a simple solution to a very common business task. It also makes use of features described in **12** and **13** above.

Example 12

Seaside Gift Shops Ltd wants to set up a worksheet to be used as an invoice template for items purchased by mail order. The invoice is to contain the following information: name and address of the shop; today's date; invoice number; item code number and name; unit price; quantity purchased; the total price for each item and the total price for all items; together with post and packaging (5% at current time with a minimum charge of £2.00); and space for purchase of 4 different items. The invoice is to look as below:

Seaside Gift Shops Ltd
123 Sea Road
HASTINGS

MAIL ORDER INVOICE

Invoice No: Date:

Item code	Item name	Price	Qty	Total price

	Total ex P&P	
5%	**P&P (min £2)**	
	Total due	

The following worksheet shows how this template could be set up. Note especially:

(a) the use of the TODAY() function (in E7) to extract the invoice date from the system (formatted to show dd-mm-yy);

(b) the nested-IF function (i.e. the use of one IF function inside another) in E15: this particular function translates as: if there is no value in E14 (the total price of the items), return 0, else if 5% of the value in E14 is less than £2 then return £2 (the minimum charge), else return 5% of the total price;

(c) to ensure that the worksheet does not display zero values (i.e. the results of formulae with no values entered) it has been formatted to "blank" zero display;

(d) the cells that are shaded in the worksheet below are those that have been protected. The user only needs to enter the Invoice No, and the item codes and quantities;

(e) the item names and prices are retrieved from a look-up table (shown partly in cells A20:A24) so that prices, in particular, can be easily updated.

	A	B	C	D	E
1	Seaside Gift Shops Ltd				
2	123 Sea Road				
3	HASTINGS				
4					
5	MAIL ORDER INVOICE				
6					
7	Invoice No:			Date:	=TODAY()
8					
9	Item code	Item name	Price	Qty	Total price
10		VLOOKUP(A10, A20:A24, 1)	VLOOKUP (A10,A20: A24,2)		=C10*D10
11		VLOOKUP(A11, A20:A24,1)	VLOOKUP (A11,A20: A24,2)		=C11*D11
12		VLOOKUP(A12, A20,A24,1)	VLOOKUP (A12,A20: A24,2)		=C12*D12
13		VLOOKUP(A13, A20:A24,1)	VLOOKUP (A13,A20: A24,2)		=C13*D13
14			Total ex P&P		=SUM(E10:E13)
15		5%	P&P (min £2)		=IF(E14=0,0,IF(B15*E14<2,2, B15*E14))
16			Total due		=E14+E15
17					
18	Lookup table				
19	Item code	Item name	Price		
20	H1001	Hastings rock	0.99		
21	H1002	Hastings keyring	1.99		
22	H1003	Hastings pencil	0.59		
23	H1004	Basket of shells	2.99		
24	H1005	Shell necklace	5.99		

A completed invoice might look as below:

Seaside Gift Shops Ltd
123 Sea Road
HASTINGS

MAIL ORDER INVOICE

Invoice No: 29345   Date: 31-Mar-1995

Item code	Item name	Price	Qty	Total price
H1001	Hastings rock	0.99	6	5.94
H1003	Hastings pencil	0.59	12	7.08
		Total ex P&P		£13.02
	5%	P&P (min £2)		£2.00
		Total due		**£15.02**

Exercise 4

(a) You have been asked to set up a template to be used as a Petty Cash book. This is to keep a record of the date each item is purchased and any monies placed in the Petty Cash box.

The first item will show the figure brought forward from the previous week and the last item the balance to be carried forward to the next week. It should also calculate the total amount spent, the total amount placed in the Petty Cash box and a running balance.

Using the worksheet below, fill in the relevant formulae so it will work effectively:

	A	C	D	E
1	**PETTY CASH BOOK**			
2	-------------- --	------------	---------------	--------------
3	*Date* *Item*	*Out*	*In*	*Balance*
4	-------------- --	------------	---------------	--------------
5	Balance b/f			
6				
7				
8				
9				
10				
11				
12	Balance c/f			
13	-------------- --	------------	---------------	--------------
14	**Total**			
15	-------------- --	------------	---------------	--------------

15. Further spreadsheet features

When developing worksheets there are a number of other useful spreadsheet features:

- *Spell checker*: Some software provides an on-line spell checker to check for spelling errors: it is just as important to ensure that spelling is correct in a spreadsheet as it is in a word processed document, so the section on *Spelling* in **2.6** is relevant reading.

- *Outliner*: This is similar to an outliner in word processing software as it can help to create the structure of a worksheet.

- *Text boxes* and *arrows*: Text boxes can often be used to display comments on the data with attached arrows and these are often available from a range of *drawing tools*.

- *Charts and graphs*: Most spreadsheet packages provide charting and graphing facilities to convert numeric data into a visual form as this is sometimes a more effective way of presenting results. However, as this aspect deserves attention in its own right it is fully discussed in Chapter 4.

- *Database* facilities: Spreadsheet software packages usually provide basic database facilities, which makes them useful for maintaining lists of data. This has been briefly demonstrated in the lookup tables shown in **12**. Tables set up in a worksheet can usually be *sorted* and *queried* and there are usually a range of *database statistical* functions to support this. For a fuller discussion of database software, however, see Chapter 5.

16. Large worksheets

If a worksheet takes up more space than fits on one screen, the screen display can be *split*, either horizontally or vertically so that two or more parts of the worksheet can be viewed in different *windows*. If necessary the screens can be synchronised so that moving up and down or to the right or left occurs in both of the screens. Similarly row and column headings can be *locked* (or *frozen*) so that they remain in place as the user moves about the worksheet.

If the worksheet is exceptionally large then the user may find the spreadsheet software becomes very slow. This is because the spreadsheet automatically re-calculates every cell any time the work is edited. Hence it is useful to select *manual* calculation whilst work is being carried out on a large worksheet. Re-calculation can then take place at the end.

Depending on the sophistication of the spreadsheet program, large or wide spreadsheets can be printed in a number of ways. DOS-based spreadsheets normally permit the worksheet to be printed using compressed text or "sideways". Windows-based software packages, however, can normally print the worksheet on A4 *landscape* rather than *portrait* and can often scale the worksheet to fit on a specified number of pages.

17. Multiple worksheets

Rather than create one large worksheet it may be more appropriate to create a number of smaller worksheets which are linked together. It may also be necessary to consolidate data from a number of worksheets created, perhaps, by a number of different users.

Multiple worksheets can usually be viewed on the screen at one time. It is then very easy to copy data from one worksheet into another. In many spreadsheet programs the data that is copied can be linked dynamically so that if any changes are made to the original worksheet the data in the second worksheet is automatically updated.

> **Example 13**
> A worksheet has been set up to work out staff expenses over the year. The totals that are created at the end of each month automatically appear in the worksheet that calculates total expenses as they have been dynamically linked.

Staff expenses			
	Jan	Feb	Mar
A	101	95	109
B	32	45	39
C	65	48	56
D	96	89	88
E	23	43	41
Total	317	320	333

Total expenses			
	Jan	Feb	Mar
Staff	317	320	333
Other	5,468	4,356	4,978
Total	5,785	4,676	5,311

If, however, a number of worksheets are being created that look identical and use the same formulae, then creating each one individually can be time consuming. A multi-page worksheet is therefore more appropriate as it allows a number of identical pages to be set up, and it is also much easier to perform calculations across all the pages. These type of worksheets are also known as *3-D worksheets* as they create an extra dimension: 2-D worksheets show rows and columns but 3-D worksheets add pages.

18. Macros

A macro is a series of recorded instructions which can be set up to automate routine tasks. At the simplest level, macros might be set up to format a value in a cell in a particular way. More complex macros can be written, for instance to place a message on the screen to prompt the user for a value or to build menus, and they can also be used to create applications in order to customise spreadsheet use.

Each spreadsheet program has its own macro language and some come with special "de-bugging" tools that allow the macro writer to work through a macro to find errors. In many software packages this macro language is just one step away from a full-blown programming development language which can be used to design application interfaces and to support integration of applications.

19. Multimedia worksheets

Some spreadsheet programs allow multimedia notes, e.g. sound files to be embedded in worksheets. Some packages even come with animated tutorials, audio commentaries and other sound effects as well as proof-readers that read back the contents of a worksheet.

20. Specialist use of spreadsheet software

It is not within the scope of this book to consider the use of spreadsheets for specialist analysis, e.g. complex financial, statistical and mathematical use. Although these are fully supported by sophisticated spreadsheet software programs they should only be undertaken if the analytical formulae and processes are fully understood by the user. If they are used incorrectly or inappropriately especially in critical worksheets the consequences could be far-reaching. Therefore this section only describes some basic and useful functions in each category.

Mathematical use of a spreadsheet might involve solving:

- algebraic problems;
- trigonometric problems;
- calculus problems.

However, some basic mathematical functions include:

INT(x)	returns the integer part of x
SQRT(x)	returns the square root of x
ABS(x)	returns the absolute value of x
EXP(x)	returns exponential e to the power of x
COS(x)	returns cosine of angle x
SIN(x)	returns sine of angle x
TAN(x)	returns tangent of angle x
PI	returns value of Π

Statistical use of a spreadsheet might include:

- calculating measures of central tendency and dispersion;
- analysis involving correlation, covariance and regression: in fact some spreadsheeet software packages provide special analysis tools for such complex statistical analysis.

Some useful basic statistical functions include:

RAND( )	displays a random number between 0 and 1
RAND( )*x	displays a random number between 0 and x
COUNT(range)	counts number of cells holding numeric values in the range
MEDIAN(range)	finds the median (the middle item) in a range
MODE(range)	finds the mode (the most frequently occurring item) in a range
VAR(range)	finds the variance of values in a range
STDEV(range)	finds the standard deviation of values in a range

Financial use of a spreadsheet (in addition to those areas already mentioned in this chapter) might include:

- the production of main accounting documents, i.e. balance sheets, profit and loss account and trial balances;
- use of a number of financial functions to calculate loans, annuities, cash flow and depreciation rates, of which the following are the most useful.

PMT(present value,interest rate,period)	calculates loan payments
PV(payment,interest rate,period)	calculates present value of a series of equal payments
FV(payment,interest rate,period)	calculates future value of a series of equal payments
IRR(guess,range)	calculates the internal rate of return of a series of cash flows
NPV(interest rate,range)	calculates net present value of a series of cash flows
SLN(cost,salvage,life)	calculates straight line depreciation

21. Further work with spreadsheet software

During the course of this chapter it has been demonstrated that spreadsheets are a very powerful business tool. They can be used to answer ad hoc problems, to model financial situations and can assist in managerial decision-making. They can also be used to create re-usable applications that rely largely on numerical analysis.

Each user will want to use a spreadsheet program for a particular reason, therefore it will be up to each individual user to develop their skill and experience in using the most appropriate features and functions of the software for their specific requirements

4

Business graphics

1. Introduction

When information tasks involve the presentation of numerical data, it may be more appropriate to do this through graphical rather than numerical means, that is by turning financial and statistical data into graphs or charts for presentation in documents or to be shown as overheads or slides.

Presenting information in graphical form has a number of advantages. In general terms graphics of all types (not just charts and graphs) can reduce the *information load* for the reader, and can provide more information in far less space. Hence the well-quoted phrase - "a picture is worth a thousand words" - is very relevant here.

Graphical information of this kind can also help to reinforce the meaning of words and makes it easier for the reader to understand the relationship between sets of figures. It is also a more appropriate way of presenting data to non-numerate people and it is also said to be easier to absorb and retain information if it is presented graphically.

Although charts are a less accurate way of presenting data than the figures themselves, this does not detract from the significant visual impact that charts and graphs have on the reader. However, there should not be too many in a document or presentation as this can overwhelm.

2. Graphing and charting software

In the past graphs and charts had to be constructed by hand, which was a laborious process and often required mathematical calculations. Nowadays, there are a number of software tools available. Spreadsheet software packages (see Chapter 3) normally have graphing facilities that can convert numeric data that has been entered into the worksheet into charts or graphs, as do integrated software packages. There are also a number of dedicated statistical graphics packages which support graphing, and most presentation graphics software packages include charting facilities (see Chapter 5).

One major problem for the user of graphing and charting software, however, is the large variety of types of graphs available for selection. To the inexperienced user the subtle differences between the different types of chart may mean nothing, and for this reason it is all too easy to select the wrong type of chart for the data just because it looks visually attractive or interesting and not because it is the most appropriate type of chart to convey the message. It should be noted that if a chart is badly created it can be more confusing than a table of figures, and it is essential, therefore, to choose the most suitable type of chart for the relationship which is being presented.

The following sections of this chapter look at how to select the appropriate type of chart (3-7) and provide general guidance on designing charts and graphs using the software together with the refinements that can be made to enhance their usability (8-11).

3.   Selecting the appropriate type of chart

There are a wide variety of charts available, the most common being *line, bar, pie* and *area* charts. Although these names are very familiar and most readers probably know what they look like and even how they should be constructed, what is not so well understood is which type of chart should be selected to convey a particular message. Sections **4-9** analyse these major types of chart in order to provide guidance in this respect.

4.   Line graphs

Line graphs display changes over time. Time is plotted along the horizontal (or x) axis, and the values that change with time are plotted along the vertical (or y) axis. Points on the chart are connected with a straight or a curved line, and hence it is easy to spot trends. The main characteristic of a line graph, then, is that it emphasises the rate of change over time.

Example 1
This line graph shows the trend in the unit sales of one product. Here the time line shows 1990-1994, and is marked in yearly intervals. The values that change over time, i.e. the number of unit sales, are plotted along the y axis. The points on the graph are connected by straight lines.

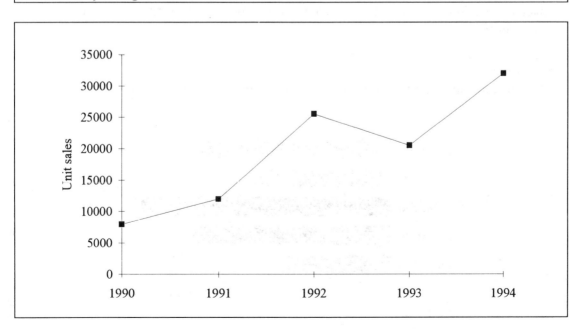

Multi-line graphs show trends for a number of related sets of figures so that comparisons can be made between them. However, they are not appropriate for more than about three sets of data, especially if the lines cross.

Example 2
This line graph shows the trend in unit sales of three products.

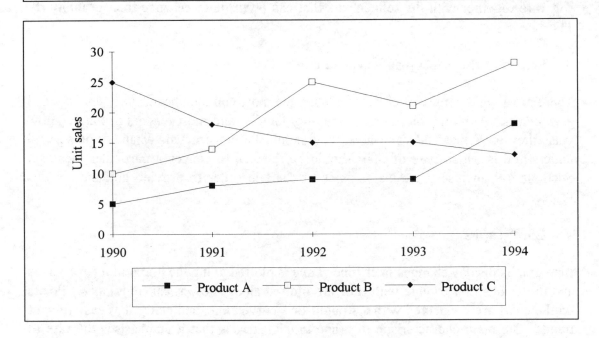

Scatter charts (or X-Y charts) are a variant of the line graph and are used to illustrate whether there is a relationship between two variables. One set of data is plotted along the x axis and one (or more) along the y axis.

5.   Bar charts

Bar charts use vertical or horizontal bars of different lengths to show the relationship between sets of data. Horizontal bar charts are commonly used to compare data at one position in time.

Example 3
This chart compares the temperature in 5 European capitals on one day in June 1994.

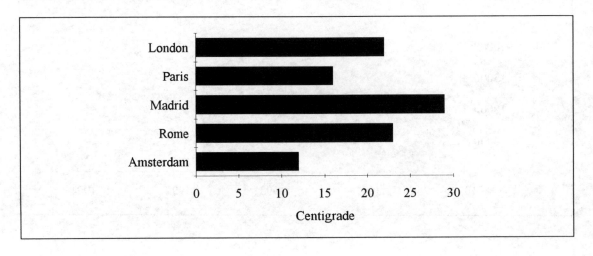

Vertical bar charts (or *column charts* as they are sometimes called) can also be used to plot variation over time and once again time is plotted along the x axis. However, the essential difference between a bar chart and a line graph is that bar charts place more emphasis on comparison of the elements rather than on the flow of time.

Example 4
This bar chart shows the increase in the use of debit cards as a percentage of total sales for a particular retail outlet for three specified years.

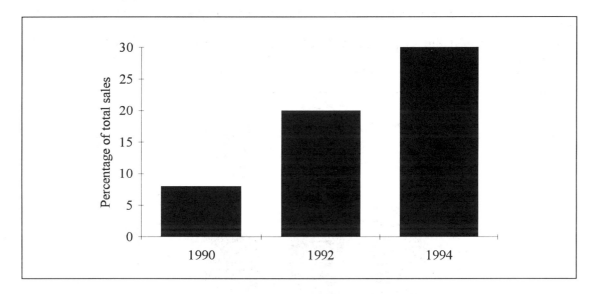

Simple bar charts show one series of data (as in Examples 3 and 4), but *multiple bar charts* present two or more sets of related figures.

Example 5
This bar chart compares three methods of payment, in terms of percentage sales, for a particular retail outlet for three unspecified years.

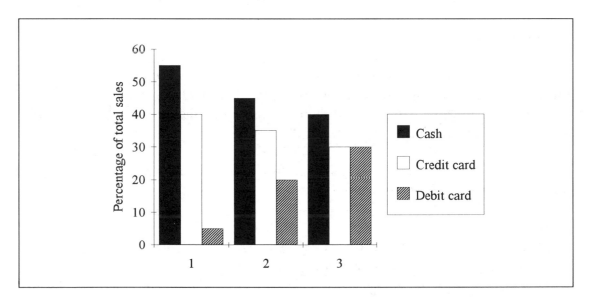

Paired bar charts are sometimes a more appropriate way of presenting two sets of related data. Here the vertical axis is placed in the middle of the chart instead of on the left so that one set of bars extends to the left of the vertical axis and the other to the right.

Stacked bar charts place the bars on top of one another. The stacked bars can use the whole of the scale, i.e. up to 100%, when they are known as *100% stacked bar* charts. This type of chart shows the data broken down into component parts and displayed as a percentage of the total. Hence all the bars terminate at the same point.

Example 6
This 100% stacked bar chart shows total sales by payment method for a particular retail outlet for three unspecified years.

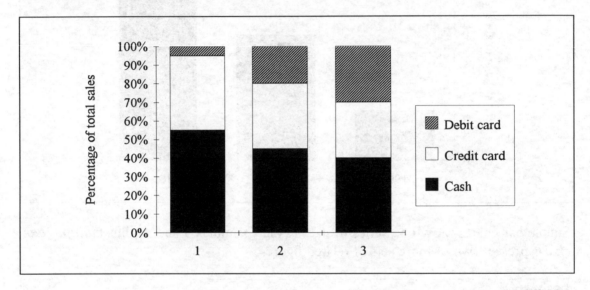

High-low charts are a type of bar chart used to illustrate fluctuations in share prices, as they can display the highest, lowest and even the average price within a given period.

6. Pie charts

When a set of data is broken down into its component parts the use of pie charts is often preferred. Each component is represented by a slice of the pie, which shows its relationship to a whole. However, if there are too many slices, each slice is too thin and any significance is lost.

To emphasise a particular slice of the pie, a slice is often "cut". This type of chart is also known as an *exploded* pie chart.

Example 7
The following pie chart shows 1994 total sales by payment method for a particular retail outlet with the Cash sales slice cut.

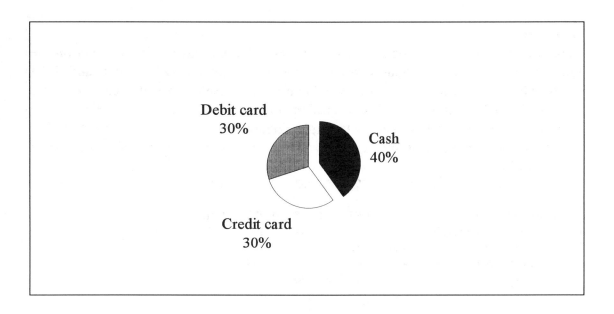

7. Area charts

Area charts are a cross between line and bar charts. They show values over time but emphasise the amount of change rather than the rate of change and this is done by shading the area under the line. Hence, they are obviously not used where the lines cross. Area charts can also be stacked and 100% stacked, like bar charts.

Example 8
This 100% stacked area chart displays the same data as the chart in Example 6 but the emphasis here is on illustrating the amount of change in the different payment methods.

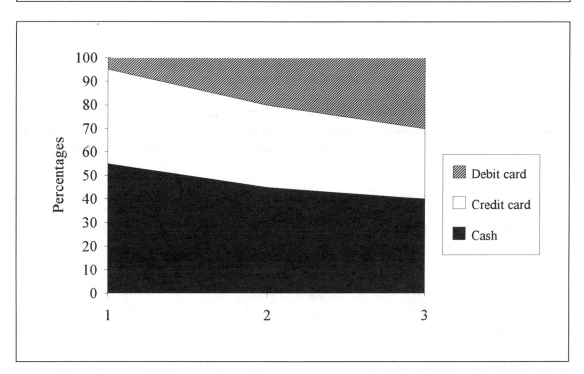

Exercise 1

You are the administrator of an independent hospital and have collected data on the number of surgical operations carried out in the hospital between 1990 and 1994 (shown below). What types of chart would you use to display the following:

(a) the breakdown of all the 1994 surgical operations; *Pie chart*
(b) to compare all the 1990 and 1994 surgical operations; *bar chart*
(c) to show the number of operations carried out in urology and ophthalmology from 1990 to 1994. *line chart*

	1990	1991	1992	1993	1994
General surgery	2,050	1,957	1,835	1,925	2,015
Ear, nose and throat	1,115	1,059	938	850	920
Gynaecology	920	869	903	935	975
Ophthalmology	456	495	475	459	483
Urology	259	293	376	392	358
Other	385	398	423	413	452

---

8. Designing graphs and charts

This section provides some guidance on creating usable charts and graphs with the aid of spreadsheet or other graphing software.

Charts created using spreadsheet software can either be set up in the *worksheet* itself (and this is particularly useful if at a later date both the data and the chart need to be printed) or *separately* in which case an automatic link is made between the two elements so that updates in the worksheet are reflected in the chart.

There are two basic steps to creating a chart or graph, although it will depend on the type of software that is being used which one is carried out first:

- enter the data; and
- select the chart type.

A rudimentary chart will then be created by the software, in which colours or patterns will automatically be assigned to each series of data in a bar, area and pie chart, and the lines on a line graph differentiated either by marking them with different shapes on the lines or else by the use of different types of lines.

Example 9

The following unit sales figures for three products sold in the UK and USA during one week in January are entered into the software:

	UK	USA
Product 1	250	300
Product 2	300	400
Product 3	250	500

A multiple bar chart is selected in order to compare these figures, and the chart is created as shown below:

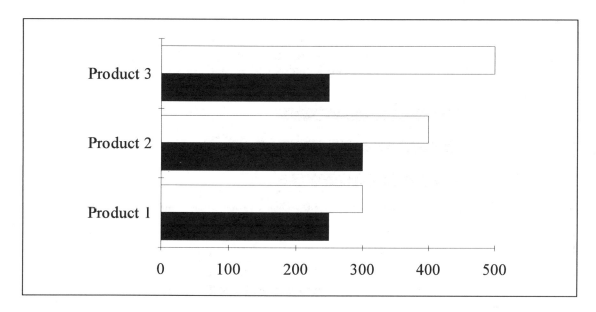

However, the chart is by no means complete: in fact is is essential to include a number of other elements to ensure that the contents of the chart are fully understandable. It should be noted, however, that the software will not necessarily prompt or remind the user that any of these further elements are required, hence the onus is on the user to remember to include them. The chart must have:

- *a key (or legend).* This will show each colour or pattern used for each data marker labelled with the relevant data name, which will normally be taken from the data entered (although the information can be added at this stage). The legend should be positioned on the chart in an appropriate position where it does not distort the shape of the chart or graph. The legend can itself be enhanced with a pattern or be shadowed to make it more prominent.
- a *title* that adequately describes the contents of the chart;
- *labels* for the horizontal (x) and vertical (y) axes; and
- an explanation of the *source* of data as a footnote (if required).

Text can be added very easily to the charts and depending on the software can be formatted in a number of ways:

The *orientation* of the headings and labels can be defined, i.e. whether they are to be displayed vertically or horizontally. It should be noted, however, that although labels are more easily readable if displayed horizontally, vertical orientation does save space.

The *alignment* of the text can be determined (i.e. right, centred or left-justified) and similarly the *typeface* and the *size* and *style* of the typeface can be changed. The sections on *Typeface* and *Alignment and Layout* in **2:7** are therefore relevant reading, especially if the worksheet is to be included in a report or other document as it is advisable to use the same or a complementary style of layout and font.

Example 10
To improve the presentation of the chart in Example 9, a title has been added to the chart, the axes have been labelled and a legend placed underneath the chart.

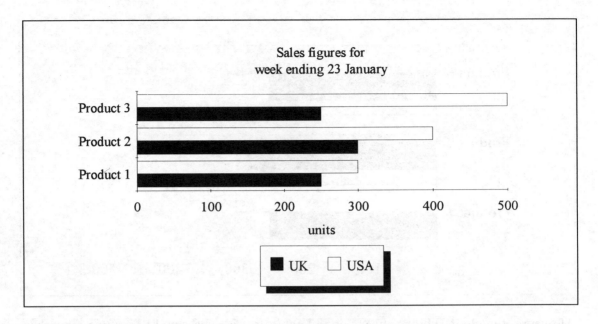

9. Refining charts and graphs

There are a number of software features that can be used to enhance graphs and charts, although to ensure that the message is not overpowered by too many different features, the designer should remember that simplicity and clarity are the key to a striking and effective chart.

Depending on the type of chart, the designer will normally have a number of different options within each type which can provide subtle enhancements to the chart, e.g. bar charts can be *clustered* (i.e. the bars presented side by side) or can be *overlapping*. Three-dimensional (*3-D*) charts can be very effective and they can also be manipulated in a number of ways, e.g. their height and rotation can be controlled. However, 3-D charts should only be used where they do not confuse the picture.

The colours and patterns of the data markers can be modified. The use of different colours can be very effective; however, too many contrasting patterns of stripes and checks may well be overkill. The width of the bars in a bar chart and the space between them can be controlled to good effect, and if it is felt appropriate, the bars themselves can be labelled.

With some charts a useful way of guiding the reader's eye to make sense of the data values is to include *gridlines*. These are lines that run across the chart horizontally or down the chart vertically (when they often known as *droplines*).

If particular data needs to be highlighted, it is often possible to add *arrows* to point to specific data on the chart and even add extra explanatory text.   In many software packages the arrow shaft and arrowhead can themselves be regulated.

Finally, if it is felt appropriate other shapes can be drawn on the chart using *drawing tools* available in the software, although it is important that they do not appear amateurish. It is also possible in some software to select images from associated *clipart* libraries to create *pictograms*.

Example 11
The chart in Example 10 has been converted into a 3-D bar chart and the legend has been moved to the right-hand side to ensure there is enough space to show the chart clearly. Gridlines have also been added for clarity, and an arrow has been used to point to the US sales figures for Product 3, together with some attached text.

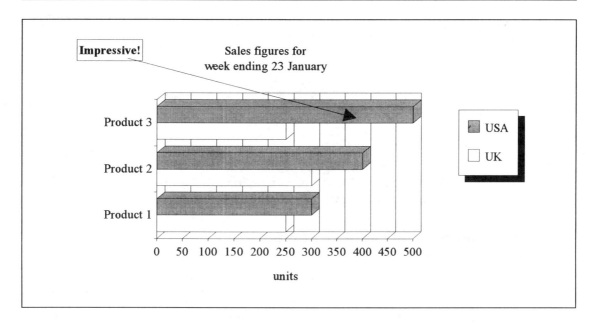

Exercise 2
Draft the design of the charts in Exercise 1.

10. Productivity tools

Some graphing packages have a number of productivity tools to assist with the production of usable charts, for example there may be:

- a *spell checker* to check the spelling of any text in the charts. The section on *Spelling* in **2:6** provides an explanation of the use of a spell checker.
- a *calculator* to carry out any intermediate mathematical calculations.

11. Multimedia charts

Multimedia charts are those that include sound, video and animation, and an example of a multimedia chart might be one that includes voice annotations instead of or in addition to textual annotations, or one that uses animation techniques to draw charts gradually on-screen pointing out relevant features.

12. Further work with graphing and charting software

Once the skill of identifying the most appropriate type of chart has been mastered, it is only a matter of time and imagination for the designer to create effective and compelling charts and graphs that convey their message to the full.

5

Business presentations

1. Introduction

Many people have to give presentations as part of their job to both small and large groups of people, e.g. to report progress to colleagues, to sell products or services to customers and clients, or to present information to delegates at conferences.

Although the most important part of a presentation is obviously the content, sometimes the presenter needs a little help in drawing the audience's attention to the main points of the presentation. Unfortunately people are not very good at just listening, they like to be provided with information visually, e.g. the key points of the presentation or the figures that are being discussed, so some kind of visual aid can be extremely useful.

There are many advantages in presenting information visually - many of which have been discussed in **4:1**. However, there are also a number of disadvantages which must be considered: visual aids, if not well-designed, can distract the audience from the content of the presentation, can confuse or even mislead the audience. It should also be remembered that visual aids are supports for the presentation not the presentation itself. In other words, the content comes first, then the visual aids.

2. Presentation graphics software

Visual aids have developed over the years with the technology. Presenters in the past relied heavily on writing on blackboards and whiteboards. They now commonly make use of overhead and 35mm slide projectors. Presentations on PCs are still in the minority but they are on the increase.

Although very basic visual aids can be produced by using word processing and spreadsheet software, e.g. to produce black and white overheads or slides, presentation graphics software provides the means of creating colour overheads and slides and the production of a PC-based slideshow. Presentation graphics software packages are also able to provide the facility of producing the supporting documentation for presentations.

This chapter looks at the process of preparing a business presentation and provides guidance on all aspects from slide production to giving the presentation.

3. Planning a presentation

Presentations like written documents need to be planned and a number of points need to be addressed before work commences. In particular the presenter should consider the following:

- the purpose of the presentation (i.e. its aims and objectives), what is to be achieved and the scope of the presentation; and
- who the audience will be (e.g. colleagues: superiors or peers; clients; other professionals) and the extent of their knowledge.

These factors will determine not only what material is to be included in the presentation but also the most appropriate way of presenting that information.

4. Structuring a presentation

There should be a well-defined structure to the presentation consisting of three main parts:

- an *introduction*, in which the audience's attention is gained, and an indication of what is to come is given;
- the *main body* of the presentation, in which the facts are presented and analysed; and
- a *conclusion*, in which the main findings are summarised. No new material should be included at this stage.

The following, unattributed, advice is useful when considering the structure of the presentation: *"Tell 'em what you're gonna tell 'em! Tell 'em! Tell 'em what you've told 'em!"*

A presenter should also bear in mind the fact that the audience will particularly remember the first things they hear and the last things they hear.

5. Designing text slides

Once the content of the presentation has been mapped out the presenter can then consider the overheads or slides that will help to convey the message. There are a number of very simple points to be remembered when designing overheads or slides for a presentation:

Each slide should be clear, concise and easy to understand. It should be uncluttered, so that each element stands out and does not compete with other elements for the audience's attention, and clear enough for the audience to see at a distance.

Text should be simplified down to a small number of key words or phrases rather than sentences and displayed as a list of items, possibly with a bullet mark (e.g. •) and there should not be more than about five or six bulleted items on a slide.

Example 1
This slide shows a simple slide with a title and 4 bulleted points

---

Slide title

- **key point 1**
- **key point 2**
- **key point 3**
- **key point 4**

Each slide should be considered as one part of the whole presentation. Therefore it is important that there should be consistency across the slides so that users can easily follow the presentation. In simple terms this means that each element of the slide should appear in the same place on the slide, and that each slide should use the same colour scheme for text, lines and background.

Presentation graphics software can support the user in both these respects as it can ensure that there is consistency by allowing the user to apply a *template* (sometimes also referred to as a *master* or *backdrop*).

Most presentation graphics packages come with a large number of templates suitable for different types of presentations, i.e. for 35mm slides, black and white or colour overheads as well as those appropriate for screen shows on PCs. These templates have been created by professional graphic designers with colour schemes that co-ordinate and with the layout of the slide already pre-defined.

Example 2
A simple black and white overhead template applied to the slide set up in Example 1 might format it to look as below:

Slide title

- key point 1
- key point 2
- key point 3
- key point 4

A template can be selected at the very beginning of the development process. i.e. before creating any slide or after a few slides have been produced or at the very end, wherever it is felt appropriate, although with some software it is more difficult to change the template after it has been adopted.

The use of a template ensures not only that consistency is maintained but also that the presenter can concentrate on the content of the presentation rather than on the layout of the slides. Hence users without inherent design skills can easily produce a set of professional slides and experienced users can also easily edit these pre-defined templates (e.g. change the colour scheme) or even create their own.

6.   Designing or amending a template

Although it is quite possible to produce a complete presentation by simply typing in the text and applying a pre-designed template, it is very likely that a user will wish to make changes to the template or even design one from scratch. In this case the following are suggestions how this might be done together with guidelines that should be observed.

Use of text

One *typeface* (or *font*) should be used throughout. A *sans serif* typeface is particularly effective as it is easier to read from a distance. The same *size of typeface* should be used for each element of the slide, e.g. titles could use 36 point and the bulleted items 24 point. Modifications to the type *style*, e.g. **bold**, *italic* and underlined should be minimal, and it should be noted that other text special effects, like shadowing and embossing, may produce unreadable text so will only be effective for slide titles. Consistent *alignment* and *line-spacing* should be maintained.

For a fuller explanation of the terms used here reference can be made to the sections on *Typeface* and *Alignment and Layout* in **2:7**.

Use of bullets

A range of different bullets will normally be available in the software, and these can be used to add interest to the text. However, there should be consistent use of bullet shape across the presentation.

Colour schemes

Presentation graphics packages vary in the number of colours they can support, i.e. from 16 to 16 million. In the latter case it is therefore very easy for the inexperienced user to create slides that use colours that clash. Contrasting colours are best and primary colours go well together, e.g. a bright blue background works well with yellow text. Colours that are too similar, e.g. pinks and reds, do not work well together. Four different colours on one slide is about the maximum number that should be used, any more and it becomes a riot of colour. Graduated or shaded background colours are also effective as they can help to draw the eye down the slide.

Layout

The layout of the slide can be modified, e.g. the title area can usually be re-positioned or re-sized. Boxes around titles can be included and extra textual elements like the date and time, or even a graphic element like the company logo, can be added to appear on every slide. However, the user should ensure that there is not too much overcrowding on a slide, since this will only distract the audience rather than enhance the slide.

7. Other types of slides

In addition to text slides the user may wish to include other types of data, e.g. tables, line graphs, bar, column or pie charts, or even other types of charts like organisation charts.

Some presentation graphics packages have a *table* facility which automates the process of creating a table slide, in which case the advice given in the section in **2:7** is applicable here. However, if a table has already been prepared in a word processed document it may well be easier to copy this in.

Similarly, if the data for *graphs* and *charts*, or even the charts themselves, have been created in spreadsheet or specialist charting software packages, then it may well be possible to copy these in too. However, most presentation graphics software packages have a *graphing* facility, and if this is used to create charts and graphs, then the advice provided in Chapter 4 is also relevant.

Organisation charts can often be produced in the software. These types of charts are used to present the hierarchical structure of an organisation.

Example 3
This slide displays an organisation chart

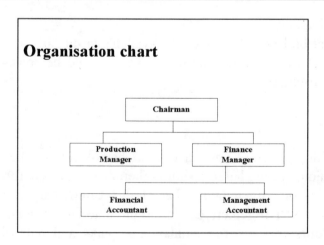

8. Enhancing slides

There are a number of ways of enhancing slides to add interest to them, although these features should be used with care to ensure that slides are not overcrowded.

Drawing tools can be used to add straight or curved lines, circles, arrows and freehand drawings to a slide. The shapes and drawings created can be further enhanced, e.g. the width of the lines can be altered, and the shapes can be *filled* with colours or patterns or *shadowed*. They can also be re-sized and manipulated, e.g. rotated.

Example 4
The following slide shows a number of examples of images drawn with drawing tools.

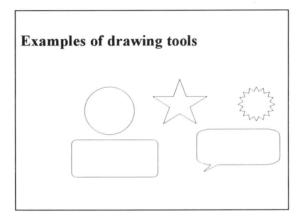

More complex graphic elements can be included. These might have been drawn in more sophisticated drawing packages or copied in from *clipart* libraries. Most presentation graphics software packages usually come with an impressive collection of clipart, e.g. drawings of people, business symbols, maps, as well as photographic images which can be included on a slide. The size of these clipart libraries is normally between 500-1,000 images although some have up to 7,000 images, in which case they are normally stored on CD-ROM. Once these images have been copied onto a slide they can be manipulated in the same way as the images created with drawing tools.

Example 5
This slide incorporates a clipart image

Extra text can be added to the slides in addition to the main text in the title and in the (bulleted) items and this can be used to provide captions, for example, or to annotate diagrams or clipart.

Example 6
This slide shows how text can be used to annotate slides

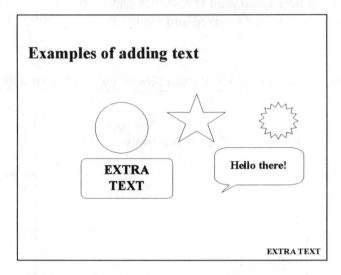

Exercise 1
You have been asked to give a short presentation on creating overheads and slides. Design (on paper) a number of slides which not only provide the information but also demonstrate the points you wish to make.

9. Developing a presentation

Most presentations can be developed one slide after another slide using the *slide-editor* which allows the user to view the appearance of the slide However, presentations can also be developed using the *outliner,* which lets the user plan and organise the presentation and also provides an alternative *view* on the presentation. The outline of the presentation can also be printed.

Example 7
The outline below shows the slides created as examples for this chapter.

1	**Slide title**
	♦ key point 1
	♦ key point 2
	♦ key point 3
	♦ key point 4
2	**Organisation chart**
3	**Examples of drawing tools**
4	**Example of clipart**
5	**Examples of adding text**

Slides can be added using the outliner and the user does need not worry about the formatting and layout as the template will take care of this. Slides can also be deleted or moved to a new position, and additionally the items in the slides can be moved into new positions (i.e. promoted or demoted). Some software packages can read in an outline developed in a word processing package and turn this into a presentation outline, or even turn a report itself into a presentation outline.

10. Speaker notes and handouts

In addition to creating the slides for the presentation the speaker may also wish to keep a note of the points to be made when each slide displays. These are often referred to as *speaker notes*. If this is done, these notes should be limited to key points - not sentences - for there is nothing worse than speakers reading from their notes.

The software normally allows the user to create such notes, placing a re-sized version of the slide on the top half of the page and allowing the user to make notes on the bottom half of the page (as shown below), although the notes area can often be increased in size if more space is required.

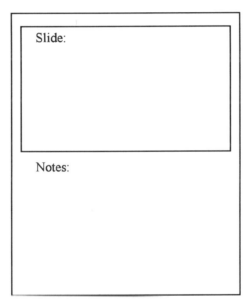

When giving a presentation it may also be necessary to provide *audience handouts*. Although some would advise that handouts should only be given out at the end of the presentation because they tend to distract the audience, it is often a good idea to provide them in advance so that the audience can make notes on them whilst listening to the presentation. Presentation graphics packages support the production of handouts by printing a number of slides on one page, e.g. three or six to a page.

Example 8
A handout which prints the 6 slides designed for this chapter is shown on page 94.

Slide title

- ◆ key point 1
- ◆ key point 2
- ◆ key point 3
- ◆ key point 4

Organisation chart

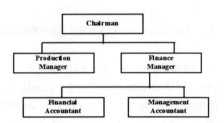

Examples of drawing tools

Example of clipart

Examples of adding text

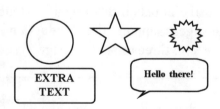

EXTRA TEXT

11. Productivity aids

There are a number of productivity tools that can help to support the creation of effective presentations:

- A *spell checker* will ensure that any spelling or typographical errors will not be displayed prominently on the screen, or appear in audience handouts or speakers notes. The section on *Spelling* in **2:7** is relevant reading.

- A *find and replace* feature can replace all instances of a word or phrase with another word or phrase.

- A *calculator* may be available to assist with mathematical calculations.

- *On-screen advisors* can provide productivity tips and design advice for users, and help to guide them through the whole process of building a presentation. In fact, it is often possible to use the default structure of a presentation and merely replace the words of the default with the user's own text.

Exercise 2
Develop the presentation begun in Exercise 1 to include further slides that demonstrate how a presentation graphics package can help to enhance and support business presentations.

---

12. Giving the presentation

Now that the presentation has been prepared, it is time to consider its actual delivery, so here are some tips on giving a good presentation.

As presenters will have spent a lot of time preparing the presentation it is important that all these efforts pay off, so they should make sure well before the presentation begins that all the necessary equipment is working. If using an overhead projector the presenter should have a spare bulb to hand, as these have a habit of blowing at the wrong moment.

Having checked the equipment works, it is also important that the presenter knows how to use it! Hunting for switches does not create a good impression or a slick performance. Similarly fumbling for notes is just as unprofessional, so all papers should be in order and in the right order.

A presenter should appear positive and enthusiastic about the subject. Unfortunately a presenter's voice can betray a less than confident attitude, so it should be controlled if at all possible. A monotonous tone should be avoided, and the pitch varied. In other words the voice should be used to good effect, for instance pausing before saying anything of significance.

Posture and gestures are also important as they can give a lot away about the presenter (since they are forms of non-verbal communication). If the speaker is nervous then it is advisable to adopt a position in which to stand in a relaxed manner, although of course some movement around the room may be required. Gestures are sometimes useful but they should not be distracting.

As far as dress is concerned, it is difficult to give guidance since what is acceptable in one environment may be totally unsuitable in another.   But suffice it to say the presenter should think carefully about what should be worn, and once again it is important to make sure that there is nothing distracting about the choice of clothes.

When addressing an audience the presenter should maintain eye contact otherwise this could be taken as a lack of confidence or even a lack of competence.   It is also essential to watch the audience's reactions so that appropriate responses can be made. For example if the audience seems to be getting bored or restless, then the pace of the presentation should be increased.   If the audience appears interested, the presenter should take advantage of this.   Above all, the main advice is that presenters need to be flexible and adaptive to their audience at all times.

Much of what has been said here only comes with experience and practice. It may therefore be useful for new presenters to rehearse their first presentations with interested parties who can help them identify problems that need to be addressed.

13. PC presentations

Although currently most users of presentation graphics software packages employ them to develop overheads and slides, the production of a PC presentation deserves special mention as this type of presentation is on the increase.   These presentations take the form of *screen-shows* or *slide-shows* which can either be viewed on one PC, displayed on a larger screen, or on a number of PCs on a network.

Most packages have a separate stand-alone *slide-viewer,* which can be used instead of the full program to display the presentation. Although the user should read the full copyright restrictions of the package, this can often mean that the presentation can be developed on the "home" computer, i.e. where the full version of the software is resident, and if the presentation is to take place elsewhere, the presentation file can be copied onto a disk together with the slide-viewer.

Preparing a PC presentation is not so very different from what has been described above, but there are a number of additional points that need be mentioned.

When developing a screenshow a further feature of presentation graphics software that is particularly useful is the *slide-sorter*. This lets the presenter view the slides in the presentation as "thumbnail" sketches or as a list of slide names, and also add, edit, delete and move slides.

There are also a number of special effects that can be employed to display a slide on the screen which are not possible in static presentations. One of these is the facility to *build* the slide on-screen, i.e. to place one (bulleted) item on the slide and then use some special effect to let the subsequent items appear.

These special effects have names like *fly in, box, split, strips* etc., and can be instructed to appear from the top, bottom, left or right of the slide. As the new item appears, it is also often possible to *dim* the previous item so that the viewer's attention is focused on the particular point in hand.

Example 9
These two slides attempt to demonstrate the build facility.

Slide title

♦ key point 1

Slide title

♦ key point 1
♦ key point 2

The slides themselves can be drawn and erased using similar special effects known as *transitions*. There is usually a demo facility to view these transitions to judge the effects. However, when setting them up it should be borne in mind that not too much emphasis should be placed on the transitions themselves as these will dominate the presentation and overshadow the content.

When showing the presentation, the default mode is to display one slide after the other when a mouse button is clicked or a key is pressed on the keyboard. However, the presenter can usually have more control than this, e.g. to move back as well as forwards through the slides.

During the presentation the presenter may be able to use the mouse pointer to point at particular features on the slide or even annotate them live, on-screen with "electronic chalk" or with a "pen" (if this is supported by the software). Some software even allows the presenter to jump to a particular slide in response to a question from the audience.

Alternatively an automated presentation can be set up that does not require the presence of the presenter. This means linking the slides so that the presentation automatically moves from one slide to the next after a stipulated *time* (in seconds). The show can also be set up to *loop* endlessly until a key, usually [Esc], is pressed.

Finally, with some software an interactive presentation can be created. This allows the user to include "buttons" on the screen for the viewer to control the presentation, e.g. to move forwards or backwards through the slides, or even branch off to other *hyperlinked* or *hotlinked* slides.

14. Multimedia presentations

Some packages allow the user to incorporate sound, animation and full-motion video to create a true multimedia presentation and this is a particularly useful application for multimedia. It can be used for example to provide narration or play background music.

Some of the presentation graphics packages include sound and video files on CD-ROM which can be included in the presentation in much the same way as still clipart images, although, of course, both sound and video and animation can be created and recorded by users themselves.

15. Further work with presentation graphics software

This chapter has provided an introduction to the design of presentations. Each user will want to use this software tool for very different purposes. Although it is very easy to create a standard presentation very quickly, designing innovative presentations requires imagination and skill. However, with time, experience and an exploration of the full potential of the software, users will discover new ways in which to produce presentations that can capture an audience's attention.

6

Data management

1. Introduction

An important information handling task in business involves the maintenance and use of a large collection of data on a particular aspect of a company's activities. Businesses commonly hold data on their customers or clients, their suppliers, their staff as well as the products they sell or services they provide. This data can then be used to provide relevant information for managers for decision-making and planning purposes.

Managing data in this way is also commonly undertaken by clubs and societies who wish to hold details of their membership, and by researchers, students and other academics to maintain their research data.

2. Database software

Traditionally data of this nature was kept in paper-based records in filing cabinets. However, database software has revolutionised the way data can be stored (i.e. it requires far less space than filing cabinets), the speed at which it can be manipulated and retrieved, as well as the ease with which it can be searched.

Database software packages vary from those that are very much aimed at the small end-user setting up a small database on their PC to assist with a particular business problem to those aimed at experienced database developers producing full-scale database applications for use on PC networks or to be connected to corporate databases held on mainframes or mini computers.

This chapter will discuss the use of databases in these contexts: A basic use of database packages is considered in sections **3-8**, which provide a definition of essential database terminology and look at the principles of database design and data entry as well as the querying and printing of the data held in the database.

Sections **9-13** discuss a more sophisticated use of database packages and this includes: the design of data-entry screens, usually referred to as *forms*; the use of *data validation* techniques to ensure that the data entered into the database is correct and the design of structured printouts, known as *reports*.

Finally, sections **14-17** look at the advanced use of powerful database packages for the design of so-called *relational databases*, the development of *customised database applications*, an understanding of how PC databases can be *connected* to corporate databases, as well as the *security* issues involved in the use of *multi-user systems*.

3.   Database terminology

This section describes the main terms that are likely to be encountered when using a database package.

The term *database* refers to a general collection of data on a particular subject. The data in a database is held in one or more *(data)files*, each of which comprises a number of *records*. Each record consists of a number of small items of data known as *fields*.

For instance, a personnel file could hold the details of the members of staff in an organisation, where each record would hold the details about each individual member of staff. Although each record would contain the same data items, e.g. name, address and date of birth, the data itself would obviously be different.

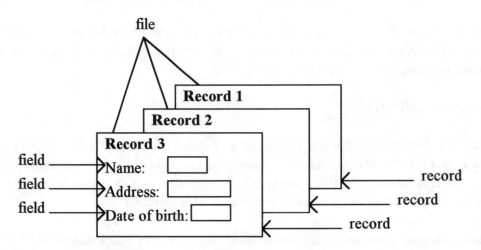

There are two main types of database software package which allow users to create databases: a *file management system*, which only allow provides the facility to create one datafile; and a *relational database management system* (or *RDBMS*)) which lets users hold data in one or more related datafiles (or *tables* as they often known).

In a table, each *record* is held in a *row* of the table and each *field* is represented by a *column*. A table holding personnel data might therefore look as below:

	Name	Address	Date of birth
1			
2			
3			

It can be seen that it will very much depend on the type of database management software that is being used which terms will be met.

4. Designing a database

Designing any database requires pre-planning. In particular, the following questions need to be asked, in order to determine what data is to be stored in the database and how it is to be broken down:

- What is the purpose or the reasons for the database?
- What is the information to be used for?
- What information is to come out of the database?

Example 1

The Personnel Officer at Kings Fashions Ltd would like to set up a small database to hold the details of employees. There are a number of reasons for this: firstly, she wants to be able to use it as a mailing list for internal documents, and secondly to provide her with ad hoc reports on the staffing situation, e.g. salaries, numbers in departments, etc.

When setting up a database the first task is to define the structure of the database. This means identifying the required data items (i.e. fields) and for each, specifying:

- a unique *fieldname*: although field names should be as descriptive as possible, some software limits the user's choice since it may only be possible to use a small number of characters and not include any spaces or lower case characters.

- the *type* of data to be held in the field: it is important to specify the right data type else the user may not be able to enter data into the field. The main data types are shown below together with the possible terms that may be used in different database software packages.

Type of data the field is to contain	Software field type names
Characters (i.e. A-Z) and/or numbers that do not require arithmetic calculations performed on them (e.g. telephone numbers)	Alphanumeric/String/Character/Text
Numbers that might require arithmetic calculations to be performed on them and no text	Numeric/Number
A sequential numbering system	Record numbers may automatically be set up by software/Counter/Numeric
Prices, i.e. monetary values	Currency/Money/Numeric/Number (This can be defined to show a specified number of decimal points)
Dates and time	Date (both British and American versions) Time (both 12 and 24-hour clock)
Logical data (e.g. yes/no; true/false)	Logical/Boolean/Yes-No
Notes, i.e. extended text	Note/Memo

- The *size* or *width* of the field: this will normally be the maximum number of characters or numbers to be held in the field so it will be necessary to look carefully at the data to be held in the field to decide on the field width. With some software, numerical data may not be defined in terms of the number of digits to be used, but by expressions like byte, integer, etc. When setting up fields of certain data types, e.g. date, logical and memo type, a default size can usually be adopted.

When identifying fields to be held in the database, the following should be considered.

- Data should be broken down into the smallest level of detail required, e.g. if a name is to be held, this might need to be broken down into firstname, surname, etc. It will very much depend on how the data is to be used in the database.
- Items of data that appear consistently in all records should not be included, since this is a waste of storage space and data entry time.
- Coding (or abbreviating) data might be appropriate if data items are frequently repeated. This will also conserve storage space as well as data entry time.

Example 2

The personnel database for Kings Fashions Ltd is to hold the following six items of data: the employee's first name, surname, date of birth, the first three letters of the department in which they work, their current salary, and whether they have had a free medical check-up. The following sample data is used to identify suitable fieldnames, data types and field widths:

    Susan, Browne, 10/11/67, Sales, £8500, no medical check
    Andy, Shah, 06/06/75, Accounts, £8000, medical
    Mary, Smith, 09/04/53, Management, £25000, medical
    Duncan, Green, 19/03/71, Packing, £6500, no medical check
    Mina, Patel, 23/08/54, Purchasing, £15000, no medical check

The structure of the database might then be defined as shown below:

Fieldname	Data type	Size
First Name	text	20
Surname	text	25
Date of birth	date	default
Department	text	3
Salary	currency	5 (no decimal places)
Medical	logical	default

It may also be possible for the designer to specify further details at this stage, e.g.

- a fuller textual *description* of the field;
- a *primary key*: this is a unique identifier for each record, and is usually a field that will contain a unique number, e.g. a reference number. Primary keys are not always essential, but data can be retrieved faster if primary keys have been set up, and they are necessary when linking tables;
- an *index*: this can be used to "sort" data and will also help speed up searches on data.

Some modern software can help to automate the process of designing databases by offering pre-designed files or tables which contain an assortment of fields, from which designers can select those most appropriate for their needs.

It is standard practice to test the database design to ensure that the expected result is achieved: subsequent modifications can then be made if required, e.g. to increase the size of fields or change the data type or to add or delete fields.

It is much easier to make changes of this nature at this stage rather than later when a large number of records have been entered, since this may cause some data to be lost and if forms and reports have been created may also mean they will have to be modified too.

Exercise 1

If an additional purpose of the database for Kings Fashions Ltd had been to use it as an external mailing list and to provide information on length of staff service and education qualifications, how might the following extra items of data be included in the database: employee's title (e.g. Mr), home address and telephone number, date of joining and educational qualifications.

Use the sample data below to make decisions on fieldnames, data types and field sizes:

Miss Susan Browne; Sales Assistant; 25 Grange Road Leighton Sussex TH4 6GH; 01767-587459; 01/01/84; 3 OLs: English; Home Economics; Maths
Mr Andy Shah; Payroll Supervisor; 87 Hardwicke Lane Creighton Sussex TH6 8JK; 01767-345912; 25/04/93; 5 GCSEs: English(2); Maths; History; French; BTEC Business and Finance
Mrs Mary Smith; Managing Director; Hampton House Kingsley Sussex TH6 9GF; 01767-673210; 06/03/72; 8 OLs, 3 ALs, BSc Economics
Mr Duncan Green; Senior Packer; 27 Leighton Road Creighton Sussex TH6 4DF; 01767-347812; 21/02/87; no qualifications
Mrs Mina Patel; Purchasing Officer; 56 Freestone Avenue Northwich Sussex TH9 8DS; 01878-345676; 23/02/92; 7 OLs, 2 ALs: English; History

---

5. Entering the data

Once the structure of the database has been finalised data can be entered. Depending on the software this might be possible in one of two ways: by use of a data-entry *table* or a data-entry *form*.

A data entry *table* (sometimes known as a *datasheet*) allows the data to be entered in a similar way to a spreadsheet, where the fields of each record are displayed in columns, and each record is entered as a row in the table. (See an example table in **3** above.)

A data entry *form*, on the other hand, displays one record at a time setting out the fields one below the other and using the fieldnames as labels for the fields like a paper-based record card. (See an example form in **3** above.)

For the designer of the database each of these two ways of entering data is as good as the other since the designer knows what kind of data is to be placed in each field.

However, if someone other than the designer is expected to enter data into it, they will require something more user friendly.

Generally, a form is the more usable way of entering data but this will depend a lot on the form itself and the software in which it was created. If a form is not set up by default, then most packages do provide a *forms designer* to create one or to improve the look and usability of the default data entry form. However, this requires more complex control of the software, so this aspect is considered separately in section **9** below.

Another important consideration when entering data into the database is ensuring that the data is correct or valid. If inaccurate data is allowed to pass into the database and is subsequently processed and presented as correct information then this might cause incorrect decisions to be made. In computing terms this is known as *GIGO* or *Garbage In Garbage Out*.

Basic validation of data is done using a field's data type, e.g. only numbers (not text) can be entered into a numeric field, but as this is not very comprehensive, further validation rules may need to be designed, e.g. only to allow a range of numbers to be entered. Data validation is discussed more fully in section **10**.

6.   Maintaining the database

Once data has been entered into the database it is important that the database is *maintained*. This is the term used to describe the task that involves ensuring that records are amended and updated as required and that new records are added and defunct records are deleted when necessary.

The software makes it easy to amend and add data, but more difficult to delete data and this is how it should be since it would otherwise be possible to delete records accidentally. Hence a number of packages insist on a two-stage process of deleting records.

7.   Querying the database

One of the most important tasks in data management is to search for particular information. This is known as querying the database. Compared to searching paper-based records searching for information in a computer-based database is much quicker, and relatively easy. All that is required is a logical approach to the task.

Example 3
Possible queries of the Kings Fashions database could include:
(a)   Which staff work in Accounts?
(b)   Which staff earn less than £15,000?
(c)   Which staff are over 40?
(d)   Which staff have had a medical check?

In order to support this task most database software packages use a *Query By Example* (QBE) tool. This is a method of locating records that match specified criteria by entering the details of the data to be found into a grid or table where each column is labelled with the field name.

There are variations on the way QBE is used in different software packages so the following provides a general guide to the use of QBE. To query a database using QBE the following items need to be specified:

- the *field* (or *fields*) to be searched; and
- the *search criteria* to be used.

It is usually also possible to specify the *fields* to be displayed as a result of the query since it is not always necessary or appropriate to display all the fields of the records as some may be irrelevant to the query.

Specifying the search criteria

When specifying the search criteria the data must be entered exactly as it is held in the database. If the software is *case-sensitive* this means ensuring that upper and lower case letters are used in exactly the same way as they are held in the database. The following operators are required in search criteria:

= equal to	< less than	> greater than
<> not equal to	<= less than or equal to	>= greater than or equal to

Below are some examples of the most frequent types of searches made of a database, categorised according to field type.

Searching text (and memo) fields

Example data to be found	Possible software notation	Explanatory notes
All occurrences of the surname Smith	=SMITH "Smith"	= sign may be required; text may need to be enclosed in quotation marks
Any surname after "S" in the alphabet	>"S"	> represents "after"; < represents "before"
Any surname other than "Smith"	<> Smith NOT Smith	

In addition, the following symbols can be used:

*	the wild card representing any series of characters
$	the symbol representing "contained within"

Example data to be found	Possible software notation	Explanatory notes
Any surname that begins with "Smi", e.g. Smith, , Smithson	"Smi" Smi* Like "Smi" $Smi	initial text may only have to be entered; wildcard may need to be used; $ symbol may be required
Any surname that ends with "son", e.g. Harrison, Jackson, Smithson	$son *son Like "son"	

Searching numeric fields

Example data to be found	Possible software notation	Explanatory notes
Any salary of £10,000	10000 =10000	= symbol may be required; £ sign and commas should not be included
Any salary greater than £10,000	>10000	
Any salary amount except £10,000	<> 10000 NOT 10000	

Searching date fields

Example data to be found	Possible software notation	Notes
1 January 1955	01/01/55 =01/01/55 ={01/01/55} =#1/01/55#	= symbol may be required; date may have to be enclosed in curly brackets or # sign
Any date after 01/01/55	>01/01/55	> represents "after" < represents "before"

Searching logical fields

Example data to be found	Possible software notation	Explanatory notes
Yes	Yes True On	
No	No False Off	

Example 4
In the personnel file set up for Kings Fashion Shops the queries shown in Example 3 might be implemented in the following ways using the QBE tool:

(a) Which staff work in Accounts?

First Name	Surname	Date of birth	Department	Salary	Medical
			="Acc"		

(b) Which staff earn less than £15,000?

First Name	Surname	Date of birth	Department	Salary	Medical
				<15000	

(c) Which staff are over 40? For a search taking place on 1 January 1995:

First Name	Surname	Date of birth	Department	Salary	Medical
		<=01/01/55			

(d) Which staff have had a medical check?

First Name	Surname	Date of birth	Department	Salary	Medical
					Yes

Exercise 2
Using the full personnel database designed in Exercise 1 how would you formulate QBE queries for the following:
(a) Which staff joined the company after 1 April 1980?
(b) Which staff have A levels?
(c) Which staff live in Leighton?

Specifying multiple criteria

It is often necessary to locate records that meet more than one criteria based on one or more fields. If the search is to be carried out on one field, then, generally, one of the following logical operators is used to link the search criteria:

- where both criteria must be met, the operator AND is used;
- where either of two criteria must be met, the operator OR is used.

If the search is to be carried out on two fields, then, generally:

- where both criteria must be met, the two criteria are placed on the same line of the QBE grid;
- where either of two criteria must be met, the second criterion is placed on the line below the first in the QBE grid.

Example 5
The following multiple QBE queries might be required of the Kings Fashions database:

(a)   Which staff were born in the 1950s?

First Name	Surname	Date of birth	Department	Salary	Medical
		>=01/01/50 AND <=31/12/59			

(b)   Which staff work in Management or Accounts?

First Name	Surname	Date of birth	Department	Salary	Medical
			="Man" OR ="Acc"		

(c)   Which staff were born before 1970 and have not had a medical check up?

First Name	Surname	Date of birth	Department	Salary	Medical
		<01/01/70			No

(d)   Which staff work in Packing or earn less than £8500?

First Name	Surname	Date of birth	Department	Salary	Medical
			="Pac"		
				<8500	

Exercise 3
Using the full personnel database how would you formulate QBE queries for the following:
(a)   Which staff joined after 1980 and work in Accounts?
(b)   Which staff have GCSEs or OLs?
(c)   Who are the female members of staff?

Specifying the sort order

With some software it is possible to have the records resulting from a search displayed in an appropriate order to help make sense of them, i.e. either in ascending order (A-Z, 0-9) or descending order (Z-A, 9-0).

Calculated fields

It is also often possible to create calculated fields. These calculations can be the result of a *mathematical calculation* (e.g. multiplying one field with another or adding two fields together) or a *combination* of *text fields* (e.g. joining three fields of an address to appear in one field). The exact notation for each of these types of calculated fields will, of course, depend on the software itself.

Example 6
(a) A QBE query to find all those earning more than £10,000, displaying a further field **New salary** to calculate a 4% increase in salary, and sorting the records in alphabetical order might first be set up as below and secondly result in the following records displayed:

First Name	Surname	Department	Salary	New salary
			>10000	[Salary]*1.04

First Name	Surname	Department	Salary	New salary
Mina	Patel	Pur	£15,000	£15,600
Mary	Smith	Man	£25,000	£26,000

(b) The same query but combining the **First name** and **Surname** of the employees in one field **Name** might be set up as shown below. (Note: the quotation marks are necessary to force a space between the two pieces of data.) The resultant records are also displayed below.

Name	Department	Salary	New salary
[First name] & " " & [Surname]		>10000	[Salary]*1.04

Name	Department	Salary	New salary
Mina Patel	Pur	£15,000	£15,600
Mary Smith	Man	£25,000	£26,000

Standard Query Language (SQL)

Many database software packages offer an additional query language called SQL. This language was intended to standardise queries across different database systems although there are now a number of variants of SQL. If a user wishes to make use of data held on a corporate database (see **17**) an understanding of SQL might be useful.

8.   Printing the data

From time to time it will be necessary to print the data in the database.   Database software provides an easy means of doing this, although sometimes this is referred to as *producing a listing* rather than printing.   However, the essential point to remember is that this printout will be very basic with very limited attention paid to its presentation, for example the fields of data will be displayed in columns with the original fieldnames used as headings.

If the printout is intended for others, e.g. managers for decision making purposes, then this is not very impressive or professional.   The solution to this problem is to create custom-designed printouts, known as *reports*, and these are discussed in more detail in section **11.**

9.   Designing forms

As mentioned above, most database software packages provide a *forms designer* to create forms. These might be required for a variety of purposes, not only for data entry but also to display data on the screen or print it out.

Although forms can be designed from scratch using a blank form, it is a good idea, especially for a new designer to use the *quick form* facility available in most forms designers. This will produce a very basic form which can then be enhanced further as required.

Depending on the sophistication of this *quick form* facility, the designer will be able to specify the fields to be included on the form as well as the layout of the form. Some software, however, will also allow the designer to choose a particular "style" or "look" for the form.

Example 7
A quick data-entry form designed for Kings Fashions database might look something like the one below, which has been used to display the first record:

```
Kings Fashions Ltd

First Name:   Susan
Surname:      Browne
Date of birth:          10/11/67
Department:   Sal
Salary:           £8,500
Medical:  ▢
```

When enhancing a basic form, or even if designing it from scratch, the designer should bear in mind the following basic points, but above all that the form should be clear, readable, consistent and effective:

The purpose for which the form is to be designed should influence its design. A form intended for data entry purposes should match any paper-based forms which might be used to collect the data.

If necessary, fieldnames should be replaced with more appropriate and descriptive labels and extra text should be added as prompts to assist the user in entering data. For instance, if the data in a field is coded, it might be advisable to provide details of the coding system. However, it is important not to clutter up the form with too many competing messages.

The data appearing in the data entry boxes should be displayed in the most appropriate format, e.g. a date might be displayed as 01-01-95, 01/01/95, 1 Jan 1995 or 1 January 1995, and a numeric value might be displayed showing commas, e.g. 10,000 or with currency signs and decimal places, e.g. £100.00.

Related fields should be grouped together and boxes or lines used to reinforce the groupings. When this has been done it may be necessary to change the order in which the cursor moves from one field to the next (known as the *tab order*), however it is important to ensure that the cursor moves through the fields in a logical rather than a haphazard way.

To ensure an aesthetically pleasing look to the form, labels should be aligned consistently, e.g. left, right or centred, and the fields themselves aligned both vertically and horizontally.

Example 8
The data entry form shown in Example 7 has been enhanced in the following ways: The data has been divided into two main groups, separated by a line. Explanatory text has been added to the Department label to prompt the user only to enter the first three letters of the department name. The Date of birth field now displays the full date. All the labels and the data entry boxes have been aligned both vertically and horizontally.

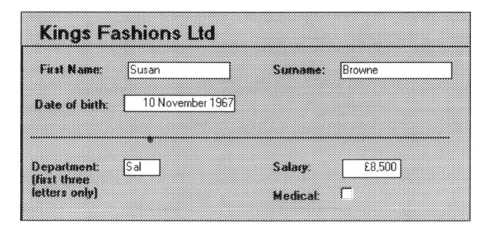

Windows-based database software provides the following extra features to enhance forms. However, it is essential that they are adopted with care for if too many are used in one form they can create an unattractive and unusable form:

Text can be formatted further, e.g. the *font* can be changed, as well as its *size* and *style*. The section entitled *Typeface* in **2:7** provides a full explanation of these terms and also provides advice on their use which is relevant to the design of forms.

Field labels and data entry boxes can appear in *shadowed* boxes or be given a *three-dimensional* look, i.e. presented in raised or sunken boxes, although features of this kind should be used carefully and consistently.

Colour can often be added to forms, and in fact, a small amount of colour can be very effective in on-screen forms, although too many bright colours can be overwhelming and should be avoided.

To assist in effective data entry and to reduce the possibility of incorrect data being entered, it may be possible to include the following additional elements:

- *List boxes*, which display all the possible selections;

- *Combo boxes*, which are list boxes that allow additional values to be entered by the user;

- *Check buttons*, which are sometimes automatically set up for logical fields. They are checked for "yes" and unchecked for "no".

- *Toggle buttons,* which can also be used for logical fields. They are pressed down for "yes" and unpressed for "no".

- *Option buttons*, which are used to select one from a group of options:

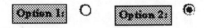

Example 9
The data entry form in Example 8 has been further enhanced: The font has been changed to Times New Roman, and a larger font size has been used for the heading; the field labels have been raised and the data entry boxes sunk. A list box has been used to display the Department names, and the explanatory text has been removed.

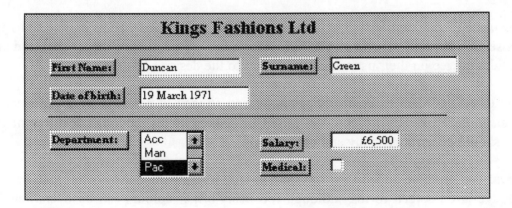

Exercise 4
Design a data entry form for the full Personnel file which makes use of some of the extra features described in this section.

10. Data validation

As explained above data validation is necessary to ensure the integrity of data entered into the database. Validation rules can be set up to specify the only data that can be accepted in a particular field together with messages to be displayed if data entry attempts to break any of these rules. In many database packages it is possible to set up both validation rules and messages when the database is designed, however, if it is not done at that stage then it should be considered here when the data entry form is designed.

The expressions used in validation rules are very similar to those used in queries (see 7) and examples of possible data validation rules and text messages are given below. One point to mention is that text messages should use consistent phrasing, i.e. either "do" or "don't", else the user will become confused.

Text fields

Valid data	Validation rule	Validation message
Only specified text	"Mr" OR "Mrs" OR "Miss" OR "Ms"	"Only Mr, Mrs, Miss or Ms permissible"

Numeric fields

Valid data	Validation rule	Validation message
A value less than or greater than a specified value	<10	"You must enter a value less than 10"
Anything but a specified value	<>0	"A zero value is not allowed."
A value within a specified range	>=1000 AND <2000	"Enter a value between 1000 and 1999."

Date fields

Valid data	Validation rule	Validation message
A date after a specified date	>=01/01/40	"Only a date from 1 January 1940 is valid."
A date before today	<= date( )	"A date after today's date is not allowed."
A date within a specified range	>=01/01/94 AND 31/12/94	"You may only enter a date in 1994."

Example 10
Data validation rules for the Kings Fashions database might include one to ensure that only a date of birth after 01/01/35 is entered (i.e. only staff under 60 are employed) and one that only allows salaries within the range £6,000 and £25,000 to be entered.

Exercise 5
What further data validation rules might be useful for the full personnel database designed in Exercise 2?

11. Designing reports

Although data can be printed out in a very basic way (as described in **9** above) it is very likely that data will need to be presented in a more attractive and understandable way. A *report* is the term given to the formatted presentation of data and reports can be designed not only to print data but also to display it on the screen. When designing reports it is important to understand that it is only the layout of the report that is being created: the data displayed in the report is extracted from the database.

A *reports designer* is usually provided in a database package and, as with a forms designer, the software normally provides the means to produce a *quick report* which can then be enhanced further.

Before creating a report, however, it is important to remember who the report is for and what its purpose is. This will very much determine what is to be included (as too much unnecessary information is irrelevant), the order in which it is to be presented, and how the information should be grouped or sorted.

Depending on the sophistication of the *quick report* facility, the designer may also be able to specify the type of layout for the report, its "style" or "look", as well as the page orientation and the line spacing to be used.

The *quick report* facility will usually present the data in columns using the fieldnames as the column headings and it will usually total all numeric data (which in some cases may be inappropriate).

Example 11
A quick report providing details of Kings Fashions' salary bill might look like the one below:

Financial report: salaries
today's date

First Name	Surname	Date of Birth	Salary
Susan	Browne	10/11/67	£8,500
Andy	Shah	06/06/75	£8,000
Mary	Smith	09/04/53	£25,000
Duncan	Green	19/03/71	£6,500
Mina	Patel	23/08/54	£15,000

			£63,000

It is very likely that the designer will want to improve the presentation of a quick report to ensure that it is more readable and more understandable. This can usually be done using the same features as available in a forms designer (see **9**). However, some advice is provided here on ways to improve the presentation of reports to enhance their usability.

If the fieldnames which have been used for the column headings are not very clear then these should be replaced or, alternatively, explanatory text added. The data in the columns should be presented in the most appropriate way and any totals should be deleted if they are not required.

The position of each column needs to be examined. If columns of data need to be read together then the designer should consider moving them closer together or even combining the data in one column.

If a report is intended to summarise data, related items should be grouped together. This will then permit calculations to be performed on the groups. These calculations might include summing, counting or finding the maximum or minimum values in the data. Boxes and lines can also be drawn around or beneath the data to highlight the groupings as well as to emphasise the calculations.

Finally, the overall look of the page needs to be considered. This can range from ensuring the most appropriate typeface, size and style are used for the different elements of the report to employing a 3-D or shadowed look to the data or the use of colour. Additionally, page numbers and other page headers and footers (see **2.10**) can also significantly enhance the usability of the report.

Example 12
A report on the status of the take up of free medical checks by the employees, grouped by the field Medical check and sorted alphabetically, and displaying full name (in one column), department and date of birth, might be designed to appear as below.

Medical checks
today's date

Medical	Name	Department	Date of birth
Yes			
	Andy Shah	Acc	6 June 1975
	Mary Smith	Man	9 April 1953
No			
	Susan Browne	Sal	10 November 1967
	Duncan Green	Pac	19 March 1971
	Mina Patel	Pur	23 August 1954

Exercise 6
Design a report based on the full personnel database, which will include the full name of the member of staff (in one column), their address (in a second column) and their home telephone number (in a third).

Exercise 7
You work for the Tourist Information Office in the fictitious town of Kory and have been asked to create a database to hold details of all the hotels in the town, so that suitable hotels can be provided for customers in the tourist office.

(a) Using the data given below, design on paper the structure of the database.
(b) Design on paper, a form to be used for data-entry purposes.
(c) Design on paper a report to display relevant hotel information for prospective customers.

Kory Hotels Information

Curzon **
Tower Street KO1 2SB
Tel: 634821
128 bedrooms
Lift, dogs allowed; no smoking areas
Conference facilities for 180
B&B single room: £80.50; double £100.50

Clifton **
9 Clifton Road KO3 6LH
Tel: 642893
18 bedrooms
Child facilities
B&B single room: £49; double £70

Harringtons ***
50 Howarth Road KO3 8LH
Tel: 642343
28 bedrooms
Child facilities
Conference facilities for 50
B&B single room: £35.25; double £70.50

Abbey **
Abbey Lane Howarth KO3 7DE
Tel: 666643
12 bedrooms
Child facilities
Conference facilities for 50
B&B single room: £35; double £60

Howarth **
13 St Mary's Howarth KO3 7DD
Tel: 675645
11 bedrooms
Dogs allowed, child facilities,
Conference facilities for 60
B&B single room: £27; double £50

Royal **
Station Green KO2 2AA
Tel: 693245
188 bedrooms
Lift
Conference facilities for 250
B&B single room: £70; double £95

Mount Vale **
23 Mount Vale KO2 2GF
Tel: 634256
25 bedrooms
Lift, child facilities
conference facilities for 25
B&B single room: £30; double £62.50

King **
125 Holgate Road KO2 4DE
Tel: 635656
15 bedrooms
Dogs allowed, child facilities
B&B single room: £35; double £55

The Mount **
125 The Mount KO2 2DA
Tel: 634556
20 bedrooms
Lift, child facilities
Conference facilities for 40
B&B single room: £40.50; double £70.50

St Mary's ***
190 Coombe Road KO4 3HA
Tel: 765342
9 bedrooms
Child facilities
Conference facilities for 12
B&B single room: £45.50, double £60

12. Mailing labels

Some report designers are able to facilitate the production of *mailing label*s which can be designed to match the user's label stationery, e.g. two or three across a page. It is often possible to insert extra spaces, punctuation and text into the addresses, if required. (The section entitled *Envelopes* in **2:12** gives some advice on designing envelopes.)

Example 13
The following shows mailing labels printed three across for the staff of Kings Fashions.

Miss Susan Browne	Mr Duncan Green	Mrs Mina Patel
25 Grange Road	27 Leighton Road	56 Freestone Avenue
Leighton	Creighton	Northwich
Sussex	Sussex	Sussex
TH14 6GH	TH6 4DF	TH9 8DS

13. Multimedia databases

In addition to text, numeric, date and logical data, some database packages allow sound and graphics, e.g. logos, photos and other graphical images, to be included in a database, thereby creating a true multimedia database. These extra objects can often be used to enhance both forms and reports.

Example 14
In the Kings Fashions database, a photograph of each employee could have been included in each record.

14. Relational databases

The discussion of databases in sections **4-13** above has concentrated on setting up a simple flat file. This is quite adequate for many small business applications. However, at the centre of most large organisations' business activities lies a substantial business database system, and such systems are more complex than a single datafile since they are based around a large number of files that have been linked together.

Much of today's PC database software can support the production of such database applications and are therefore very powerful tools. However, the design of sophisticated database applications is a specialist task which should not be undertaken unless the designer has some background in database design, since if it is not done with care it might cause serious problems in the processing of data.

However, a few of the most significant points of designing relational databases are presented here as it is possible that a user will wish to design a small relational database. In order to do this, a common small business application is taken as an example.

> **Example 15**
> Pandora's Box is a small mail order company selling jewellery items. It wants to set up a database to keep control of its products, customers and their orders. In addition to creating mailshots it also wants to be able to create forms to be used as invoices.

Firstly, the designer needs to identify not only the data items (i.e. the fields) in the database but also the different tables that are required. However, this is not as easy as it sounds. One important requirement is that data is not duplicated in the different tables as this can create errors of integrity, e.g. if the user updates the data in one table and not in another.

Secondly, it is necessary to consider how the data in one table is related to another. When determining the relationships between data, this must be approached from both ends of the relationship. There are three basic types of relationship:

One to one

In a one-to-one relationship each record in one table has one corresponding record in a second table and each record in the second table has one corresponding record in the first table. For example, for each customer in a customer table there is an equivalent record in a credit ratings table and vice versa.

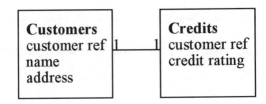

A one-to-one relationship type normally means that only one table is required. However, there are times when it is appropriate to create two linked tables of this type.

One to many

In a one-to-many relationship a record in one table has many corresponding records in a second table, but a record in the second table has only one corresponding record in the first, e.g. one customer places many orders, but each order only comes from one customer.

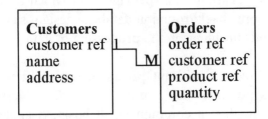

This is the most common type of relationship in relational database design.

Many to many

In a many-to-many relationship a record in one table has many corresponding records in the second table, and a record in the second table has many corresponding records in the first, e.g. an order can be for many products, and a product can appear on many orders.

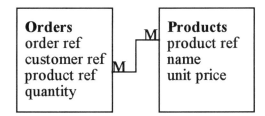

However, this type of relationship is problematic since it would result in the duplication of data held in the database. The solution is to create a third table, e.g. an order items table that holds the details of one item on an order. The two many-to-many relationships can then become two one-to-many relationships.

For instance, a one-to-many relationship can be set up with the orders table, such that an order can consist of many order items (but each item only appears on one order), and a one-to-many relationship can be set up with the products table such that a product can appear on a number of order items (but each order item only refers to one product).

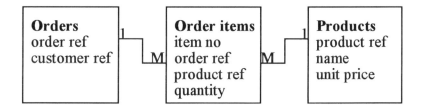

Example 16
Pandora's Box database should therefore consist of four tables, linked as shown below.

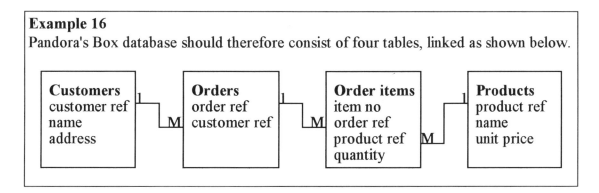

Queries

Once the tables have been designed and linked, queries can be made of the database in the same way as described in 7 above, although, in addition, it will be necessary to specify the tables in which the fields appear.

Forms and reports

In a similar way both forms and reports can be designed using data from one or more linked tables. However, it will depend very much on the software how this is achieved in practice. For instance, a form using data from two tables which have a one-to-many relationship might be achieved by creating a main form using the data from the "one" end of the relationship and a sub-form, using the data from the "many" end of the relationship. On the other hand, creating a form or report that is taken from more than two tables might need to be created in some other way, e.g. from a saved query.

Example 17
A form might be created for Pandora's Box to be used as an invoice. In addition to the main data that comes from the linked tables, the Invoice date is extracted from the system, and the Total price, Sub-total, VAT and Total are calculated fields: i.e. Total price = Quantity*Unit price, Sub-total =Sum(Total price), VAT =Subtotal*17.5%, and Total = Subtotal+VAT

Pandora's Box
123 High Street   Whitelea   Surrey   BT34 6TG
Tel: 01896-678945
INVOICE

To: Mrs J Livingstone
      Laverstock Lane
      Heathfield
      East Sussex
      TN24 7RW

Order ref: 10456

Invoice date: 25 March 1995

Item No	Product Ref	Product name	Quantity	Unit price	Total price
1	BW89	16" Gold necklace	2	£39.75	£79.50
2	AB56	Brooch	1	£29.95	£29.95
				Sub-total	£109.45
				VAT	£19.15
				Total	£128.60

Example 18

A report for Pandora's Box to display summary information about sales of products might look as below. The data has been grouped by Product ref and shows the quantity sold as well as the name and address of the purchasing customer. It also shows the number of each item sold as well as the total sold.

Pandora's Box: Product sales
today's date

Product ref	Product name	Quantity sold	Customer's name and address
AB1	**Brooch**	1	Mrs J Livingstone, 67 Haverstock Lane, Heathfield, East Sussex
		1	Miss T Green, Farrow Grove, Hamble, Hants
	Total sold	2	
AW1	**Horse charm**	3	Mrs J Brown, Highfield Road, Leeds, Yorks
		1	Mrs K Norris, 23 George Road, Hastings, E Sussex
		2	Miss F Rose, 89 Highbrooms Road, Norwich
	Total sold	6	
AW2	**Cloverleaf charm**	5	Mrs K O'Hare, Ivy Cottage, Malahide, Dublin
		2	Miss M Weeks, 654 New Road, Lincoln
	Total sold	7	
	Total items sold	**15**	

Exercise 8

Metropolitan Properties is a small property management business that looks after a large number of residential properties in London. Its clients are both individuals and companies, and many of them own more than one property. The services offered by Metropolitan Properties include advertising properties for rent, vetting prospective tenants, setting up the Tenancy Agreements and collecting rent.

(a) Design the structure of a small relational database comprising three linked tables: one holding details of the landlords; a second holding details of their properties; and a third holding details of the tenants.

(b) Design a form to be used as a monthly rent demand for tenants paying by cheque or cash.

(c) Design a report to produce a list of all unoccupied properties showing the landlord's details.

15. Automating a database application

In this chapter the different aspects of the design and use of a database have been described separately. This was acceptable from both a designer's and a learner's point of view in order to understand how to use them and how to get the most out of them.

However, for someone merely using a database application, e.g. to enter, query or print data, the whole process needs to be made far less complicated. Hence, if creating a database for   others to use a designer should consider automating the database application. The application can then be activated from an initial start-up screen where either a text-based menu system or button control can be used to move to the different parts of the system.

Example 19
The database designed for Pandora's Box might be automated to run from the following start-up screen. Pressing the first button would take the user to a data entry form to add new customer's details (not yet created); pressing the second, to a data-entry form to add new orders (not yet created); pressing the third, to print invoices using the form (designed in Example 17); and pressing the final button, to quit the database.

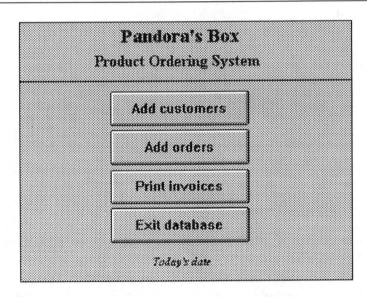

Depending on the software, creating a customised application can be achieved in a number of ways which are described below.

- *Application generators*, as their name suggests, can automatically generate an application by setting up the database data-entry forms and reports to work together.

- *Macros* are a series of actions that can be set up by the designer to be carried out automatically, literally "at the touch of a button". With many software packages it is possible to *record* macros by carrying out the tasks themselves, rather than writing a *script* (a textual description of the commands using the macro language). In this context a macro would be attached to a button to display the relevant form or print a report as required.

- *Programming* facilities are not available in all database packages, but where they exist, are very powerful and provide even greater control over the database. To write a program requires in-depth knowledge of the programming language, but once this has been mastered, it can be used to automate and customise the database system significantly.

Exercise 9

How might the relational database designed for Metropolitan Properties be set up as a working application? Design the start up screen.

---

16. Multi-user systems and security

With single-user database applications, i.e. where the database is kept on one PC and only used by one person, there are no significant problems as far as use and security are concerned. However, if the application is to be used on a multi-user system, e.g. across a network, this requires significant control of the system and especially its security.

Although it is quite possible for a number of users to work on different files at the same time, one problem concerns a number of users who want to access or change the same data at the same time. Most of the relational database packages which allow multi-user access have *file- and record-locking* facilities, which means that only one user can edit a record at one time. It is therefore good practice not to spend too much time editing records as this can hold up other users.

The second problem concerns the integrity of the data held on the system and this means ensuring that unauthorised users do not gain access to the data and that those who do have access to the system can only perform tasks they are allowed to do. (See **13:9** for more advice on unauthorised access.)

Normally, a database system administrator is responsible for the security of the system, and with a sophisticated database system, the system administrator will be able to create *accounts* for all the users of the database, allocate each user a *user number* and *PIN* (personal ID number) as well as a *password*. The administrator will also assign *permissions*. This means allowing certain users the ability only to view datafiles and forms, whereas other users may be able to modify datafiles and forms, and yet others will have full permissions. The software may also allow *guests* to be able to use the database system.

For further database security, software may provide the facility for files to be encrypted (i.e. made indecipherable) to protect the contents being viewed, say in a word processing software. If a database is being designed that is to hold personal data of living individuals then the implications of the Data Protection Act should also be considered (see **13:15-17**).

17. Connectivity

In a multi-user computing environment, it may be necessary for a PC database to use data created in other databases or spreadsheets. With most PC database software packages this is often possible by *importing* other databases or worksheets. Data created in databases can also be used in word processing software for mailmerge activities.

If further connectivity is required however, e.g. to the corporate database held on a mainframe or mini-computer, then this is usually only possible with the most sophisticated PC database software packages on the market. When data is accessed from another platform, this is usually done using SQL, hence so-called *SQL-compatibility* is important in a PC software package if corporate connectivity is required, although there are a number of other proposed standards for corporate connectivity, e.g. Microsoft's *ODBC (Open Database Connectivity)*.

18. Further work with database software

This chapter has covered a vast amount of the functionality associated with sophisticated database software packages and has described how to design and set up the different elements of a working database application. Although using the minimal features available it is possible to design an effective database application, it must be reiterated that to create a complex relational database system that is to be used as the hub of an organisation's information processing activities does require significant experience and time.   However, as PC database users become more and more experienced with the software and fully understand the concepts involved they will be able to create some extremely powerful applications.

Part two

Practical guidelines

7

Getting started with PCs

1. Introduction

Before beginning to use any of the types of software described in this book you should read this chapter. It will give you the essential information you need to be in a position to start work on your PC as well as provide you with a firm foundation on which the material in the other chapters in this section is based. Further important information will also be found in Chapters 13 and 14.

However, before you turn on your PC you should take some time to get to know your computer system and find out what makes it effective.

2. Understanding a personal computer system

A personal computer system like any other "system" is composed of a number of elements which together make a usable whole. There are three main elements to a personal computer system:

- the *hardware*, which is the generic name given to all the physical components of the computer;

- the *software*, which are the programs that instruct the hardware to carry out particular tasks; and

- the *user* (often termed the *liveware*), who is in overall control of the hardware and software.

Each of these three main elements of a computer system is described further below.

3. The user - the liveware

You, the user, are an invaluable part of your computer system as you are in control. It is therefore in your hands whether your computer system is an effective productivity tool or is used inappropriately and inefficiently to little practical purpose.

The following chapters take you step-by-step through the process of learning to use PC software effectively to carry out common business tasks. You are advised to work through the material slowly, taking time to absorb it and put what you have learnt into practice. You should also relate what you learn in one application to what you learn in another. Much of what is said is applicable in many situations, so as you progress through the book, there will be less to learn.

As a new user you may be a little anxious and apprehensive about using the computer. But you should not feel inhibited to experiment as this is an important part of learning, and there is usually more than one way of doing things.

If you are motivated, enthusiastic and prepared to put in some effort to learn how to use the software, you will become an effective part of your computer system.

4.   The hardware

The term *hardware* is used to describe all the physical components of the computer. These are outlined briefly below, but if you are interested in finding out more about the technical details, then Chapter 15 provides a good starting point.

The main *system unit* houses all the electronic components, e.g. the *processor* as well as the *hard disk* (which holds both the software and data) and at least one *floppy disk drives* (the doors of which you will see on the front of the system unit).

The *screen* (also known as a monitor or VDU, i.e. a visual display unit) is attached to the system unit by a cable and displays what is often referred to as a *soft copy* of your work.

A *keyboard* is used to control and enter data into the computer. As you will be making considerable use of the keyboard to interact with it, this is a good time to familiarise yourself with its layout. With word processing software, in particular, you will have to use the keyboard extensively for text entry, so familiarity with the main keys will pay off. The keyboard has the same alphanumeric keys and spacebar as a typewriter but note also:

- the Enter key, marked [↵], which is used, for example, to send instructions to the computer;
- the Shift keys, marked [↑], on the left and right of the alphabetic keyboard, which when held down with an alphanumeric key will produce a capital letter or the character shown on the top half of the numeric and other keys;
- the [Caps Lock] key, which when depressed will light up the *Caps Lock* light on the top right hand corner of the keyboard and will allow you to type continuously in capitals (thus obviating continuous use of a Shift key);
- the [Esc] key, which can often be used to escape from an activity;
- the function keys, labelled [F1] to [F12] along the top of the keyboard, which are used by some software packages as short-cuts for some commands;
- the [Ctrl] and [Alt] keys which are used in combination with other alphabetic or function keys for package-specific use;
- the cursor (or arrow) keys, which are used to move the cursor (a position marker) around the screen, and the keys marked [Home], [End], [Page Up] and [Page Down], which are for moving to the beginning or end of a document or screen;

- the keys marked [Insert] and [Delete] which can be used in certain software to insert and delete data; and
- the numeric keypad on the right hand side which can be used in place of the numeric keys on the alphanumeric keyboard, but only when the *Num Lock* light is on. (You may need to press the [Num Lock] key to turn it on.)

When you use the keyboard you should raise the feet underneath the back of the keyboard, resting the palms of your hands in front of the keyboard and your fingers lightly on the keys. ("Touch-typists" will know where to place their fingers on the "home keys" for optimum movement around the keyboard.) When working at the computer, it is very important to sit comfortably, especially for extended periods, to ensure you do not suffer from any health problems. (See **13:18** for more information.)

A *mouse* is another means of interacting with the computer. You will need to keep the mouse flat on the desk with the buttons at the top. Your right hand should rest on top of the mouse with your palm around the body of the mouse and your thumb and small finger gripping the sides of the mouse. Your index finger should rest lightly on the left button as most of the operations will take place on this button. Eventually you will need to learn how to move the mouse around to control a pointer on the screen and how to *click, double-click* and *drag* the mouse to carry out certain operations. You should note that although the mouse will probably have been set up for a right-handed person, it is possible to change it to a left-handed mouse (see **14:8**).

A *printer* is also a necessary part of a computer system in order to provide you with a *hard copy* of your work. This may be sited next to your computer or elsewhere in the building.

5. The software

Although the hardware is important you will not be able to do anything useful with your PC unless you have some *software* installed on it. The software you use will be of two types: *applications software* for carrying out specific tasks like word processing for document production, spreadsheets for analysing numerical data; and *systems software,* e.g. the operating system which controls the operation of the system. Applications software is dealt with in depth in other chapters of this book, but the operating system needs to be considered here.

Every computer has to have an operating system and the standard operating system for PCs is called *MS-DOS* (short for Microsoft Disk Operating System) often known simply as DOS. However, another piece of software called *Windows,* which is an extension of DOS, offers significant advantages over DOS. Applications software either works directly with DOS (and is generally termed "DOS-based software") or with Windows (hence "Windows-based software").

Although you will have most contact with the applications software packages, you will still need to understand the basics of DOS or Windows to be able to carry out some tasks that are usually not possible with the applications software. In order to learn about DOS and Windows, the best way is to start up the computer and see them in action.

6.   Starting up the computer

Turn on your PC at the mains as well as the switch on the system unit itself. The screen may come on automatically or you may have to turn that on separately. Watch the screen as a number of messages appear: this is the computer *booting up* and carrying out a number of diagnostic checks.

Once these have been completed and the operating system has fully loaded, what appears next will depend on whether you are working on a single-user system or on a network.

Single-user system

If you are working on a single-user system you will see one of the following:

- a blank screen except for the letter **C:\>** with the cursor flashing beside it. This means that DOS has loaded and you are working *at the DOS prompt*. (If this is the case you can skip the rest of this section and move directly to **7**); or

- the Windows logo, which means that the computer has been set up to load Windows automatically when the computer is turned on. (If this is the case you can skip the next section and move to **8**); or

- something else, in which case you should see if you can select either Windows or DOS. For example, if the *DOS Shell* loads, then press [Shift]+[F9] to move to the DOS prompt. (If you are now at the DOS prompt, go on to **7**, if Windows has loaded move to **8**.)

Networked system

If you are working on a network you will probably have to log on to your computer using a password and only then, once you have been accepted as a bona fide user, will you be allowed to work on the system. (Remember, you must log out at the end of your session too.) You should then see one of the following:

- the letter **C:\>** or some other letter of the alphabet with the cursor flashing beside it, which means that DOS has loaded and you are working *at the DOS* prompt. (If this is the case, you can go directly to **7**); or

- the Windows logo, denoting that Windows has loaded (which means you can go to **8**); or

- a menu system offering you a number of choices, in which case you should choose Windows (and then move to **8**) or if this is not available, choose DOS (and go to section **7**).

7. Understanding DOS

With the **C:\>** prompt visible on the screen, you are ready to start work with DOS. Note the letter "C" means that you are working on the hard disk of your computer, i.e. that you are in a position to load software from the hard disk or save work on to it. (If you are using a PC network and you see some other letter, e.g. "D" or "E" or "F" this means you are initially working on the hard disk of another computer on the network, known as the *file server*.)

In order to proceed further you will have to type in a DOS command beside the prompt. The DOS command language uses a strict vocabulary of nouns and verbs, syntax, punctuation and spacing. You will learn some basic DOS commands in this chapter. However, you should note that any deviation from the correct format of the command will not be recognised by the operating system and an error message will appear on the screen. In this chapter you will also meet some of the common error messages (although you should note that further messages are explained in **14:6**).

To run a particular applications software package, you will have to type in the command to load the software. So you will need to know the exact command to load the software you want to use. For instance, the command to load Windows from the DOS prompt is **WIN**. If you try this and see **Bad command or file name** on the screen, then this is one of the error messages mentioned above and means the operating system could not find Windows. You should first check that you typed the command in correctly, and if not re-type it. However, if the operating system still cannot find Windows it can be assumed, for the time being at least, that it is not on your system, although this still does not necessarily mean that it is not there. In section 9 you will have a further opportunity to look for it, so if Windows has not loaded you can skip the next section and move directly to **9.**

8. Understanding Windows

After the Windows logo disappears, you will see a screen full of graphical information. Windows is known as a *graphical user interface* (or *GUI* for short) because it uses graphics rather than text to display information. Such an interface is also known as a *WIMP* interface. Although this term is a little outdated, it does help to explain the component parts of such an interface, because WIMP is an acronym standing for *Windows-Icons-Mouse-Pull down menus*. These terms are explained below in relation to the Windows screen you will see in front of you, and an example of which is shown overleaf. (Do not worry if your screen does not look exactly like this. It will depend what software is installed on your computer and how the *desktop* (as the screen of information is known) has been set up.)

The *windows* are the areas of the desktop which hold different applications or tasks. At this point you may only be able to see one large window showing the **Program Manager**, or (as in the desktop shown below) you may be able to see a number of smaller windows holding different types of information. Windows can overlap one another (as shown below) and they can also be re-sized and moved to new positions on the desktop.

The *icons* are the small graphical representations of applications and tasks. You may only be able to see icons that represent *groups* of programs, (e.g. the **Accessories** group on the desktop below), or you may be able to see individual program icons within the groups, (e.g. the **File Manager** and **Print Manager** icons in the **Main** group of programs).

Windows applications software are normally set up in their own groups, (e.g. **Word for Windows**, and **Excel**) although a number of application programs may have been set up in one group (e.g. **Applications**).

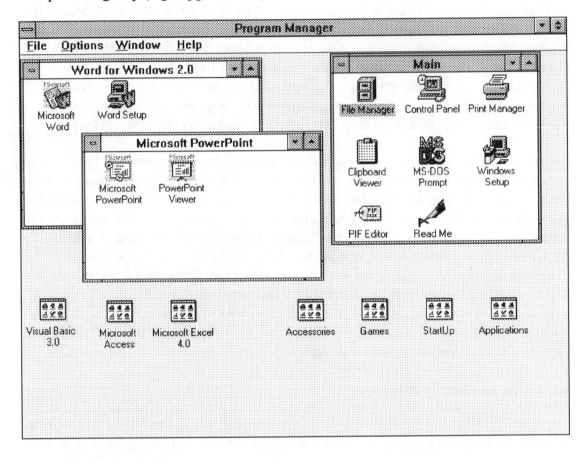

In order to open a group or start an application you need to move the pointer to the relevant icon and then double-click the *mouse*.

When a window is open, two or three buttons will be visible at the top right hand corner. Clicking on the down arrow will *minimise* (or *iconise*) the application (i.e. turn it into an icon), clicking on the up arrow will *maximise* it (so that it takes up the whole screen), and clicking on the double arrow will *restore* it to a previous size.

The *pull-down menus* appear on the top of the desktop. In the **Program Manager** you will see the following pull-down menus: **File** **Options** **Window** **Help** If you want to pull-down any of these menus you should either move the pointer to the relevant menu name and click the mouse, or hold down the [Alt] key and press the relevant underlined letter. Once you have pulled down a menu you can select items from the menu in the same way.

In order to gain a basic understanding of how Windows works and how to use the mouse, you are strongly advised to work through the Windows tutorial, by carrying out the following:

- select the **Help** pull-down menu;
- select **Windows Tutorial**.

A lot of software has been written to work with Windows, and it is particularly popular because it is easy to use and you can carry out tasks in much the same way in all Windows-based software, e.g. there are always **File**, **Window** and **Help** pull-down menus. So once you have understood the basic structure and processes used in Windows, you will quickly be able to get to grips with any Windows-based software.

9. Storing your work

Before you can start using the software, however, you will need to decide where you will store the work you will be creating, e.g. the letters or reports you write. On a single-user system you will have the choice of storing your work on either the hard disk or on a floppy disk. If you are working on a PC network, however, you may not have a choice and will be required to keep all your work on a floppy disk, but you should find out the position from your Network Manager. Once you have decided where to store your work you will need to prepare the disk. However, first of all you need to understand the concept of files.

10. Understanding files

All software programs as well as the work that you create using the software are held in *files*, hence there are program files and datafiles. In order to understand the concept of a file, take a look at the files already on the hard disk of your computer.

(Note that, on this and subsequent pages, instructions for DOS-users are shown on the left-hand side of the page whilst the instructions for Windows-users appear on the right-hand side of the page. Note too, that these instructions only show one way of carrying out the tasks, there may be other possible ways.)

DOS-users:	Windows-users:
Type: **DIR**	Select the **Window** pull-down menu;
(Note: you must always use the Enter key [↵] at the end of a DOS command)	Select the **Main** group of files; Double-click the **File Manager** icon.

DOS-users might see a list something like the one below:

```
DOS                <DIR>            08/01/93      12:00
WINDOWS            <DIR>            15/06/93      13:15
LOTUS              <DIR>            23/03/94       9:39
AUTOEXEC    BAT           487       29/05/94      17:25
COMMAND     COM        54,619       30/09/93      12:00
CONFIG      SYS           490       29/05/94      16:24
     6 file(s)        55,596 bytes
                   8,067,567 bytes free
```

Such a DOS listing displays all the files showing their *filenames*, *file extensions*, *size* and the *date* created or modified, whereas with Windows you may only see (in the right hand window of the screen) some of this information. However, it is worth understanding all the *attributes* of files because with Windows it is possible to view all the attributes of the files.

Filenames describe the contents of files and are between 1-8 characters long. They do not include any spaces or commas or characters like \ (which are reserved for other uses), e.g. the main DOS file is called COMMAND.

File extensions describe the type of file and are 3 characters long. In the Windows listing they are separated from the filename by a full stop, whereas in the DOS listing they appear in a separate column.

Examples of program file extensions include .COM, .EXE, .BAT and .SYS:

- .COM is short for *compiled*, e.g. the COMMAND file;
- .EXE (pronounced "exy") is short for *executable* file;
- .BAT is short for *batch* file. This type of file holds a number of DOS commands that are automatically carried out when the batch file is run. The most important batch file is the AUTOEXEC.BAT file which runs automatically when the computer is switched on and explains why Windows is often loaded automatically, since the WIN command is one of the DOS commands.
- .SYS is short for system file. The CONFIG.SYS file is an example and this is used to configure (i.e. set up) the computer when it is turned on.

Examples of datafile extensions include .DOC for documents created by some word processing packages, .XLS for spreadsheet worksheets, and .DBF for database files.

Windows-users should note that file types are also denoted by the icons displayed to the left of the file name.

The *size* of each file is shown in bytes, one byte being equivalent to one character, e.g. the AUTOEXEC.BAT file shown above is 487 bytes in size. The *date* and *time* of the last modification of the file are also displayed, and at the bottom of the file listing there is an indication of the number of files displayed, as well as the amount of disk space free (again in bytes).

There are a number of other ways of viewing files which are very useful if there are more files in the list than can be displayed on one screen.

DOS-users:	Windows-users:
For a wide listing of files (that only shows filenames), type: **DIR/W**	From the **File Manager:** Select the **View** menu; Select **All file details** (to display all the file details as described above).
For a full listing of files that is displayed one screen at a time, type: **DIR/P** You will be prompted to: **Press any key to continue . . .** to move to the next screen.	Select **Name** (for the file and file extensions only).

When looking at the list of files, DOS users will probably have noticed files that have the <DIR> sign after them and no extensions, and Windows-users will probably have noticed files at the beginning of the list that also have no extensions or other details. These are known as *directories* and require fuller explanation.

11. Understanding directories

Because the hard disk can hold hundreds if not thousands of files, the use of directories is essential to keep track of related files. All the files on a particular subject, e.g. all the program files for a word processing software program are normally installed in one directory. Directories can themselves contain directories and these are known as sub-directories. The structure of directories, sub-directories and further sub-directories can be represented by an upside-down tree, hence the first directory is known as the *root*.

C:\> is therefore the root directory, and from this directory there are usually a number of directories holding various sets of files, e.g. DOS files, Windows files, word processing program files, etc. To view the directories on the hard disk:

DOS-users:	Windows-users:
Type: **TREE**	In the **File Manager:** Select the **View** menu; Select **Tree only**

A hard disk tree which displays all the directories and sub-directories may look something like the one below:

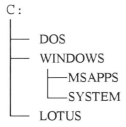

```
C:
├── DOS
├── WINDOWS
│     ├─MSAPPS
│     └─SYSTEM
└── LOTUS
```

Although it is very much up to the user to decide how to keep files on the hard disk, it is advisable that a user does not keep any files other than the essential system files (i.e. AUTOEXEC.BAT, COMMAND.COM and CONFIG.SYS) in the root directory, and that data files are kept together in a directory or sub-directory distinct from the one that holds the software application that was used to create them. There are also limitations on the number of files that can be stored in the *root* directory of a hard disk (i.e. 512 files) and this might be filled up quite quickly.

Even if you are working on a single-user PC you are advised to set up a directory for your own data files and if more than one user keeps files on a single PC then each user should have a separate directory for their work files. If you are working on a PC network, you should find out from the Network Manager if you can set up a directory for your files, or whether you should keep your datafiles on a floppy disk. If the latter is the case you can skip the next section and move directly to **13.**

12. Creating a directory on the hard disk

If you want to create a user directory on your PC this section will explain how to do so by creating a sub-directory USER within the root directory. (You can of course replace the word USER with your own or any other name as long as it only has up to 8 characters and no spaces or odd characters.)

This section will also show you how to move into that directory and create a further sub-directory (called WPDOCS) to hold files for word processed documents that you create. Once you have understood these basic tasks you will be able to set up further directories and sub-directories as required.

DOS-users:	Windows-users:
Ensure you are in the root directory, by using the CD (change directory) command to move to the root, represented by the \ character Type: **CD**	In the **File Manager**: Ensure you are in the root directory by clicking on the **C** at the top of the directory tree in the left hand window of the File Manager
Use the MD (make directory) command to make a directory (called USER). Type: **MD USER**	To create a directory (called USER): Select the **File** menu Select **Create directory ...** In the Name box, type: **USER**
Use the CD command to move into the new directory. Type: **CD USER**	Select **OK**
The DOS prompt should now show: **C:\USER>** which means you are in the new directory.	To move into the new directory, select USER in the tree in the left-hand window.
	The right-hand window should show there are
If you use the **DIR** command to find a list of files in this directory, you will see two special files that hold details of the directory, marked by . and ..	no files in the USER sub-directory.
	To create a sub-directory (called WPDOCS):
Use the MD command to make a new directory (called WPDOCS). Type: **MD WPDOCS**	Select the **File** menu Select **Create directory ...** In the Name box, type: **WPDOCS** Select **OK**
Use the CD command to move into the new directory. Type: **CD WPDOCS**	To move into the new directory, select WPDOCS in the tree in the left-hand window
The DOS prompt should now show: **C:\USER\WPDOCS**	
Notes: To move back one directory at a time, type: **CD..**	**Notes:** To move from the root to sub-directories and back, select the relevant directory and sub-directory names in the tree in the left-hand window.
To move to the root directly from any sub-directory, type: **CD**	
To move directly to the WPDOCS sub-directory from any other directory, type: **CD\USER\WPDOCS**	

DOS-users:

This is an opportune time to point out that in order to run a program that is stored in a sub-directory you either have to enter the DOS command to do so whilst in the relevant directory or if you are at any other point in the tree, you must also type in the full *path* to the program. For example, to run Lotus 1-2-3, you can either type **123** in the LOTUS directory itself, or if you are at any other position, type **\LOTUS\123**

However, to obviate the need to type such a command every time you wish to run Lotus (or any other program), the PATH command, e.g. **PATH C:\LOTUS**, should be entered into the AUTOEXEC.BAT file on your computer. This means that the path to Lotus is then set up from the outset, and hence typing 123 anywhere in the tree will load Lotus.

Consequently, if you can see a WINDOWS sub-directory in your tree, and the WIN command did not run Windows, then it is most likely that the relevant path command has not been included in the AUTOEXEC.BAT file. Try typing: **\WINDOWS\WIN** to see if you can run the WIN.EXE file. If you can you should go back to **8** and start again from there.

Notes:

It should be pointed out, however, that in most systems that have software pre-installed on them, PATH commands will have been set up in the AUTOEXEC.BAT file already. However, if this is not the case, **14:7** describes how an AUTOEXEC.BAT can be created or amended.

13. Preparing floppy disks

Floppy disks are a useful place to store data files as they can be kept securely away from the PC, and they also allow for portability, i.e. they can be used on different PCs. Even if you intend to use the hard disk to store your files, you should also prepare a number of floppy disks as you will need them to keep back-up copies of your files.

The first thing to do is to make sure that you obtain and use the correct size and density of floppy disks for your PC, so you should find out what *size* and *density* you need to acquire. Floppy disk drives come in two basic sizes: 5¼" and 3½" (although 3½" drives are the current standard) and two density types: *double* and *high*.

Before you can save any work on your disks you will have to prepare them. This preparation process is known as *initialisation* or *formatting*. The default process of formatting assumes that you wish to format the correct type of disk for the drive. Although it is possible to format double density disks in high density drives, it is not possible to format high density disks in double density drives. If you try to do this you will have problems with the storage and subsequent retrieval of your data.

Note, too, that you need only format a disk once and that if you format a disk that has work on it, this work will be erased.

To format a floppy disk you should carry out the following instructions shown overleaf:

DOS-users:	Windows-users:
Use the FORMAT command to format the disk in drive A. Type: **FORMAT A:**	In the **File Manager:** Select **Disk**; Select **Format Disk**.
If all goes well you will see the message: **Insert new diskette for drive A; and press ENTER when ready ...** When you do this, a message showing the **percent of disk formatted** will appear, and once the formatting is finished, a further message will appear: **Format complete** **Volume label (11 characters, Enter for none)** You can press Enter. The final message will be: **Format another (Y/N)?** Type in **Y** or **N** as appropriate.	You will then have an opportunity to change the drive name (e.g. **A** or **B**) and the capacity of the drive (e.g. 720K is double density and 1.44Mb is high density for a 3½ disk); Select **OK** If all goes well a message should appear showing that formatting is taking place. When this is complete, a further message will confirm the formatting details, and state: **Do you wish to format another disk?** You should select **Yes** or **No** as appropriate.
If you see one of the following error messages there is a problem:	Once the disk has been formatted, you can view the contents by selecting the **A** drive icon just above the left-hand directory tree window.
Invalid media or track 0 bad - disk unusable. **Format terminated.** This means that you are using the wrong type of disk, so you will need to amend the format command. If you are trying to use a 3½" double density disk in a hard density drive, type: **FORMAT A:/n:9/t:80** and if you are trying to use a 5¼" double density disk in a hard density drive, type: **FORMAT A:/4**	
Bad command or file name This suggests you have either typed the command incorrectly or DOS cannot find the FORMAT command. The FORMAT command is one of the DOS external commands (see **14:5**) so if you have been unable to format the disk it is because the path has not been set up to access the command. You will need either to move into the directory in which it is stored, probably called DOS, or type **DOS**\ before the command.	
Once the disk has been formatted, you can view the contents, either by changing drives, e.g. **A:** and then typing **DIR** or at the C prompt, by typing **DIR A:**	

It is a good idea to format a number of disks at one time so that they are readily available when you need them. You may even want to use a different disk for the different types of files you will be creating using the software, although if you need to integrate data from a datafile with one on another disk it will be a little more difficult - although not impossible (see **14:2**).

Floppy disks have root directories like hard disks and it is possible to set up directories on floppy disks in the same way as for the hard disk, although with the small amount of disk space on disks there is no real reason for doing this, unless you wish to hold more than the number of files that is permitted in the root directory. For double density disks this is 112 files, and for high density disks this is 224 files.

Once you have formatted the disks you should label them immediately using the supplied sticky labels. This is for a number of reasons: firstly, so you can identify them as *formatted* disks and secondly, so that you can identify them as *your* disks. Disks should then be looked after carefully (see **13.5** for further advice on care of disks).

14. Loading the applications software

You are now ready to load the software. With DOS-based software you will need to find out what command you must type at the DOS prompt and with Windows-based software what icon you need to select from Windows.

DOS-users	Windows-users
If you do not know what DOS command to use, you should move into the directory that holds the application program files, and locate a file that has the file extension .EXE or possibly .BAT Then type in the filename as this is the command to load the software, e.g. 123.EXE is the Lotus 123 program file, so just type **123**	If you do not know which icon to activate in Windows, search through the different groups of programs in the **Window** pull-down menu of the **Program Manager**.

Quitting the software

Once the software is loaded, the first thing you should find out is how to quit the software properly as it may be necessary for you to leave the software prematurely. You should not simply remove the disk and turn off the machine as you will be almost certain to lose some if not all of your work.

15. Using the on-line tutorial

You should then find out if there is an on-line tutorial. In Windows-based software this is usually found in the **Help** pull-down menu. With DOS-based software, you may be invited to try the tutorial package automatically, if not you could try using the [F1] function key. If this does not work, then you should quit the software, and see if you can locate a separate tutorial program, possibly in a sub-directory, and type in the command to load the tutorial.

If you have located the tutorial, then you should run through some of the early lessons of the tutorial in order to familiarise yourself with the package. It is not worth trying to take in too much at one time as you are unlikely to remember it and anyway you can always go back at a later date to try the intermediate and advanced lessons.

Part of the familiarisation process of using the tutorial is for you to find out the answers to the following questions:

Do I use the keyboard or the mouse or both?

You will need to find out whether you can only use the keyboard or whether you can also use the mouse. If you are working with a Windows-based software package there are usually a number of "keyboard short-cuts" to avoid a long series of mouse selections. This is useful because experienced users sometimes find it irritating to have to type the text in using the keyboard but control the software using the mouse. On the other hand, for the first-time user it will be much easier, initially at least, to use the mouse.

Is there on-line help?

If available, most packages seem to have standardised on the use of the [F1] key to activate help. (Windows-users can also locate Help in the **Help** pull-down menu.) Help systems may be context-sensitive, i.e. they will give you help relevant to what you are doing at the time you activate help. There may also be a search facility which will let you find help on a given topic. You may even be able to print the Help topic. (Note: if you are unable to find any help on a given topic, you should try a different term for the feature you are seeking.)

You should make extensive use of the help facility to find out how to carry out the tasks and exercises in the following chapters, and you are encouraged to make notes in this book as it is intended to be a useful resource for future use. Some software packages provide more than just a help system, they offer *on-line advisors*, which take you step-by-step through tasks using your own data, so look out for these.

What information is provided on the screen?

How much information is provided on the screen will depend on the particular software package. Some DOS-based packages, for instance display almost a blank screen, whilst Windows-based software will provide you with a lot of information. Here you will see, at least, *a menu bar* that shows the main groups of pull-down menus, with generic names like **File, Edit, Format**, etc., and one or more *tool bars* that display icons that represent common tasks and which can be activated by using the mouse. For instance, an icon of a disk might represent "saving", and an icon of a printer might represent "printing".

You should watch the screen at all times as you will not only find assistance how to carry out tasks, but messages will also be displayed there.

How do I save my work?

Saving your work is vital, since whilst you are typing in data you are only working in the computer's temporary storage area and it is not being saved onto the disk. You should therefore make sure you save your work frequently, especially before you print, but certainly every 10-15 minutes. With some software it is possible to set up the software to save your work automatically. (You should also not change disks in the middle of working on a file, as this may cause problems with saving.)

16. Naming files

When you save your file for the first time you will need to give it a name. There are a number of conventions for naming files (many of which have already been mentioned earlier in **10**):

Firstly, you should specify the *drive* (or *directory*) in which you wish to hold your data file. You can either prefix the name of the file with these details, e.g. **A:** (for the floppy drive) or the relevant hard disk directory, e.g. **C:\USERS\WPDOCS**, or you may be able to select the relevant drive or directory from a list.

Secondly, you will need to give your work a *filename*. This must be between 1 and 8 characters long and not include any spaces or strange characters like * or $ or £. You can, however use the dash [-] or underline [_] keys to separate parts of the filename, e.g. EX-1 or EX_1

Thirdly, you may need to provide a *file extension*. To do this you will have to type in a full stop immediately after the filename followed by three characters that describe the type of file. However, file extensions are normally allocated to the files by the software itself, e.g. a word processed document might automatically be given the file extension .DOC It is therefore easier to leave the file extension out unless you know what you are doing, as some software will not be able to locate files automatically if they have the wrong file extension.

You will have to name a datafile the first time you save it, but subsequently the software program will always save it with this name. However, if you want to save a second copy of your work under a different name this is also possible, e.g. Windows-based application software users can select the **Save As** command.

17. Using the default settings

In order for you to get started on the package straightaway, the software will have been installed with a number of *default settings*. Examples of such default settings include, for example in word processing software, the size of the paper to be used and the width of left and right margins. You can change any of these default settings at any time and these new settings will be saved with your work. However, for any new pieces of work you start the software will revert to the default settings.

If you would like to change the default settings permanently, then you should consider *customising* or *changing the setup* of your software (see **14:11**). Note that if you are working on a network, you will probably not be able to customise the software permanently on an individual basis.

18. Problem solving

If you do encounter problems, for instance if you do not understand an error message, you should endeavour to solve it using the on-line help. If you cannot find an immediate answer to your problem, you may need to search for another term.

Very occasionally, the computer may "hang up", e.g. the screen may seem to "freeze", and pressing keys will only cause the computer to beep at you. If this happens, and unless it resolves itself within a few minutes for it might just be accessing the disk or carrying out some other task you set it, you will have to *re-boot* the computer which will mean that you will lose all the work you have typed in since the last save. There are two ways to re-boot the computer:

- Carry out a *warm boot* by typing **[Ctrl]**+**[Alt]**+**[Del]**   (A warm boot will not cause the computer to carry out the diagnostic checks.) However, if the keyboard has hung up, it will not be able to accept this command, so you will have to carry out the second option.
- Carry out a *cold boot* by either pressing the **Reset** button on the system unit, or else turning off the computer, waiting a few seconds and then turning it back on again.

19. Using the chapters in this section

The practical guidance you are going to find in this section of the book is generic. This means that it is not specific to any one software package. The purpose of the book is for you to learn general concepts and principles, rather than package-specific instructions.

Another purpose of this book is for you to learn transferable skills so that you will be able to apply these general concepts and principles to any software package. You will therefore be given guidance on what to discover in the software, and it will be up to you to investigate (mainly using the on-line tutorial or help) how to put this into practice in your specific software package.

You should also work through each of the practical software chapters (8-12) in conjunction with the relevant theoretical chapters (2-6). The practical chapters should not be studied in isolation because the theoretical chapters will provide you with all the necessary knowledge and terminology required to carry out the tasks effectively using the software.

20. Remaining effective in your work

You are now ready to start to use this book to learn how to use the applications software to carry out common business information tasks. However, in order to ensure that you remain effective in your work there is still more to learn. You should therefore read Chapter 13 on how to avoid problems whilst working with your PC, and Chapter 14 on how to use DOS and Windows for further vital tasks, in particular how to make back-up copies of your files as well as how to integrate material created in different applications software programs.

8

Word processing software

1. Getting started

Before beginning to use your word processing package it is essential that you read Chapter 7 so that in particular:

- you are familiar with the use of both the keyboard and the mouse;
- you know how to start up the computer; and
- you have prepared your disks ready to hold your work.

2. Getting to know your word processing software package

You should refer to **7:14-15** for advice on getting to know your word processing package by finding out

- how to load the word processing software;
- if there is an on-line tutorial;
- whether you will need to use the keyboard or the mouse or both;
- if there is on-line help and how to access it;
- what information is shown on the screen; and
- how to quit the package.

3. Basic principles

You need to find out how to carry out the following basic operations:

Start your document: With some packages you may be in a position to type text straight in. With others you will have to start a *new* file or document, which you may have to name at this stage. (See **7:16** for advice on naming files.)

Save your document: With some programs you must save your work before you print, with others you can print before you save. However, whichever is the case, you should save frequently to ensure you have no problems with losing data. (Some software can be set up to save your work automatically for you - say every 10-15 minutes.)

The first time you save your work you will need to give it a name (see **7:16** for advice on naming files) but when you subsequently re-save it the software will use the same name, although it should be possible to save the file with a different name.

Print your document: Your software will probably have been set up to work with a particular printer and A4 size paper so you can print straightaway. However, you should be able to choose whether you want to print:

- the whole document;
- the current page;
- a specified page or pages; and
- how many copies you want.

You should also find out how to *preview* your work on the screen before printing.

Finally, you need to find out how to *close* your document and later how to *retrieve* (or *open*) it.

Use wordwrap: Now that you are ready to type in text you should keep in mind that you do not need to press [Enter] at the end of each line of a paragraph as the word processing software will automatically start the new lines for you when necessary. (You only need to press [Enter] at the end of a paragraph and at the end of headings and other short lines.) It is essential that you do not use the [Enter] key inappropriately otherwise the software will not be able to re-adjust your work if you subsequently edit it.

Exercise 1
(a) Type in the piece of text that appears below. Remember, you do not need to press [Enter] at the end of each line, only at the end of each paragraph.
(b) Make sure you leave at least one clear line space after the heading and between each paragraph, by pressing [Enter] again.
(c) Do not worry if you make any typing mistakes, you can correct them later.
(d) Save, print and close the file.

WORD PROCESSING

There's no such thing as 'the best' word processor. The right one depends on the user's temperament.

Some users don't care about aesthetics, but want to be able to process text as fast and efficiently as possible. Some users insist on the latest GUI version that has every possible utility and every fancy typeface.

But the user has to consider what the word processor is to be used for and how powerful the PC to run it is.

Source: "Word on the Street", Personal Computer Magazine, July 1993.

4. Basic error correction techniques

You should find out how to carry out the following basic error correction techniques:

Delete text: The backspace key [←] removes text, spaces, etc., to the left of the cursor/insertion point and the [Delete] key deletes the character under the cursor or to the right of the insertion point. Other key combinations can often be used to delete words and lines.

With Windows-based word processing software a piece of text can be *selected* using the mouse and then deleted using the [Delete] key. Double-clicking the mouse will normally select a word, and in some packages treble-clicking the mouse will select a sentence and quadruple-clicking the mouse will select a paragraph, although in others you will have to select sentences and paragraphs in the normal way.

Insert text: Text is inserted to the left of the cursor/insertion point, but to do this you will need to be in Insert mode (possibly shown by the message INS on the screen). If you are not in Insert mode, press the [Insert] key.

Replace text: In order to replace text, you will need to be in Overtype or Typeover mode (possibly shown by the message OVR on the screen). If you are in Insert mode you will have to press the [Insert] key to move into Overtype mode. Alternatively, with Windows-based word processing software the text to be replaced can be selected using the mouse and then replaced simply by typing the new text - the old text is automatically deleted.

Use the Undo facility: In some word processing software there is a feature that allows you to reverse your last action or a number of previous actions. An *action* might be, e.g. the typing of a word or the deletion or insertion of a piece of text.

Exercise 2
(a) Retrieve the work you saved in Exercise 1 and make the following amendments as well as correct any typing mistakes you may have made.
(b) Save and print your work.

WORD PROCESSING

There is no such thing as "the best" word processor. The right one depends on the user's temperament.

Some users do not care about aesthetics, but want to be able to process text as fast and efficiently as possible. Some users insist on the latest Windows-based version that has every possible utility and every fancy typeface.

But the user also has to consider what the word processor is to be used for and how powerful the PC it is.

Source: "Word on the Street", Personal Computer Magazine, July 1993.

5. Text revisions

You should find out how to carry out the following text revisions:

Split a paragraph into two or more shorter paragraphs: Insert two [Enter]s at the beginning of the sentence that is to be the start of the new paragraph. (Note: one [Enter] will split the paragraphs and the second will ensure there is a blank line between them.)

Join two paragraphs: Move the cursor to the beginning of the second paragraph and delete the [Enter]s between the paragraphs using the backspace key. (Note: you may need to enter some [space] to separate the last sentence of the old first paragraph from the first sentence of the old second paragraph.)

Copy or move text: You will have to find out how to select or mark the text and then how to move or copy it to another part of the document. In Windows-based software moving text is done by *cutting and pasting* whilst copying text is done by *copying and pasting*. An alternative technique for moving text in Windows-based packages is by use of the *drag and drop* facility, if available.

Search for a piece of text and replace it with another piece of text: You can use the *find and replace* facility to do this, however as this is a very powerful editing feature you should check every instance of the text being replaced to ensure it does not make any unforeseen changes. For instance, if you want to replace "in" with "on", unless you are careful, it might also change "pin" to "pon" and "window" to "wondow".

(This facility can also be used to search text downloaded from computer-based sources for [Enter]s at the end of each line and replace them with [space]s, unless an *autoformat* facility is available in the software.)

Exercise 3
Retrieve the work you saved in Exercise 2, and replace all instances of the term *word processor* with the term *word processing software*. Make the other revisions marked below. Save and print.

WORD PROCESSING

There is no such thing as "the best" word processor ~replace~ The right one depends on the user's temperament. *move* *join*

Some users do not care about aesthetics, but want to be able to process text as fast and efficiently as possible. Some users insist on the latest Windows-based version that has every utility and every typeface. *split paragraphs here*

But the user also has to consider what the word processor is to be used for and how *replace* powerful the PC is.

Source: "Word on the Street", Personal Computer Magazine, July 1993.

6. Proofing tools

You should find out if the following on-line proofing tools are available:

Spell checker: You can use the spell checker to check the spelling of one word, a marked selection of words or the whole document. If the spell checker finds a word that is not in its dictionary, it will present this to you as a possible mis-spelling and may:

- offer you suggestions of other words to adopt;
- let you make your own changes;
- let you ignore or bypass the spelling of that particular instance or all occurrences of the word; or
- let you add the word to the dictionary.

If the spell checker locates instances of double words it will let you delete one of them from the text.

Thesaurus: An on-line thesaurus will provide you with synonyms of the word on which the cursor is placed. You can then select a word from a list provided and replace the original word in the text. You may also be able to select antonyms.

Grammar checker: An on-line grammar checker will review your sentences and identify possible grammatical, stylistic or punctuation errors. It may offer you:

- suggested corrections;
- let you enter your own corrections;
- let you ignore the grammatical error;
- give you more information on the nature of the error;
- let you de-select certain rules or adopt "general" or "business" rules.

Your grammar checker may also provide you with readability statistics.

Exercise 4
Using the work you saved in Exercise 3.
(a) Use your on-line thesaurus (if available) to find alternatives for the words "temperament", "aesthetics" and "utility".
(b) Spell check your work.
(c) Check your work for grammar and style (if available).
(d) Find the reading level of the passage through the readability statistics. (Compare your statistics with those in Appendix 2.)
(e) Save and print.

---

7.   Text formatting

You can format the text either (a) as you type it in or (b) after you have typed it in. In the case of (a) it means selecting the particular text formatting feature before the text is typed in and then de-selecting it after use. In the case of (b) it involves selecting the text to be formatted first of all and then the appropriate feature.

In DOS-based word processing software text formatting features are normally displayed as embedded printer commands (which in some software can be hidden) or as changes in text colour. In Windows-based software the text is displayed on the screen as it will appear when printed.

Once a particular text format has been adopted it can easily be removed or changed. With DOS-based software this generally involves removing (and then replacing) the embedded printer commands before and after the text, with Windows-based software it involves selecting the relevant text, de-selecting the particular text formatting feature, and then if required, selecting a different feature.

Text formatting can be made at a number of levels: character, paragraph and page.

8.   Character formatting

You should find out how to apply the following basic character formatting:

- *underlining*
- **bold**
- *italics*
- CAPITALISATION
- different typefaces and sizes

Exercise 5
Using the work saved in Exercise 4 make the following simple text enhancements. Save and print.

<u>**WORD PROCESSING**</u> ← bold + underlined

There is no such thing as "the best" word processing software. The right one depends on the user's temperament. But the user also has to consider what the word processing software is to be used for and how powerful the PC is. Some users do not care about aesthetics, but want to be able to process text as fast and efficiently as possible. Some users insist on the latest Windows-based version that has every utility and typeface.

But the user also has to consider what the word processing software is to be used for and how powerful the PC is.

⌐underlined   ← italics →
<u>S</u>ource: "Word on the Street", *Personal Computer Magazine*, Issue 65, July 1993

9. Paragraph formatting

You will need to understand and apply the following types of paragraph formatting:

Alignment: By default, paragraphs are normally unjustified although you should find out how to select justified, centred or right-justified alignment.

Layout: Blocked paragraphs are the easiest to create: you simply start typing all paragraphs at the left hand margin. *Indented* paragraphs can be produced by using the [Tab] key (but NOT the spacebar) to indent the paragraph. However, creating paragraphs that are indented from both the left and right margins and *hanging* paragraphs requires more control. With Windows-based software, however, this can often be done by dragging *indent markers* into place on the ruler line.

Line spacing: You should find out how to change the line spacing from the default (i.e. single) line spacing to 1.5 or double-line spacing.

Exercise 6
Type in the following piece of text. Use blocked paragraphs, justified text and single line-spacing. Save and print the file.

Information Management

In all organisations, commercial or otherwise, information is an important resource. Traditionally, the resources of an organisation have been named as: money, machinery and manpower. But it is now recognised that information should be added to the list.

Organisations require information about themselves, their customers, their suppliers and their competitors in order to remain competitive in their market. Within the organisation, the information is required for three main purposes: decision-making, planning and control.

Peter Drucker (1955) in his classic text on management, *The Practice of Management,* said that "information is a specific tool for the manager with which he motivates, guides and organises people to do their own work".

In an organisation, there are three broad levels of management decision making: strategic (top); tactical (middle) and supervisory (or operational). The type of information required by each level will vary in terms of its source, accuracy, scope and detail.

References

Drucker, Peter. (1955) *The Practice of Management,* Heinemann.

Exercise 7
Change the line spacing of the main text in Exercise 6 to 1.5 or double. Save the file.

10. Tables

Tables can easily be set up to display information in columns and rows.

Tab key: Use the [Tab] key to move across the line to pre-set tab positions. If you type in text at the tab stops, this, by default, will be left-aligned. Note: you should not use the space bar to move across the line as this will not necessarily align the work in columns for you.

Exercise 8
Set up the following two-column table shown below. Make sure you use the [Tab] to move to the second column which should be about ¼ way across the screen, say at about 4 cm.

<u>Information Technology for Managers</u>

Conference Programme

09.30 - 10.00	Registration and Coffee
10.00 - 11.15	"Information, IT and Managers" *Speaker: Peter Donaldson*
11.15 - 11.30	Coffee
11.30 - 12.45	"Improving your Effectiveness" *Speaker: Anne Shaw*
12.45 - 14.00	Lunch
14.00 - 15.15	Word processing workshops *Workshop leaders: Frances Wilson and Tony Pearce*
15.15 - 15.30	Tea
15.30 - 17.00	Spreadsheet workshops *Workshop leaders: Bill Woods and Angela Hammond*

Setting tab stops: You should find out how to set new tab stops. These can be left, right, centred or decimal tabs (i.e. ones that allow you to position figures under the decimal point or the implied decimal point). With Windows-based software this can often be done by dragging "tab markers" into position on the ruler line.

Note: Anything more than a simple two-table column will require some pre-planning.

Exercise 9
Set up the two-table column below, right-aligning the figures in the second column.

Employment in UK transport in June 1993

	1993 Thousands
Railways	125.5
Other inland transport	400.7
Sea transport	31.2
Air transport	67.7
Other	271.4
All transport	869.5

<u>Source</u>: *Social Trends 24*, 1994

Table facility: You should find out if your software has a table facility to automate the production of a table. You will then have to specify the number of columns and rows in the table. You may also be able to select *gridlines* to guide you as you work and if you want to increase or decrease the width of these columns you should be able to drag the *gridlines* (or *column markers)* into different positions. The text in the table can then be formatted on a row, column or individual cell basis.

Exercise 10
(a) Retrieve the file saved in Exercise 6, and insert the following centred sub-heading after the last paragraph and before the References: *Information Needs of Management*
(b) Use the table facility (if available) to set up the following table with four columns and five rows, and use the gridlines to guide you in entering the data into the correct columns and rows as shown below. (Note: you do not need to draw lines around the boxes.)
(c) Save and print.

Type of information	*Strategic level*	*Tactical level*	*Supervisory level*
Source	External	External and Internal	Internal
Accuracy	Low	Medium	High
Scope	Wide	Medium	Narrow
Detail	General	Medium	Specific

Maths facility: You should find out if you have a *maths* facility which will perform basic mathematical calculations for you, e.g. to add up rows wand columns. You should check what symbols you should use for the mathematical operators: probably + (for add), - (for subtract); * (for multiply) and / (for divide).

11. Page formatting

You should find out how to format your document in the following ways:

Force a new page: Page breaks are determined by the pre-set page length (which is measured either in numbers of lines or in inches or centimetres). However, you should find out how to start a new page before you reach the actual end of the page.

Page numbering: Page numbering may be either on or off by default. However, you should find out how to control page numbering in the following ways:

- omit page numbering on the first page;
- select its position on the page, i.e. bottom or top, left, centre or right-aligned; and
- start the page numbering at a different place other than at 1.

Headers and footers: You should find out:

- where to enter the text to be used as the header and footer since this information is usually kept separately from the main document;
- how to incorporate the system date, time and page number automatically, e.g. to create a footer with the word "Page" followed by the relevant page number; and
- how to control headers and footers so that there are different headers or footers on the first page and on odd or even pages.

Footnotes or endnotes: Footnotes can easily be added to a document, where they will be numbered automatically and marked in the text with a reference number or another character like an asterisk [*]. The software will then place the footnote, according to your instructions at the end of the page to which it refers, at the end of a section, e.g. a chapter or at the end of the whole document.

Footnotes can often be cross-referenced, and if footnotes are added or deleted then the others are re-numbered and any cross-referencing is automatically updated.   The software will also adjust the text on the page so that there is room for the footnote(s) relevant to that page and also separate the text from the footnotes by a short line.

Bullets and/or numbering system: Numbering may be numerical or alphabetical with or without a separator, i.e. brackets, full stops, e.g. A B C, a b, c, or (a) (b) (c) or [a] [b] [c]; or 1 2 3, or I II III, or i ii iii, or (i) (ii) (iii).

The bulleting facility may give you a choice and size of bullets, e.g. • • ◆ ■ ☐

Exercise 11
(a) Type up the draft report shown on page 153.
(b) Set the page numbering to start at page 100.
(c) Display the page number as a left-aligned footer preceded by the word: Page:
(d) Save and print.

The future of business computing

Introduction

This report provides a brief history of business computing, it describes the present state of computing in business and then makes some suggestions as to the likely future of computing in business.

History of business computing

Although the first computers were developed in the 1940s, they were very large and very expensive and it was not until 1951 that the first computer was used for commercial activities. This was LEO - Lyons Electronic Office.

The present state of business computing

The personal computer (or PC as it is known for short) is now prevalent in many businesses and work has been transformed by:

- productivity tools like word processing, spreadsheet and database software; and
- PC networks which support the sharing of vital business information and resources.

The future of computing

With PCs becoming increasingly more sophisticated, future developments in computing will be in *multimedia* together with systems that can support *workgroups*. Multimedia systems are already on the market, but in the future prices will drop and the multimedia PC will become the standard piece of equipment on office desks.

Conclusion

Through a discussion of the history and present state of computing in business this report has identified the main areas of computing that will develop in the future.

---

12. Productivity aids for long documents

You should find out if the following features are available:

Paragraph styles: These can normally be defined either before or after text has been entered into them. Paragraph styles are named, stored globally, and then selected and applied as required.

Templates: Templates can be selected from pre-defined templates (although it is likely they will be of the US variety), set up from scratch or converted from existing documents.

Outliner: You should find out how to use this feature to enter headings and sub-headings to structure a document, and also how to re-organise the structure by demoting or promoting headings.

Table of contents and *index:* These can be produced once the document has been completed:

- for a *table of contents* you will need to identify the text to be included in the table of contents, the starting page number or range, and the style of leader dots (if any);
- for an *index* you will need to identify the text to be used in the index (and any sub-entries), the page number and the range or text to be used;

Word count: You should find out how to count the number of words in a document or a selected part of the document. In some software a word count may be done automatically after using the spell checker, or this information may be held in the *statistical information* maintained in the document.

Exercise 12
Count the words in the document in Exercise 11.

---

13. Correspondence

Letters, memos and fax cover sheets can be set up using many of the features described above, but the following additional features are particularly useful:

Page set up: You should find out how to alter the left, right, top and bottom margins in order to take account of any pre-printed letterheads.

Date: You should find out how to insert the date automatically from the system.

Envelopes and labels: You should find out how to create an envelope automatically in the software (for your size of stationery) and if it can be saved with the document. If you have already typed the name and address of the recipient into the letter this can usually be used for the envelope. You should also investigate if you can include a return address on the envelope.

Glossary: You should find out how to set up a glossary of common names and addresses and standard paragraphs for recall into later letters.

Exercise 13
(a) Type up the following full-blocked letter.
(b) Use the page set up feature to allow 2" for the printed letterhead.
(c) Insert today's date from the system.
(d) Use open punctuation and justified paragraphs.
(e) Save and print.
(f) Print an envelope (on plain paper).

(today's date)

J M Parker & Sons Ltd
45 High Street
GRAVESEND
Kent
GR1 4AB

Dear Sirs

PC software training

Please allow us to introduce ourselves. We are a recently established company that specialises in PC software training.

Please find enclosed a leaflet that describes the standard training courses that we currently offer. However, we would be very pleased to provide any tailor-made training on request, either on your own premises or in our modern PC training room.

If you feel that we could be of assistance in your future PC training needs, please do not hesitate to contact us.

Yours faithfully

Joanna King
Managing Director

Enc

Exercise 14
(a)   Prepare the following memo format using a bold, sans serif typeface like Arial or Helvetica type face (if available). Save it as a template.

MEMORANDUM

To: **From:**

Date: **Subject:**

_____

(b) Use the memo template for the following memo from Joanna King to Tony Brown concerning a proposed mailshot. Insert today's date. Leave a couple of line spaces under the separating line before you type in the text and use blocked paragraphs and justified text.

We have had a good response for training courses from the companies we have contacted directly. I therefore think it would be a good idea for us to carry out a large mailshot of companies in the area who might be interested in software training.

Could you therefore draw up an initial list of 200 companies who you feel we should contact in the first mailshot together with the names of individuals in the company to whom the letter should be addressed.

Exercise 15
(a) Prepare the following fax cover sheet using a bold, sans serif typeface like Arial or Helvetica (if available). Save as a template.

Fax Cover Sheet

To:
Company: **Fax No:**

From:
Company: **Fax No:**

Date: **Pages including this one:**

Message

(b) Use the fax cover sheet to send a one page document from Joanna King of King Training Consultants, 01634-887766 to Kelly Smith of Parry Computers Ltd, 0171-0035-989. Insert today's date.

14. Mail merging

This facility is available in most word processing software. There are three steps to mail merging, described below, although you may find that this whole process has been automated.

- Create a *form letter* (also known as the *main* document or the *primary* file): This file contains the standard text to be used in all the letters together with the *merge codes* where the variable items are to be entered into the fixed text.
- Prepare the *data file* (also known as the *address* file or *secondary* file): This contains the variable data, i.e. all the names and addresses and other items of data that are to be included in the document.
- Merge the two files: At this point the variable data for each addressee is placed in the correct position in each letter. Depending on your software you may be able to select criteria for the merge. The documents can then either all be printed or saved in a new file for viewing and printing at a later date.

Exercise 16

Prepare a form letter by adapting the letter saved in Exercise 13 in the following way:

(a) Replace the complimentary close and salutation with "Dear" and "Yours sincerely"

(b) Remove the inside address and insert the merge codes for the letter. These are marked here with an * but you must use the merge codes specific to your software.

(today's date)

title *firstname* *surname*
position
company
address1
address2
KENT
address3

Dear *title* *surname*

PC software training

Please allow us to introduce ourselves. We are a recently established company that specialises in PC software training.

Please find enclosed a leaflet that describes the standard training courses that we currently offer. However, we would be very pleased to provide any tailor-made training on request, either on your premises or in our modern PC training room.

If you feel that we could be of assistance to you in your future PC training needs, please do not hesitate to contact us.

Yours sincerely

Joanna King
Managing Director

(b) Prepare a data file using the names and addresses of the following 4 companies (the data items are shown here separated by commas):

Mrs, Pamela, Brown, Personnel Officer, Theyrock Ltd, 54 High Street, GRAVESEND, GR1   4AB
Mr, John, Hoskings, Managing Director, Mannering Brothers Ltd, 89 Thames Road, GRAVESEND, GR2 8GH
Miss, Andrea, Harris, Proprietor, Pots 'n Pans, 23 Swan Lane, DARTFORD, GR2 6GK
Mr Sandeep, Patel, Senior Personnel Officer, Harrington Textiles PLC, DARTFORD, GR3 9JY

(c) Merge the files.

15. Special text effects

You should find out if the following special text effects are available:

- <u>double underlining</u>
- superscript and subscript (Note: in some software you may need to decrease the size of the type of the superscript or subscript);
- the extended character set;
- shadowing and outlining;
- special typefaces;
- special text display, e.g. vertically, angled or rotated.

You should also find out how to:

- centre material vertically on the page;
- align material with either the top or bottom margin;
- change the orientation of the page to landscape or portrait.

Exercise 17
Create the following logo using the special effect shown below or another available in your software.

16. Graphics

You should find out if the following features are available in your software:

- *set of symbols*;
- *drawing tools*;
- *clipart library.*

17. Lines and boxes

You should find out how to:

- draw a *line* at the top, bottom, or to the left or right of text or graphics;
- change the *line width* and *style*;
- control the *amount of space* between the line and the text;
- *shadow* boxes.
- *shade* boxes: there are usually a number of different shading patterns.

Exercise 18
Set up the following invitation. Use a typeface like Book Antiqua for the main text and Coronet for the name. Place a double-line box around the invitation.

King Training Consultants

request the pleasure of the company of

Mrs Pamela Brown

at the opening of their new training room

on Wednesday 14 June 1995

The Manor House
Arrowbridge
Kent DA23 8NY   RSVP

Exercise 19
Set up the form shown below using the table facility (if available). Draw a box around the gridlines and shade the bottom row. Use a 12 point serif typeface, e.g. Times or Times New Roman font.

King Training Consultants
The Manor House
ARROWBRIDGE
Kent DA23 8NY

To book a place or places on the courses listed, please fill in and return this form together with a deposit for 10% of the total fees due.

Course No	Course Name	Date	Name of delegate	Fee
			Total fees due:	

You should see if there are any pre-designed forms that come with your software, and whether you can include check boxes or drop-down lists.

18. Parallel columns

You should find out how to use the parallel columns (or table facility) to set up two or more parallel columns.

Exercise 20
Set up the six-page brochure shown on pages 161-2 in the following way:
(a) Set the page orientation for landscape.
(b) Set up page margins of 1" at the top and bottom and ½" at the left and right.
(c) Set up three parallel columns - you may have to adjust the width of the middle column to ensure that you have three columns of equal width when you print out.

---

19. Newspaper columns

You should find out how to:

- select the *number* of columns required: you can usually type in the material in the normal way and then format it into the required number of columns or else you can select the number of columns before you type it in;
- add *vertical* and *horizontal* lines;

Exercise 21
Set up the newsletter shown on page 163 in the following way:
(a) Create the masthead using 24 or 25 point bold Times New Roman font.
(b) Place a box around the masthead. Leave at least one line space between the masthead and the columns.
(c) Select three newspaper columns of default size.
(d) Select vertical lines between each column.
(e) Type in the main body of the text using 12 point Times New Roman and unjustified paragraphs. Leave the rest of the formatting until later.
(f) Select a horizontal line at the end of the page.
(g) Type the final line under the horizontal line in 10 point.
(h) Format the sub-headings as bold and in 18 point size.
(i) Embolden the two paragraphs after the sub-heading "Emphasis", and shade the last paragraph.
(j) Insert a clipart graphic after the paragraph beginning "It also includes ..." and enclose it in a box

---

- adjust the *gutter*;
- control the *leading*;
- use the *automatic hyphenation* facility: you should be able to alter the area in which words are hyphenated (known as the *hot zone* or *hyphenation zone*). The smaller the area, the less ragged the margins but more hyphens will be required.

Exercise 22
Improve the presentation of the newsletter created in Exercise 21 by hyphenating the text, adjusting the gutter and controlling the leading.

KING TRAINING CONSULTANTS

PC Software Training

PC TRAINING
CONSULTANTS

King Training Consultants

Return the slip overleaf to the address below for details and dates of the courses listed in this leaflet or for a meeting to discuss your personal requirements.

Joanna King
King Training Consultants
The Manor House
ARROWBRIDGE
Kent DA23 8NY

Tel: 01634-886745
Fax: 01634-887766

Word processing

Spreadsheets

Presentation graphics

Desk Top Publishing
(DTP)

Beginners courses

Intermediate courses

Advanced courses

Tailor-made courses
also available
on your premises
or ours

For further details please complete the slip below and return it to the address overleaf.

Name:
Company:
Address:

Telephone:

I am interested in receiving information on the following courses:

Word processing ☐
Spreadsheets ☐
Databases ☐
Presentation graphics ☐
DTP ☐

I would like to set up a meeting to discuss our company's specific training needs ☐

THE NEWSLETTER

Purpose

The purpose of this exercise is to demonstrate how a simple newsletter might be presented.

It is an example of how a number of the advanced presentation techniques described might be used to prepare a piece of work of publishable quality.

The text in this Newsletter appears in three columns with a vertical line between each column.

Graphic

It also includes a graphic which has been inserted into the text below.

In this example the graphic was obtained from a clip art library that accompanied the word processing software

However, it could easily have been drawn in a graphics package or scanned in from a photo. The graphic is enclosed within a border or box.

Headings

The Newsletter has a main heading, which in this instance uses the Times Roman font, emboldened, and is in 25 point size. The sub-headings are in 18 point size.

Main text

The main text is in 12 point size and the text at the bottom of the newsletter is in 10 point size, although it could be in a smaller size as it is not as important as the rest of the document.

Emphasis

The text in these two paragraphs has been emboldened, whilst the text at the end of the Newsletter has been shaded.

Both of these are ways of emphasising text.

There are of course other ways of emphasising text, and the designer of the document should try these out. The Print Preview facility of the word processing software should be used frequently to view the document.

Design

However, it should also be remembered that too many different techniques detract from the overall appearance of the document rather than add to it. Simplicity is often the key to a striking document.

This Newsletter was designed and printed by (insert your name here)

20. Multimedia documents

Provided you have the relevant hardware in place you should investigate if you are able to include:

- *sound*: you may want to use pre-recorded sound files stored on CD-ROM which can be read in as clipart, or else record your own sound;
- *video or animation*: these will probably be pre-recorded files which you could use to annotate your documents.

21. Macros

You should find out how to create macros by either:

- recording the macro as you execute it, stopping the recording and then playing back the macro; or
- writing macros using the macro language

You should also find out how to store macros: usually they can be stored in the document to which they refer or globally.

22. Further features

You should find out if you have the following features:

- *File management facilities:* i.e. features that allow you to copy and delete files without having to resort to DOS or Windows;
- *Document protection:* i.e. how you can set up different types of protection, e.g. to make your documents *read-only* or *password-protected*.

23. Integrating data

Using the information provided in **14:10** you should investigate the most appropriate way to:

- include text from a document prepared in another word processing software package: many word processing software packages can convert documents created in other formats;
- copy a spreadsheet worksheet or graph or chart into a word processed document;
- include data held in a database.

Integrated Exercise
(This exercise uses material to be created in the Integrated Exercises in Chapters 9, 10 and 12.)
You are the Finance Director of a small company. At the recent meeting of the Board of Directors you were asked to present a forecast of expenditure for the next year.

(a) Set up the memo that appears overleaf:

MEMORANDUM

To:	(leave blank)
	Board of Directors
From:	(your name)
	Finance Director
Date:	(today's date)

At the recent meeting of the Board of Directors last week I was asked to prepare a forecast of expenses for the coming financial year.

In the table below I show the figures for the last two years together with an indication of the likely figures for next year.

The following bar chart shows the projected costs for the next financial year:

(b) After paragraph two incorporate the relevant worksheet set up in the Integrated Exercise in Chapter 9.

(c) After paragraph three include the relevant graph, designed in the Integrated Exercise in Chapter 10.

(d) Use the database set up in the Integrated Exercise in Chapter 12 to merge this memo with all the names of the members of the Board of Directors.

9

Spreadsheet software

1. Getting started

Before beginning to use your spreadsheet package it is essential that you read Chapter 7 so that in particular:

- you are familiar with the use of both the keyboard and the mouse;
- you know how to start up the computer; and
- you have prepared your disks ready to hold your work;

2. Getting to know your spreadsheet software package

You should refer to **7:14-15** for advice on getting to know your spreadsheet package by finding out:

- how to load the spreadsheet software;
- if there is an on-line tutorial;
- whether you will need to use the keyboard or the mouse or both;
- if there is on-line help and how to access it;
- what information is shown on the screen; and
- how to quit the package.

3. Basic data entry

Starting a worksheet: When the spreadsheet package has loaded you may be in a position to start entering data straightaway. However, with some software you will have to create a *new* worksheet first.

You should find out how to enter the different types of data (described below) into the *active cell.* Once you have entered the data, you can then either press [Enter] or the relevant arrow key to move the cursor in the direction you wish to work, e.g. along a row or down a column.

Values: Examples of valid numeric values include 0, -1, 77, 1000, £25, 99%, 23.25. With some software you can type in values using the required format, e.g. £1,000, with others you will have to type in the value, e.g. 1000 and then format it later. Values will, by default, appear right-aligned in the cell.

Labels: Data beginning with an alphabetic character is normally recognised as being a label by most spreadsheet software, although with some packages it will have to be preceded by ' (apostrophe character). This will also be necessary in all software if the label begins with a numeric character.

Labels will, by default, appear left-aligned in the cell. If the label is longer than the column width it will spill over into the adjacent cell(s), however if anything appears in an adjacent cell, the full label will not be visible. In this case the column will have to be widened (see **9**).

Formulae: With most spreadsheet software you will have to prefix a formula with a character so that the program recognises that it is a formula and not a piece of text you have typed. Depending on your software this might be the relevant operator e.g. + or -, or the = character. If you see the formula displayed in the cell rather than the result this is because you have not prefixed it with the correct symbol. Note: you can usually type in formulae in either upper or lower case characters.

Functions: Functions begin with an @ sign or an = sign depending on your software. Functions usually require an *argument* in brackets. If the argument of the function is a range of cells, there are a number of ways that this can be entered:

- by typing in the beginning cell reference followed by a "to" symbol, usually the colon sign or two dots followed by the end cell reference, e.g. A1:A5 or A1..A5 or
- by *selecting* (or *pointing to*) the range of cells on the screen.

Note: if you are typing in the cell range yourself, do not forget to close the brackets of the argument, although some software will do this automatically for you.

For the most common function, the SUM function, there may be an *autosum* feature, marked by the Greek sigma sign, Σ This feature will automatically sum the relevant range or if it is not able to identify an appropriate range leave you to fill in the argument in the brackets.

You should find out if there is a facility in the software that lists the available functions for you to make your selection. This list, if available, will probably arrange the functions by category and should also show you the format of the argument for the function.

If you see a *circular reference* error message this means that you have included in the range, the cell in which the calculation takes place. You will therefore need to make the necessary corrections.

Exercise 1
Set up the following worksheet which will give you practice in basic data entry. (Note: in the worksheet below the formulae are shown in the cells, although of course you will see the results displayed.) Do not clear your work as you will need it for Exercise 2.

	A	B
1	MATHS	
2	100	25
3	Add	=A2+B2
4	Subtract	=A2-B2
5	Multiply	=A2*B2
6	Divide	=A2/B2
7	Total	=SUM(B2:B6)

4.   Correcting and editing data

Whilst you are working in the active cell you can edit data by using the backspace [←] key to delete the characters one by one. Once you have entered data into the cell, there are a number of ways of amending it:

- *replacing data:* simply move to the relevant cell and retype the new data;
- *erasing* data: select the cell or range of cells and either use the [Delete] key or a DELETE, ERASE or BLANK command;
- *editing* data: you can edit the data on the *entry line.* (With DOS-based software you may need to use a function key to return the data item to the entry line. With Windows-based software it should automatically appear on the entry line.) Then you can either insert, delete or overtype the data as appropriate although you may have to press the [Insert] key to move between insert and overtype mode;
- *undoing* the typing in a cell: if there is an Undo facility available you should use it immediately after you make a mistake to reverse your previous action or data item that you typed in.

Exercise 2
In the spreadsheet you set up in Exercise 1, change the value in B2 (using the most appropriate method) from 25 to 10 and watch the values change in the other cells.

---

5. File operations

You should find out how to carry out the following file operations:

Save your worksheet: you should save your work frequently to disk, so that you do not lose any data. The first time you save your work you will need to give it a name (see **7:16** for advice on naming files) but when you re-save it, the software will use the same name although it should be possible to save it with a different name.

Clear the current worksheet from the screen: this may involve *closing* a file or using a ZAP or ERASE command.

Retrieve your worksheet: once saved to disk you may need to *open* or *retrieve* your file at a later time.

Exercise 3
Save the work from Exercises 1 and 2 and then close the file.

---

6. Copying data

You should find out how to copy labels and values:

With DOS-based software this will probably mean:
- using the COPY command;
- identifying the cell (or range of cells) to be copied;
- identifying the cell (or the first cell of the range) in which the copy is to be held.

With Windows-based software this will probably mean:
- selecting the cell (or range of cells) to be copied;
- selecting the *copy* feature;
- selecting the cell (or the first cell of the range) in which the copy is to be held;
- selecting the *paste* feature.

Alternatively, with Windows-based software there may be a *fill down* or *fill right* feature, or even an *autofill* facility which will let you drag the cell (or cells) to copy them.

You may also be able to use this copying facility to create a *series of data*, e.g. Monday, Tuesday Wednesday, although if the series is not easily recognisable, e.g. Product 1 ... Product 10, you will need to type in the first two data items so that the program can recognise the increment. Otherwise, you can use the *series* facility.

Exercise 4

Create a worksheet for the Hadley Cricket Club to calculate match statistics.

(a) Create a series of data for the batsmen, by typing "No 1" in A4, "No 2" in A5 and then copying the series down to A14. Add a row for the "Extras".

(b) Type in the number of runs scored by each batsman as well as the extras.

	A	B
1	HADLEY CRICKET CLUB	
2		
3	Batsman	Number of runs
4	No 1	91
5	No 2	103
6	No 3	64
7	No 4	17
8	No 5	76
9	No 6	0
10	No 7	39
11	No 8	5
12	No 9	23
13	No 10	19
14	No 11	3
15	Extras	20

7. Basic statistical functions

You should find out how to use the following basic statistical functions:

- the AVERAGE function, e.g. AVG(range) or AVERAGE(range);
- the MAX function, e.g. MAX(range);
- the MIN function, e.g. MIN(range).

Exercise 5

Using the worksheet begun in Exercise 4:

(a) Add the following labels and functions shown below in cells B16 to B20. You should see the values displayed in the cells rather than the functions.

(b) Save the file if it looks like the one in Appendix 2, and then close the file.

16	MATCH STATISTICS	
17	Total	=SUM(B4:B15)
18	Average	=AVERAGE(B4:B14)
19	Max runs	=MAX(B4:B14)
20	Min runs	=MIN(B4:B14)

8. Copying formulae

You should find out how to copy formulae and functions. This can normally be done in the same way as copying data described above. However, you will need to look carefully at the worksheet to see whether you will need to use relative, absolute or mixed addressing. With most software the use of the dollar character $ is used in absolute addressing to specify the cell address that must not be adjusted. However, with some DOS-based software it is possible to use a modified COPY command to instruct the program to retain a specific cell address.

If you have made a mistake and not used the correct addressing mode, then there may be a *reference* facility which will allow you to convert a selected reference to relative, absolute or mixed.

Exercise 6

Set up the following simple worksheet for Flexi Company Ltd to calculate the number of hours worked by 4 temporary staff in one week, together with their gross pay.

	A	B	C	D	E	F	G	H
1	FLEXI COMPANY LTD							
2	Pay rate:	4.25						
3	Name	Mon	Tues	Wed	Thu	Fri	Total	Gross
4							hours	pay
5	Amy	7	8	7	8	8		
6	Bob	6	5	6	7	6		
7	Claire	8	8	9	8	8		
8	David	6	6	7	6	7		
9	Total							

(a) In G5, use the SUM function to calculate the total hours Amy worked in a week, e.g. **=SUM(B5:F5)** Copy this formula down to G6, G7 and G8 for Bob, Clare and David. As this requires all cell addresses to be adjusted copying this formula as it stands will do this.

(b) Similarly, in B9, use the SUM function to work out the total hours worked on a Monday, e.g. **=SUM(B5:B8)** and copy this formula across the rest of the days of the week, to calculate the total hours worked in the week as well as the Total hours and the Gross pay (i.e. to C9, D9, E9, F9, G9 and H9).

(c) To work out the Gross Pay for each employee, the rate of pay (in B2) needs to be multiplied by the number of hours worked. Hence the formula to calculate Amy's gross pay in H5 should be **=$B$2*G5** so that when it is copied down to the other 3 members of staff, B2 is not adjusted.

(d) If the worksheet looks as below, save it as you will need it for the next exercise.

	A	B	C	D	E	F	G	H
1	FLEXI COMPANY LTD							
2	Pay rate:	4.25						
3	Name	Mon	Tues	Wed	Thu	Fri	Total	Gross
4							hours	pay
5	Amy	7	8	7	8	8	38	161.5
6	Bob	6	5	6	7	6	30	127.5
7	Claire	8	8	9	8	8	41	174.25
8	David	6	6	7	6	7	32	136
9	Total	27	27	29	29	29	141	599.25

9.   Formatting a worksheet

Format numeric values: You should find out how to format numeric values to display: *integers*; a specified number of *decimal* places; a *comma* separating the thousands; *currency*, i.e. with two decimal places and a preceding £; or *percentages* (%).

Change the alignment of labels: You should find out how to adjust the alignment of labels, i.e. to left, centred, right, justified or word-wrapped text.

Adjust column widths: If labels or values do not fit into cells, you will need to widen the whole column: a cell containing values that is too narrow will display a series of characters like **** or ####. With DOS-based software this will normally mean specifying the width of columns in characters. With Windows-based software you can either drag the column markers to the right to widen columns or select the column width feature. It may also be possible to choose a *best fit* option. A number of columns can also be adjusted at the same time.

Create a line: This might be achieved in a number of ways: by repeating a character across a cell (or row) using one of the following characters - , = , or * to produce a row of ---- or ==== or ****; or by preceding the character with a *repeat* key; or by *filling* the cell.

Exercise 7
Retrieve the worksheet saved in Exercise 6.
(a) Type the full names of the staff in the relevant cells: Amy Browning; Bob Deeds; Clare Freeman; and David Harris. Increase column A to the most appropriate width.
(b) Decrease columns B-F holding the days of the week to the same width.
(c) Right align the labels in the range B3-H4.
(d) Format column H and cell B2, to accept currency (i.e. £ sign and 2 decimal places.)
(e) If the spreadsheet looks as below, save it. You will need it for the next exercise.

	A	B	C	D	E	F	G	H
1	FLEXI COMPANY LTD							
2	Pay rate:	£4.25						
3	Name	Mon	Tues	Wed	Thu	Fri	Total	Gross
4							hours	pay
5	Amy Browning	7	8	7	8	8	38	£161.50
6	Bob Deeds	6	5	6	7	6	30	£127.50
7	Clare Freeman	8	8	9	8	8	41	£174.25
8	David Harris	6	6	7	6	7	32	£136.00
9	Total	27	27	29	29	29	141	£599.25

Before printing the worksheet you should investigate the following features:

- how to control the printing of the *row and column borders*: if they are removed by default you should find out how to retain them, if desired;
- how to use *headers and footers*: usually these have three distinct areas in which data can be entered: the left hand side, the centre and the right hand side. You should also find out how to include (or delete if entered by default) the file name, the page number and the current date;
- how to control the *page set up* details, e.g. the page orientation, or use the scaling option to fit the worksheet on the page;
- how to print the *cell formulae*;
- how to print the whole document or *specified pages*.

You should also find out how to use the *print preview* facility to preview the results of your work before printing.

10. Further formatting features

You should investigate how to achieve these further formatting features:

- *change the typeface (font), size and style:* this may mean column widths or row heights will need to be adjusted;
- *remove the gridlines for all or part of the worksheet*: this feature is often controlled separately for both the screen display and the printout;
- *enclose the whole or part of the worksheet in a box:* this is confusingly referred to by some software as a border;
- *shade* cells:

Exercise 8
(a) Make the following enhancements to the worksheet:
•   Use Times Roman typeface throughout: 14 point for the heading (in A1), 12 point for the labels and values in row 9, and 10 point for the rest of the data.
•   Use bold for the heading (in A1), labels (in rows 3 and 4) and labels and values (in row 9).
•   Use italics for the data in row 2.
•   Use shading for row 9.
•   Remove all gridlines.
(b) Print the worksheet ensuring there are no borders. Save the worksheet as you will need it for the next exercise.

	A	B	C	D	E	F	G	H
1	**FLEXI COMPANY LTD**							
2	*Pay rate:*	*£4.25*						
3	**Name**	**Mon**	**Tues**	**Wed**	**Thu**	**Fri**	**Total**	**Gross**
4							**hours**	**pay**
5	Amy Browning	7	8	7	8	8	38	£161.50
6	Bob Deeds	6	5	6	7	6	30	£127.50
7	Clare Freeman	8	8	9	8	8	41	£174.25
8	David Harris	6	6	7	6	7	32	£136.00
9	**Total**	**27**	**27**	**29**	**29**	**29**	**141**	**£599.25**

Exercise 9
Print the worksheet showing the cell formulae and check it with the one in Appendix 2.

11.   Extending a worksheet

You should find out how to extend a worksheet using the following features:

Insert rows and columns: With DOS-based software you can use an INSERT command, with Windows-based software you can select the area where the new rows or columns are to be inserted and then use the *insert* facility. You should note that if you insert a row or column into a range used in a formula, it is best to do this between the first and last items else the formula may not include the data from the inserted row or column.

Delete rows and columns: In DOS-based packages this is achieved using a DELETE command and in Windows-based packages by selecting the rows and columns to be deleted and then using the *delete* facility. You should note that if you delete rows and columns that are the first or last items in a range in the argument of a function, you may have to adjust the range.

Move data: With DOS-based software this will be done by means of the MOVE command and with Windows-based software this is done using the *cut and paste* facility, or by the *drag and drop* facility, i.e. by dragging the cell or cells into new positions.

Exercise 10

Retrieve the spreadsheet and extend it in the following ways: :

(a) Insert a row between Amy Browning and Bob Deeds for a further employee, Ian Jones. Copy formulae into H6 and I6 to calculate his total hours as well as his Gross Pay. Check that the functions for Total hours worked each day include those worked by Ian Jones. Enter the data for Ian: 6, 7, 8, 6, 7.

(b) Insert a new column at G to show the hours worked on a Saturday with an appropriate width. Label it "Sat" (in G3) and copy into G10 the formula to calculate the total hours worked on Saturday. If the functions (in column H) do not include the hours worked on a Saturday, amend and copy as necessary.   Enter the data for Saturday: Amy 3, Ian 3, Bob 4, Clare 3, David 3.

(c) Depending on your software, either insert a new row between rows 2 and 3 and draw a line across it or else draw a box around the titles, the data and the total row.

(d) Print the worksheet and save the file as you will need it for Exercise 11.

	A	B	C	D	E	F	G	H	I
1	**FLEXI COMPANY LTD**								
2	*Pay rate:*	*£4.25*							
3	**Name**	**Mon**	**Tues**	**Wed**	**Thu**	**Fri**	**Sat**	**Total**	**Gross**
4								**hours**	**pay**
5	Amy Browning	7	8	7	8	8	3	41	£174.25
6	Ian Jones	6	7	8	6	7	3	37	£157.25
7	Bob Deeds	6	5	6	7	6	4	34	£144.50
8	Clare Freeman	8	8	9	8	8	3	44	£187.00
9	David Harris	6	6	7	6	7	3	35	£148.75
10	**Total**		**33**	**34**	**37**	**35**	**36**	**16**	**191**	**£811.75**

12. Logical functions

You should find out how to use the IF function: in particular, the structure of the function's argument.

Exercise 11

Retrieve the spreadsheet saved in Exercise 10. In this exercise you worked out the Gross Pay for the 5 temporary workers at Flexi Co Ltd. This company actually pays overtime over 40 hours at the rate of time and half. Hence the formulae in the Gross Pay column need to be amended to check if the employee worked more than 40 hours and if so pay time and a half for the hours worked over 40.

(a) So for Amy Browning the formula in I5 should be something like: **=IF((H5<=40),H5*$B$2,((H5-40)*1.5*$B$2)+40*$B$2)**   [This means: IF (the number of hours in H5 is less than or equal to 40 then multiply the number of hours in H5 by the pay rate in B2, else subtract 40 from the number of hours in H5 and multiply this by 1.5 times the pay rate and then add this to 40 times the payrate).]

(b) Copy this function down for the other workers.

(c) If the spreadsheet looks as below, print and save it.

Do not delete this file as you will need it later.

	A	B	C	D	E	F	G	H	I
1	**FLEXI COMPANY LTD**								
2	*Pay rate:*	£4.25							
3	Name	Mon	Tues	Wed	Thu	Fri	Sat	Total	Gross
4								hours	pay
5	Amy Browning	7	8	7	8	8	3	41	£176.38
6	Ian Jones	6	7	8	6	7	3	37	£157.25
7	Bob Deeds	6	5	6	7	6	4	34	£144.50
8	Clare Freeman	8	8	9	8	8	3	44	£195.50
9	David Harris	6	6	7	6	7	3	35	£148.75
10	**Total**	**33**	**34**	**37**	**35**	**36**	**16**	**191**	**£822.38**

13. Date and time functions

You should find out how to use date and time functions as follows:

- how to *enter* dates and times: you may be able to type them in using the required format or you may have to use a date or time function;
- how to *format* dates and times to your specific requirements;
- what *function* to use to extract the system date and time, e.g. **=TODAY()** and **=NOW()**
- how to create a *series* of dates or times.

> **Exercise 12**
> Create an appointments calendar for a week in the following way:
> (a) In B1, type: Monday and create a day series along the row to F1. Centre the days.
> (b) In B2 type: 26/6/95, and create a date series along the row to F2. Centre the dates.
> (c) In A3 type: 09:00 and create an hour series down the column to A11
> (d) Increase the column width and row height to allow room to write in text.
> (e) Print the calendar on A4 landscape, if possible scaled to fit on the whole page.

	A	B	C	D	E	F
1		Monday	Tuesday	Wednesday	Thursday	Friday
2		26/6/95	27/6/95	28/6/95	29/6/95	30/6/95
3	09:00					
4	10:00					
5	11:00					
6	12:00					
7	13:00					
8	14:00					
9	15:00					
10	16:00					
11	17:00					

14. Worksheet protection

You should find out how to use the most appropriate method of protecting data in your worksheets:

- *hide columns and rows*: with DOS-based software this will mean using a HIDE command. With Windows-based software you should be able to drag the right-hand column border to the left of the left-hand column border, thereby hiding the column and for rows drag the bottom row border up to the top of the row border;
- *hide cells*: to display the values rather than the formulae;
- *lock cells*: to protect them from being edited;
- *protect the file with a password;*
- *create a read-only* file.

15. Large worksheets

You should find out how to:

- *lock* or *freeze titles* on the screen, either horizontally, vertically or both;
- *split* the screen and, if necessary synchronise;
- turn on *manual* calculation, and later *re-calculate* or return to *automatic* calculation;
- *print wide* spreadsheets by printing either the whole or a specified part of worksheet, by specifying row and column titles to appear on each page; and by scaling the page to fit on a specified number of pages.

Exercise 13

You would like to set up a small PC training and consultancy business and want to model the activities of the business over the next year to find out the best way of financing the business. You have a small amount of cash in the bank and income will come from training courses, consultancy as well as any interest on money in the bank. Outgoings will consist of an initial purchase of equipment, monthly overheads, salary, any loan repayments or overdraft payments.

(a) Set up a worksheet, using the model shown on page 177. Use the labels given in column A. In B2 use today's date formatted to show month and year only.

(b) Create a series of 12 months across row 2 to M2.

(c) As the spreadsheet is now too large to appear on one screen, freeze the titles horizontally at row 2 and vertically at column A.

(d) Set up the logic of the model by entering, firstly the following general formulae:

- In B5 to calculate total cash in bank: **=B3+B4**
- In B11 to calculate total income: **=SUM(B8:B10)**
- In B19 to calculate total outgoings: **=SUM(B14:B18)**
- In B21 to calculate cash to bank at end of month. **=B5+B11-B19**
- In C4 to show the cash carried forward from last month: **=B21**

(e) Copy these formulae along the rows to the last month.

	A	B
1	CASH FLOW	
2		Apr-95
3	Loan	
4	Cash in bank	
5	Total cash in bank	
6		
7	INCOME	
8	Training courses	
9	Consultancy	
10	Interest on cash in bank	
11	TOTAL INCOME	
12		
13	OUTGOINGS	
14	Equipment	
15	Overheads	
16	Salary	
17	Loan repayments	
18	Overdraft payments	
19	TOTAL OUTGOINGS	
20		
21	To bank	

(f)   Enter the following specific formulae:

• The income from training courses is estimated to be the same amount each month for the next 12 months as you have a guaranteed booking for at least the first six months. The estimated figure will appear in B8, therefore in C8 enter **=B8.**

• It is hoped to increase consultancy by 5% each month. In C9 enter **=B9*1.05** or a similar formula. Copy the formulae in B8 and B9 across the rows.

• Monthly estimates for overheads and salary will appear in B15 and B16, so in C15 enter **=B15** and in C16 enter **=B16** and copy these formulae across the row.

(g) Enter the following formulae to calculate interest on cash in bank, and loan and overdraft repayments.

• Interest on cash in bank (for the purposes of this exercise) is paid at 5% on balances over £2,000. Therefore in C10 enter the following function: **=IF(B5>=2000,(B5*0.05)/12,0)** Copy this function across the row.

• Loan repayments on a 12-month loan would be (for the purposes of this exercise) twelve monthly repayments at a special 5% annual business interest rate. In C17 enter the following formula: **=($B$3*1.05)/12** Copy this formula across the row.

• Overdraft payments are at the rate of 5% per annum with a minimum overdraft fee of £50. In C18 enter the following function: **=IF(B5>=0,0,IF((-B5*0.05)/12<50,50, (-B5*0.05)/12))** Copy this formula across the row.

(h)   Test the logic of the model.

(i)   As only estimates are to be used format all cells in the range: B3:M21 to display integer values and showing separating commas but not £ signs. Can you spot any rounding errors?

(j)   Protect all cells that hold formulae or functions as well as B10, B17 and B18.

CASH FLOW	Apr-95	May-95	Jun-95	Jul-95	Aug-95	Sep-95	Oct-95	Nov-95	Dec-95	Jan-96	Feb-96	Mar-96
Loan												
Cash in bank	3,000	-9,800	-7,563	-5,361	-3,132	-875	1,413	3,734	6,137	8,591	11,093	13,643
Total cash in bank	3,000	-9,800	-7,563	-5,361	-3,132	-875	1,413	3,734	6,137	8,591	11,093	13,643
INCOME												
Training courses	4,000	4,000	4,000	4,000	4,000	4,000	4,000	4,000	4,000	4,000	4,000	4,000
Consultancy	500	525	551	579	608	638	670	704	739	776	814	855
Interest on cash in bank		13	0	0	0	0	0	0	16	26	36	46
TOTAL INCOME	4,500	4,538	4,551	4,579	4,608	4,638	4,670	4,704	4,754	4,801	4,850	4,901
OUTGOINGS												
Equipment	15,000											
Overheads	800	800	800	800	800	800	800	800	800	800	800	800
Salary	1,500	1,500	1,500	1,500	1,500	1,500	1,500	1,500	1,500	1,500	1,500	1,500
Loan repayments		0	0	0	0	0	0	0	0	0	0	0
Overdraft payments		0	50	50	50	50	50	0	0	0	0	0
TOTAL OUTGOINGS	17,300	2,300	2,350	2,350	2,350	2,350	2,350	2,300	2,300	2,300	2,300	2,300
To bank	-9,800	-7,563	-5,361	-3,132	-875	1,413	3,734	6,137	8,591	11,093	13,643	16,244

(k) To view the position without a loan, enter the data for the first month:
- Cash in bank: 3000
- Income: training courses - 4000; consultancy - 500
- Outgoings: equipment - 15000; overheads - 800; salary - 1500.

(l) Print the cash-flow analysis, scaled to fit on one page of A4 in landscape mode. It should look the one on page 178.

(m) What would be the effect if:
- you took out a £10,000 loan? or
- you increased consultancy work to an estimated £1000 from the first month?

(Compare your worksheets with those in Appendix 2)

16. Lookup functions

You should investigate what LOOKUP functions are available and how to use them. You should note that, in the argument of the function, when you refer to the column from which the data is to be retrieved, the first column of the lookup table will either be 0 or 1, depending on your software.

You should also note that some software may not be able to look up text, so this may have to be both entered and looked up as a text value, e.g. in the format **("text")**

Exercise 14

In this exercise you are going to set up a template for Simpson's Travel, a travel agent dealing with foreign exchange. It will work out the amount to be paid to the customer when the Agency buys foreign currency and print a payslip to confirm the transaction. The following data needs to be shown: the country, currency and rate of exchange, the number of units being bought from the customer, the amount due, the commission (2%, minimum £2.50) and the amount due to the customer. (The data on country, currency and rate of exchange will be held in a vertical lookup table.)

(a) Set up the labels as follows, using appropriate column widths.

	A	B	C	D	E	F	G
1	SIMPSON'S TRAVEL						
2	Foreign Exchange: Buying						
3							
4	Country	Currency	Rate	Number	Amount to	Less	Total to
5				bought	Customer	Commission	Customer
6							

(b) For the moment leave cells A6-C6 free, these will be dealt with later. D6 is the figure to be entered by Simpson's, so it remains blank at this stage.

(c) In E6, the formula to work out the Amount will be the Number/Rate so long as the value in D6 is not 0 (i.e. **=IF(D6=0,0,D6/C6)**

(d) In F6 the commission must be calculated at 2% of E6 or £2.50 if this is greater, hence it requires a formula like: **=IF(E6=0,0,IF((2%*E6)<2.5,2.5,(2%*E6)))**

(e) In G6 the amount due to the Customer will be Amount-Commission so long as the value in D6 is not 0 (i.e. **=IF(D6=0, 0, E6-F6)**

(f) Format cells E6-G6 for currency.

(g) Protect the cells in rows 1 to 5 and cells B6, C6 and E6-G6.
(h) Set up a lookup table to hold the rates of exchange as shown below:

	A	B	C
7	Currency LOOKUP table		
8	Country	Currency	Rate
9	Austria	Schilling	17.00
10	Belgium	Franc	51.60
11	Denmark	Krone	10.04
12	France	Franc	8.47
13	Germany	D Mark	2.43
14	Greece	Drachma	342
15	Italy	Lira	2345
16	Portugal	Escudo	250
17	Spain	Peseta	195
18	USA	US$	1.46

(i)   Now enter the details in A6-C6: when the customer comes in, the clerk enters in A6 the country of the currency (this is to ensure there are no difficulties with similar currency names, e.g. francs) so A6 remains blank.
(j)   The spreadsheet will then look up the country in the lookup table (A9:C18) and extract the Currency and the Rate of Exchange, and place these in B6 and C6. Hence in B6 enter a formula like =IF(A6=0,0,VLOOKUP(A6,A9:C18,2)) This will ensure that an error message is not displayed in B6 if there is nothing in A6.
(k) Similarly, in C6 enter a formula like =IF(A6=0,0,VLOOKUP(A6,A9:C18,3))
(l)   Blank the zero display.
(m) When the customer's details are entered a printout of the transaction will be given. Hence you need to improve the presentation of the first part of the spreadsheet only (i.e. A1:G6), in a similar way to that shown below:

	A	B	C	D	E	F	G
1	SIMPSON'S TRAVEL						
2	Foreign Exchange: Buying						
3							
4	Country	Currency	Rate	Number	Amount to	Less	Total to
5				bought	Customer	Commission	Customer
6							

(n) Save the file as a template called FOREXBUY.
(o) Print out transaction slips (i.e. cells A1:G6) for the following transactions:
•   600 German Deutsch Mark;
•   55 Danish Krone; and
•   500 US Dollars.
(Compare your transaction slips with those in Appendix 2.)

17. Multiple worksheets

You should find out how to work with a number of different worksheets by:

- *viewing* two or more different worksheets on the screen at one time, e.g. by using the *arrange* facility;
- *copying* data from one worksheet to another;
- *linking* data in one worksheet so that when the original worksheet is amended, the linked worksheet is automatically updated.

Exercise 15

In this exercise you are going to use the part-time hours worksheet you saved in Exercise 11 to link the Gross Pay figures to a second worksheet which keeps details of all staff working for Flexi Company Ltd and works out their pay after deductions. (For the purposes of this exercise the calculations for the deductions are kept relatively simple.)

(a) Set up the following worksheet to calculate the net pay of both full-time and part-time staff. You should make any further changes to the presentation of the worksheet that you feel are necessary and effective.

	A	B	C	D	E	F	G
1	**FLEXI COMPANY LTD**						
2	**PAYROLL**						
3							
4	**Full-time staff**	**Annual**	**Monthly**	**Tax**	**National**	**Other**	**Net**
5		**salary**	**gross pay**		**Insurance**	**deductions**	**pay**
6	Katy Green	£12,000				£20.00	
7	Chris Stone	£15,250					
8	Jonathan Wong	£8,000				£50.00	
9	**Part-time staff**		**Weekly**	**Tax**	**National**	**Other**	**Net**
10			**gross pay**		**Insurance**	**deductions**	**pay**
11							
12							
13							
14							
15							

(b) Use a formula in C6 to work out Monthly gross pay for the full time staff, i.e. Annual salary/12. Copy this to the other full time staff, i.e to C7 and C8.

(c) Use a formula in D6 to work out Tax payable (for the purposes of this exercise assume a 25% rate), i.e. 25%*Gross pay. Copy this down to both the full-time and five part-time staff.

(d) Use a formula in E6 to work out the National Insurance payable by staff (for the purposes of this exercise assume NI is calculated at 9% of gross pay), i.e. 9%*Gross pay. Copy this down to all staff.

(e) Use a formula to work out Net pay (i.e. Gross pay less all deductions). Copy this down to all staff. If the worksheet looks as overleaf, save it.

	A	B	C	D	E	F	G
1	**FLEXI COMPANY LTD**						
2	**PAYROLL**						
3							
4	**Full-time staff**	**Annual**	**Monthly**	**Tax**	**National**	**Other**	**Net**
5		**salary**	**gross pay**		**Insurance**	**deductions**	**pay**
6	Katy Green	£12,000	£1,000.00	£250.00	£90.00	£20.00	£640.00
7	Chris Stone	£15,250	£1,270.83	£317.71	£114.38		£838.75
8	Jonathan Wong	£8,000	£666.67	£166.67	£60.00	£50.00	£390.00
9	**Part-time staff**		**Weekly**	**Tax**	**National**	**Other**	**Net**
10			**gross pay**		**Insurance**	**deductions**	**pay**
11				£0.00	£0.00		£0.00
12				£0.00	£0.00		£0.00
13				£0.00	£0.00		£0.00
14				£0.00	£0.00		£0.00
15				£0.00	£0.00		£0.00

(f) Retrieve the worksheet saved in Exercise 11 and if possible arrange the worksheets so that they appear in different windows on the screen.

(g) Copy the following data so that the two worksheets are linked:

• the names of the part-time staff in A5:A9 of the part-time worksheet into cells A11:A15 of the Payroll worksheet; and

• the gross pay of the part-time staff shown in I5:I9 of the part-time worksheet into cells C11:C15 of the Payroll worksheet.

	A	B	C	D	E	F	G
1	**FLEXI COMPANY LTD**						
2	**PAYROLL**						
3							
4	**Full-time staff**	**Annual**	**Monthly**	**Tax**	**National**	**Other**	**Net**
5		**salary**	**gross pay**		**Insurance**	**deductions**	**pay**
6	Katy Green	£12,000	£1,000.00	£250.00	£90.00	£20.00	£640.00
7	Chris Stone	£15,250	£1,270.83	£317.71	£114.38		£838.75
8	Jonathan Wong	£8,000	£666.67	£166.67	£60.00	£50.00	£390.00
9	**Part-time staff**		**Weekly**	**Tax**	**National**	**Other**	**Net**
10			**gross pay**		**Insurance**	**deductions**	**pay**
11	Amy Browning		£176.38	£44.10	£15.87		£116.41
12	Ian Jones		£157.25	£39.31	£14.15		£103.79
13	Bob Deeds		£144.50	£36.13	£13.01		£95.37
14	Clare Freeman		£195.50	£48.88	£17.60		£129.03
15	David Harris		£148.75	£37.19	£13.39		£98.18

(h) Return to the Part-time worksheet. Delete the names of all the part-time staff and all the hours worked between Mon and Sat, and enter the new hours:

Amy Browning: 7,7,8,7,6,0;   Bob Deeds: 7,7,8,9,7,4

Clare Freeman: 7,7,5,6,8,0   Mina Patel: 0,0,7,7,7,3

Donald Wise: 8,8,8,8,8,0

The two worksheets should now look as below:

	A	B	C	D	E	F	G	H	I
1	**FLEXI COMPANY LTD**								
2	*Pay rate:*	£4.25							
3	**Name**	**Mon**	**Tues**	**Wed**	**Thu**	**Fri**	**Sat**	**Total**	**Gross**
4								**hours**	**pay**
5	Amy Browning	7	7	8	7	6	0	35	£148.75
6	Bob Deeds	7	7	8	9	7	4	42	£182.75
7	Clare Freeman	7	7	5	6	8	0	33	£143.55
8	Mina Patel	0	0	7	7	7	3	24	£102.00
9	Donald Wise	8	8	8	8	8	0	40	£170.00
10	**Total**	**29**	**29**	**39**	**40**	**35**	**11**	**174**	**£747.05**

	A	B	C	D	E	F	G
1	**FLEXI COMPANY LTD**						
2	**PAYROLL**						
3							
4	**Full-time staff**	**Annual**	**Monthly**	**Tax**	**National**	**Other**	**Net**
5		**salary**	**gross pay**		**Insurance**	**deductions**	**pay**
6	Katy Green	£12,000	£1,000.00	£250.00	£90.00	£20.00	£640.00
7	Chris Stone	£15,250	£1,270.83	£317.71	£114.38		£838.75
8	Jonathan Wong	£8,000	£666.67	£166.67	£60.00	£50.00	£390.00
9	**Part-time staff**		**Weekly**	**Tax**	**National**	**Other**	**Net**
10			**gross pay**		**Insurance**	**deductions**	**pay**
11	Amy Browning		£148.75	£37.19	£13.39		£98.18
12	Bob Deeds		£182.75	£45.69	£16.45		£120.62
13	Clare Freeman		£143.55	£35.89	£12.92		£94.74
14	Mina Patel		£102.00	£25.50	£9.18		£67.32
15	Donald Wise		£170.00	£42.50	£15.30		£112.20

18. Multi-page (or 3D) worksheets

You should find out if it is possible to create 3-D worksheets in your software by setting up the formatting features and formulae to appear on each of the pages. You should also find out how to consolidate the data from each of the pages of the worksheet

---

Exercise 16

In this exercise you need to set up a 3-page worksheet to record the sales figures for each of the three sales regions: North, South and West.

(a)   Create three identical pages using the formatting shown in the example below. You should also create formulae to total the three different branch sales figures for each month.

	A	B	C	D	E	F	G
1	Sales region:						
2	Branch	Jan	Feb	Mar	Apr	May	Jun
3							
4							
5							
6	Total						

(b) In the worksheet set up for the West sales region create a further row where you can show the grand totals of all the sales regions for each month.

(c) Enter the following data for each of the sales regions together with their January sales figures:

North		South		West	
Leeds	2345	London	2456	Cardiff	1890
Manchester	2356	Brighton	2567	Bristol	1678
Liverpool	2678	Portsmouth	2678	Bath	1567

The worksheets should look as below, together with the grand totals

	A	B	C	D	E	F	G
1	Sales region:	North					
2	Branch	Jan	Feb	Mar	Apr	May	Jun
3	Leeds	2345					
4	Manchester	2356					
5	Liverpool	2678					
6	Total	7379					

	A	B	C	D	E	F	G
1	Sales region:	South					
2	Branch	Jan	Feb	Mar	Apr	May	Jun
3	London	2456					
4	Brighton	2567					
5	Portsmouth	2678					
6	Total	7701					

	A	B	C	D	E	F	G
1	Sales region:	West					
2	Branch	Jan	Feb	Mar	Apr	May	Jun
3	Cardiff	1890					
4	Bristol	1678					
5	Bath	1567					
6	Total	5135					
7							
8	Grand total	20,215					

19. Productivity aids

You should check your software to see if the following facilities are available:

- *spell checker*;
- *outliner*;
- *text boxes and arrows.*

20. Macros

You may find there are some sample macros that accompany your software, so take a look at these to see what is available. You should then find out how macros can be created in your spreadsheet software:

- how to *record* macros and how to stop the recording;
- how to *play* back a macro;
- how to *write* macros using the macro language;
- how to *store* macros: they can normally be stored either in the application to which they refer or globally.

21. Charts and graphs

If your spreadsheet software can produce charts and graphs, you should work through the exercises in Chapter 10.

22. Statistical functions

You should find out how to use the following basic statistical functions:

- to create a *random number*. Note: the values created by the RAND() function are continuously updated as you edit the worksheet;
- to *round* figures to a specified number of decimal places, i.e. the ROUND() function;
- to calculate measures of *central tendency*: e.g. the mean, median and mode;
- to calculate measures of *dispersion*: e.g. variance and standard deviation.

Exercise 17

(a) In A1 generate a random number between 1 and 100 (rounded to two decimal places) by using, for example, the following function **=ROUND(RAND()*100,0)**

(b) To stop the worksheet re-calculating the random number, select manual calculation.

(c) Copy the function in A1 into the range A1:G9. (This will give you a range containing exactly the same value as appears in A1.)

(d) Set up functions to:
- count the number of items in the range, e.g. **=COUNT(A1:G9)**
- find the median, e.g. **=MEDIAN(A1:G9)**
- find the mode, e.g. **=MODE(A1:G9)**
- find the variance, e.g. **=VAR(A1:G9)**
- find the standard deviation , e.g. **=STDEV(A1:G9)**

(e) Re-calculate the worksheet. It should look something like the one on page 186, although of course the numbers generated by the random number function will be different:

	A	B	C	D	E	F	G
1	14	62	18	17	45	29	66
2	3	76	92	2	88	18	64
3	15	4	97	95	76	100	74
4	51	31	67	17	29	36	12
5	97	8	70	8	53	68	23
6	72	98	92	15	43	65	51
7	30	57	76	1	30	6	65
8	36	96	4	37	52	73	35
9	66	28	91	33	5	35	67
10							
11	count:	54	median:	40	mode:	76	
12	variance:	1028.052	standard deviation:	32.06325			

23. Financial functions

You should find out what financial functions are available in your software and in particular the arguments to be used with them.

Exercise 18

Set up the following worksheet to calculate annual and monthly loan repayments:

	A	B	C	D	E	F
1	Loan repayment schedule					
2						
3	Loan amount:		Interest rate:		Period in years:	
4						
5	Annual loan repayments:			Monthly loan repayments:		

(a) Format cells B3, C5 and F5 for currency (no decimal places) and D3 for numeric value with two decimal places;
(b) Shade (and protect) the cells as shown above.
(c) In C5 enter the PMT function to work out the annual loan repayments. Note: the argument may be in the form **(amount,rate,period)** or **(rate,period,amount)** and also that you may have to type **-amount** to force a positive figure.
(d) In F5 enter a formula to work out monthly repayments, e.g. **=C5/12**
(e) Use the following data to calculate loan repayments:
•   amount: £25,000; interest rate: 8.5%; period: 10 years
•   amount: £12,000; interest rate: 11%; period: 3 years
(Check your calculations with those in Appendix 2.)
(f) Extend the worksheet to produce a 25 year loan repayment schedule, showing the interest and principal paid each year together with the balance outstanding (as shown below) for a loan of £120,000 at 6.75% interest rate. (Check the result in Appendix 2.)

	A	B	C	D	E	F
7	Year	Interest paid		Principal paid		Balance
8	1	=D3*B3		=$C$5-$B8		=B3-D8
9	2	=$D$3*F8		↓		=F8-D9
10	↓	↓				↓

24. Multimedia worksheets

Provided you have the relevant hardware in place you should investigate if you are able to include:

- *sound*:   you may want to use pre-recorded sound files to annotate your worksheets or else record your own sound;
- *video or animation*: these will probably be pre-recorded files which you might wish to use to annotate your worksheets.

25. Integrating data

Using the information provided in **14:10** you should investigate the most appropriate way to:

- read a worksheet created in another spreadsheet program: many spreadsheet packages are able to convert worksheets created in other formats;
- copy a worksheet into a word processed document;
- read data from a database package or copy data to a database package.

Integrated Exercise
(This exercise uses material to be created in the Integrated Exercises in Chapters 8, 10 and 11.)
You are the Finance Director of a small company. At the recent Board of Directors meeting you were asked to present a forecast of expenditure for the next year.

(a) Create a worksheet that shows the expenses for 1993 and 1994

	1993	1994
Salaries	994,000	1,108,000
Council tax	12,850	13,450
Electricity	6,925	7,865
Maintenance costs	5,395	7,655

(b) Estimate the 1995 expenses based on the same percentage increase experienced between 1993 and 1994.
(c) Copy this worksheet into the word processed document set up in the Integrated Exercise in Chapter 8.
(d) Copy this worksheet into the PC presentation set up in the Integrated Exercise in Chapter 10.

10

Charting and graphing software

1. Getting started

Before beginning to use your charting and graphing software package, whether it be a spreadsheet package or a dedicated statistical package, it is essential that you read Chapter 7 so that in particular:

- you are familiar with the use of both the keyboard and the mouse
- you know how to start up the computer; and
- you have prepared your disks ready to hold your work.

2. Getting to know your charting and graphing software package

You should refer to 7:14-15 for advice on getting to know your charting and graphing package by finding out:

- how to load the charting and graphing software;
- if there is an on-line tutorial;
- whether you will need to use the keyboard or the mouse or both;
- if there is on-line help and how to access it;
- what information is shown on the screen; and
- how to quit the package.

3. Basic principles

In order to create any chart you should find out how to carry out the following:

Select the required chart type: With some software you need to select the chart type first, with others you type the data in first and then select the type of chart (normally from a gallery). A gallery will show either thumbnail sketches or names of charts.

Enter the details of the x and y axes: You should find out how to enter the details of the horizontal (x) axis (i.e. the time line) and the vertical (y) axis. In spreadsheet software the data for the x axis is usually entered across a row.

Preview the chart: As some software does not allow you to see the chart being created, it is a good idea to preview (or "draw") the chart on the screen to ensure that it is being created as you require.

Print the chart: The software will probably already have been set up to work with a particular printer, but depending on your software, print options may include the following: print quality; size of printout and number of copies. It is also often possible to print a number of charts on one page.

Save the chart: You should save your work frequently to disk, especially before printing. The first time you save your work you will need to give it a name (see **7:16** for advice on naming files) but when you re-save it, the software will use the same name although it should be possible to save it with a different name.

4. Line graphs

You should investigate the different types of line graphs you can produce, e.g. to show the line(s) only, or the data markers only, or to show both the lines and data markers.

Exercise 1
Draw a line graph (showing the lines only) to display Gold Computer Supplies' yearly sales figures (in £millions) from 1985 to 1994 at their two offices: London and Birmingham. If the chart looks as below, save it.

	85	86	87	88	89	90	91	92	93	94
London	1.5	2.0	2.5	3.3	3.5	4.0	4.4	4.5	4.0	4.3
Birmingham	0.8	1.0	1.2	1.5	1.8	2.3	2.5	3.0	2.5	3.3

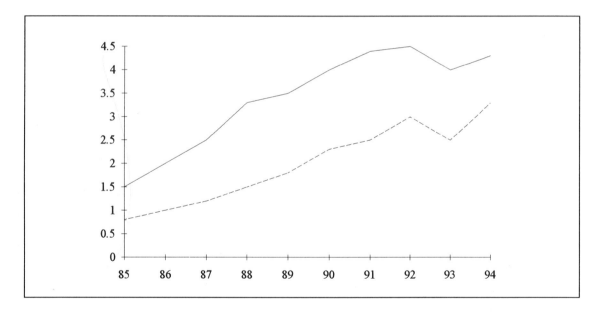

Text labels: You should find out how to enter a chart title and label the axes. (Note: in Windows-based software you can normally create a second line of a title by pressing [Ctrl]+[Enter].) You may have to change the orientation of the data and the alignment of the labels to look right and fit well.

Exercise 2
(a) Add a chart title: **Gold Computer Supplies** and sub-title: **Sales figures 1985-1994**
(b) Label the Y axis: **£m**   No x axis title is required here.

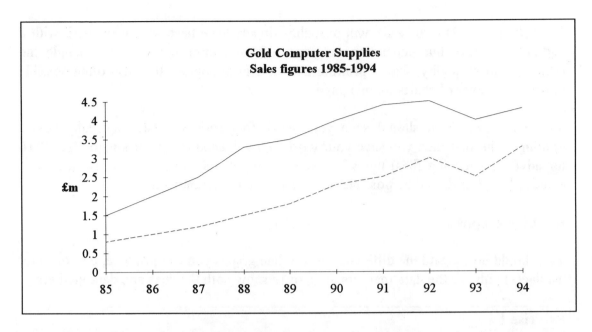

Legend: Unless a legend is automatically added to the chart, you should find out how to add one yourself.

Exercise 3
Add a legend and place it in its default position. Re-save the chart if it looks as below.

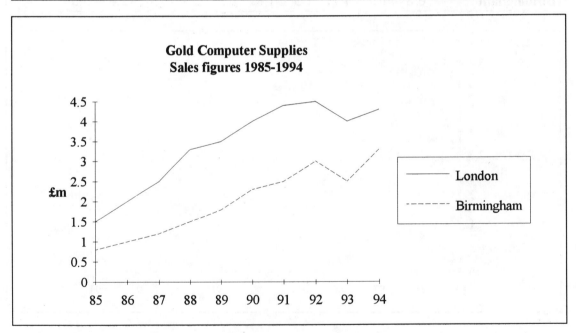

Formatting the legend: You should find out how to:
- move the legend to a new position, i.e. above, below or to the right or left of the chart;
- change the border of the legend, e.g. add a pattern, or change the width of the border or shadow it;
- change the shading (i.e. pattern) of the legend area.

Exercise 4
Move the legend under the chart and shadow its border. Re-save the chart.

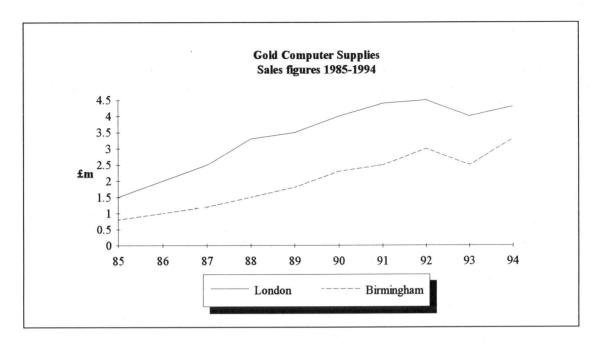

Text formatting: You should find out if it is possible to format the text of the different elements of the chart in the following ways:

- change the typeface (or font);
- increase or decrease the font size;
- alter the type style;
- change the colour of the text;
- alter the alignment of the text;
- place a box or border around the text.

These features may be alterable both on a global basis and on an individual basis.

Exercise 5
Increase the font size of the title and sub-title and italicise the text in the legend. If the chart looks as below, re-save it and then print it.

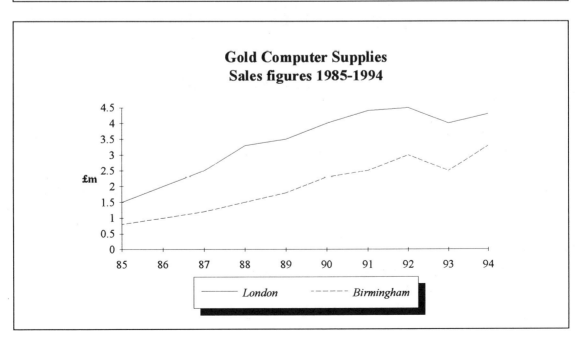

5.   Bar charts

You should investigate the different types of bar charts that you can produce using the software: there should be simple, cluster, stacked, 100% stacked charts as well as a range of 3-D charts.

Data marker labels: You should find out how to add labels to all or selected data markers.

Exercise 6

(a) Draw a simple bar chart to show Gold Computer Supplies' sales figures (in £'000s) for the first quarter of 1995 at their two offices:

	Jan	Feb	Mar
London	465	374	256
Birmingham	365	325	380

(b) Use the chart title: **Gold Computer Supplies** and the subtitle: **Sales figures: first quarter 1995** and embolden these. Label the values on the y axis: **£'000s**

(c) Add a shadowed legend underneath the chart.

(d) Add data markers labels to the London data.

(e) If the chart looks as below, save it.

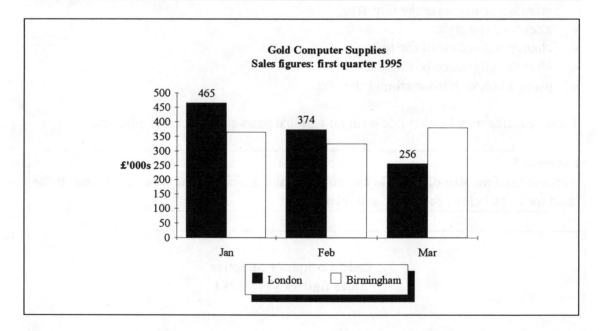

Formatting data markers: You should also be able to change the patterns of the data markers, modify their widths and control the amount of any overlap.

Gridlines: You should find out how to add horizontal gridlines (or vertical droplines) to a chart.

Exercise 7

(a) Convert the chart into a 3-D bar chart with gridlines.

(b) Remove the data markers.

(c) If the chart looks as below, save it again.

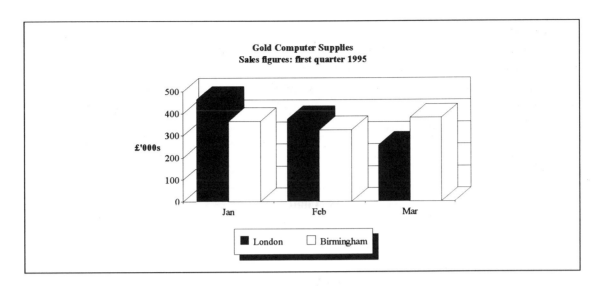

Arrows: You should see if it is possible to add an arrow to the chart, to modify the width or length of the arrow shaft as well as change the shape of the arrowhead.

Attach text: You should also find out if you can add extra text to the chart and how this can be formatted in the ways described above.

Exercise 8
(a) Remove the gridlines in the chart.
(b) Change the colours or patterns of the data markers.
(c) Add an arrow pointing to London's March data. Attach a piece of text: **Poor March figs**
(d) Place a border around this text.
(e) If it looks as below re-save it and then print it.

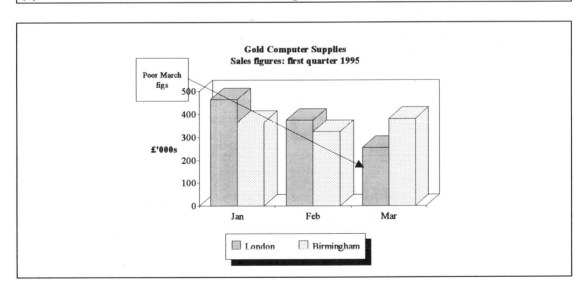

6.   Pie charts

You should investigate the type of pie charts that are available in your software. You will probably find a variety of pie charts that display the slices with or without labels, values or percentage marks (%). There will probably be a range of 3-D pie charts and stacked column pie charts too.

Exercise 9
(a) Create a 3-D pie chart to display Gold Computer Supplies 1994 unit sales:
PCs 25000; Printers 20000; Modems 7500; Scanners   2500
(b) Each slice should be labelled with its name and percentage value only.
(c) Use the chart title: **Gold Computer Supplies** and the sub-title: **1994 unit sales**
(d) If the chart looks as below, save it.

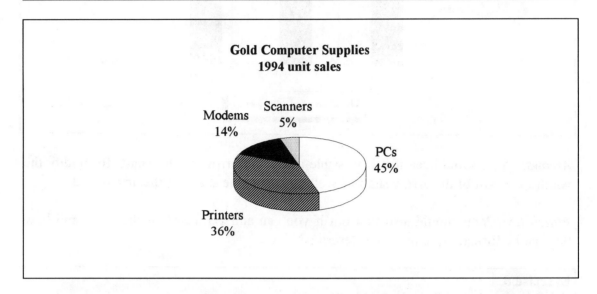

Exploded pie charts: You may either be able to select an exploded pie chart from the gallery (where normally the first slice is "cut") and/or be able to *drag* slices in and out of any pie yourself. You should note, however, that with some software you will not be able to cut a 3-D pie-chart.

Exercise 10
(a) Amend the pie-chart to cut the PC slice.
(b) Delete the labels and percentage markers and add a legend.
(c) Re-save the chart if it looks as below and then print it.

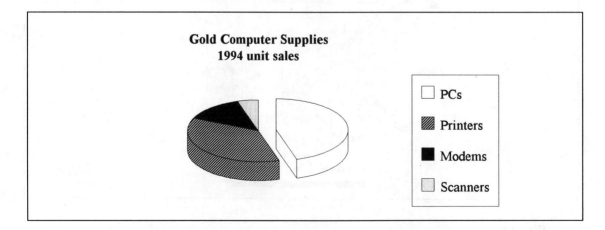

Linked pies: Once a slice has been cut, you should find out if it is possible to link the cut slice of the pie-chart to a second (proportionally smaller) pie to demonstrate the breakdown of that slice.

7.   Area charts

You will probably find that you have a number of area chart options both 2-dimensional and 3-dimensional, with or without gridlines or droplines. You should also be able to select whether you wish to label the areas rather than use a legend.

Exercise 11
(a) Convert the chart created in Exercise 5 into an area chart (retaining the legend) with both vertical and horizontal gridlines.
(b) If it looks as below, save it with a different name.

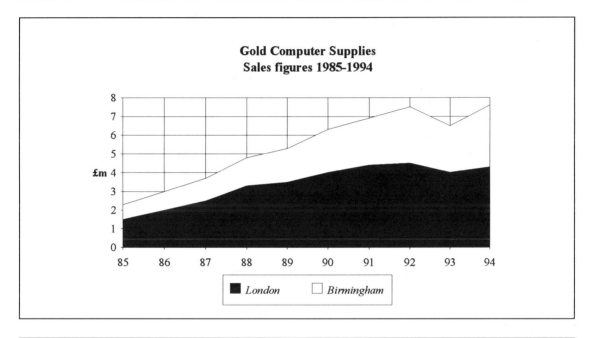

Exercise 12
(a) Remove the gridlines and the legend, and label the areas.
(b) Save the chart if it looks as below, and then print it.

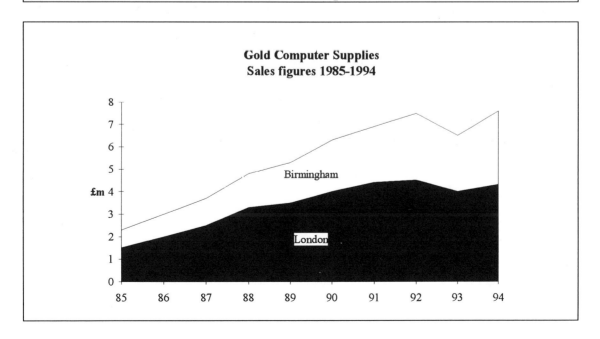

8.   Further features

You should find out if the following tools are available in your software and how to use them:

- *spell checker;*
- *calculator;*
- *clipart library.*

9.   Multimedia charts

Provided you have the relevant hardware in place you should investigate if you are able to include:

- *sound*: you may want to use pre-recorded sound files stored on CD-ROM which can be read in as clipart, or else record your own sound;
- *video or animation*: these will probably be pre-recorded files which you could use to annotate your documents.

10. Integrating data

Using the information provided in **14:10** you should investigate the most appropriate way to:

- copy a graph or chart into a word processed document; and
- copy a graph or chart into a presentation file.

Integrated exercise
(This exercise uses material to be created in the Integrated Exercises in Chapters 8, 9 and 11.)
You are the Finance Director of a small company. At the recent meeting of the Board of Directors meeting you were asked to present a forecast of expenditure for the next year.

(a) Using the 1995 expenses figures calculated in the Integrated Exercise in Chapter 9, convert them into a bar chart.
(b) Copy this chart into the word processed document created in the Integrated Exercise in Chapter 8
(c) Copy this chart into the presentation created in the Integrated Exercise in Chapter 11.

11

Presentation graphics software

1. Getting started

Before beginning to use your presentation graphics software package it is essential that you read Chapter 7 so that in particular:

- you are familiar with the use of both the keyboard and the mouse;
- you know how to start up the computer; and
- you have prepared your disks ready to hold your work.

2. Getting to know your presentation graphics software package

You should refer to **7:14-15** for advice on getting to know your presentation graphics package by finding out:

- how to load the presentation graphics software;
- if there is an on-line tutorial;
- whether you will need to use the keyboard or the mouse or both;
- if there is on-line help and how to access it;
- what information is shown on the screen; and
- how to quit the package.

3. Basic principles

Before beginning to create your presentation you need to understand how to carry out the following basic operations:

Create slides (or charts): You will need to find out whether your software requires you to create (and save) each slide as individual files or whether you can create (and save) the presentation as one file.

Select the required slide type: With some software you will find one basic type of slide where you can enter text or graphs, whereas with other software you will have to select the relevant type of chart first.

Preview the slide: Note that some software does not allow you to see the slide being created, if this is the case then it is a good idea to preview (or "draw") the slide on the screen to ensure that it is being designed as you require.

Save the presentation: You should save your work frequently to disk: at least after you have created each slide, but perhaps also before you try out anything new. You may not need to save before you print, but you are strongly advised to do so in case there is a problem whilst printing. For advice on naming your file, see **7:16**.

4. Creating a text slide

You may find that you have a choice of different styles of text slides e.g. with or without bullets, or you may only have one slide on which you can display all types of text.

Generally, there are two main parts to a slide, the *title* and the *body* and you may have to select the particular part you wish to work on before you can type anything in.

Exercise 1

You are the leader of the sales team of a computer supplies company called Gold Computer Supplies. Create a text slide with bullets to be used as a slide to show the overview of a presentation. Use the title **Gold Computer Supplies** and the bulleted items shown below:

Overview of presentation

- **1985-1994 figures**
- **Top selling PCs**
- **1994 unit sales**
- **Top selling software packages**
- **March 1995 sales figures**
- **Where do we go from here?**

You should also find out how to create a *new* slide and how to move backwards and forwards through the slides that you have created.

5. Applying a template

You should find out what *templates* are available with your software. They may be divided up into different categories, i.e. for black and white overheads, colour overheads, and for video screens, i.e. for PC presentations. It should be possible to view each of the different templates, probably as a thumbnail sketch in order to make a choice.

Exercise 2

Apply a template to your presentation suitable for colour overheads. Choose a layout and a colour scheme that you like. (For the purposes of these exercises the following simple black and white overhead template has been selected - yours will probably look very different to this.)

Overview of presentation

❑ **1985-1994 figures**

❑ **Top selling PCs**

❑ **1994 unit sales**

❑ **Top selling software packages**

❑ **March 1995 sales figures**

❑ **Where do we go from here?**

6.   Using the outliner

You should find out how to:

- *view* your presentation using the outline facility. With Windows-based software you should be able to identify the types of slides (listed in the outline) by the icons at the left hand side of each slide;
- *add* further slides by simply typing in the text for the title and the (bulleted) items.

Exercise 3

Select the outliner view and add the following text slide in this view:

Top selling PCs
❑ **Dell**
❑ **Compaq**
❑ **Olivetti**
❑ **IBM**

---

7.   Drawing tools

Back in *slide view* you should find out how to:

- add lines, circles, arrows, and other shapes to slides by selecting the relevant *drawing tool* (possibly an icon on a tool bar);
- *increase the width of lines* drawn with these tools;
- *fill the shapes* with a colour or shading pattern;
- *shadow the shapes* or place a *border* placed around them; and
- *re-position, duplicate* or *re-size* these drawings.

Exercise 4
Create a new slide with the title: **Where do we go from here?** showing an up arrow,
which you should shadow.

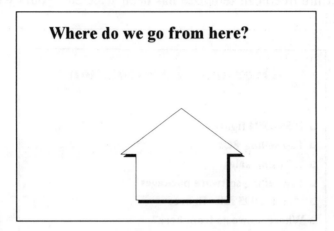

8.   Clipart

You should find out:

*   if your presentation graphics package has a library of clipart images which can be
    used in slides. It should be possible to view each of the images in the library as a
    thumbnail sketch;

*   how to copy your selected image onto your slide, where it should also be possible
    to re-position it, re-size it and manipulate it in the same way as the objects created
    by the drawing tools.

Exercise 5
(a)   Create a new slide.
(b)   Give the slide the title: **Gold Computer Supplies**
(c)   Find an appropriate clipart image for the slide and copy it into the slide.

9. Working with text

You should find out how to add extra text to a slide, for example to provide captions, and how to format it in the following ways:

- select a different *typeface* (or *font*) or *size*;
- make modifications to the type *style* or use special effects like shadow or emboss;
- alter the *alignment* of the text;
- adjust the *line spacing*;
- *remove* the bullets or *change the shape* of the bullet.

Note: the same formatting changes can be made to the main text in the slides - but beware of creating an inconsistent slide.

Exercise 6
(a) Add some text inside the arrow in the slide created in Exercise 4: **We must increase sales!**
(b) Change it to italics and choose a font size that fits neatly into the shape, or else "size the object to fit".

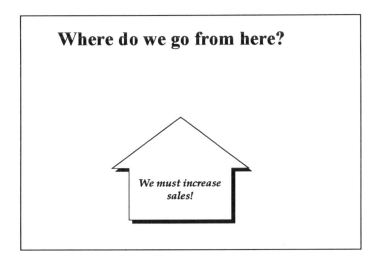

10. Further text slides

You should investigate how to create the following further types of text slides:

Title charts: A title chart may be created automatically for you at the beginning of the presentation. If it is not then you can create one yourself. This will probably mean formatting some or all of the text in a different way to that used in the template.

Exercise 7
If the software has not already created a title slide for you, set one up as below:
(a) Use the text **Gold Computer Supplies** as a centred heading at the top.
(b) Use large bold text: **Sales Presentation** underlined and centred in the middle of the slide
(c) Add your name, either embossed or shadowed, and centred at the bottom of the slide.

Gold Computer Supplies

<u>Sales Presentation</u>

Your name

Table charts: You should find out how to create a table slide, this may be possible in a number of ways:

- you may be able to select a table chart or a table facility;
- you may have to create a table yourself, in which case the Tab key will be useful as it will let you move across the screen in small "jumps" so that you can align the columns of text. (You may be able to view a ruler line to see the default tab stops and even be able to change them to your own requirements);
- you may be able to copy in a table that has been created in a word processed document.

Exercise 8
Create the table chart shown below. Note: you may have to decrease the size of the font of the text in the table to fit it onto the slide.

Top selling software packages

<u>Word processing</u>	<u>Spreadsheets</u>	<u>Databases</u>
Word for Windows	Excel	Access
WordPerfect for DOS	Lotus 123	dBASE IV
Ami Pro for Windows	SuperCalc	Approach

11. Graphs and charts

You should find out how to create graphs and charts as there are a number of ways that are possible depending on your software:

- you may have to select the type of chart that you require and then simply add the data; or
- you may have to select a graphing facility and enter the data into a datasheet and then convert this data into the appropriate type of chart; or
- you may be able to read the data from a spreadsheet package (or similar) into the *datasheet* or even read the chart in directly itself.

Exercise 9
Create a new slide showing the line graph that appears in Exercise 5 of Chapter 10.

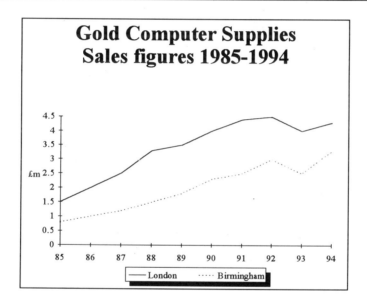

Exercise 10
Create a new slide showing the column chart that appears in Exercise 8 in Chapter 10.

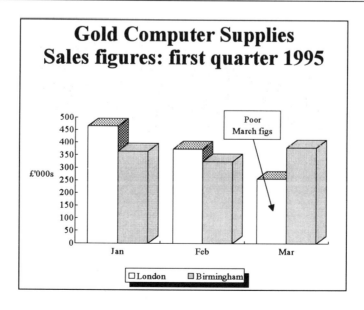

Exercise 11
Create a new slide showing the pie chart that appears in Exercise 10 of Chapter 10.

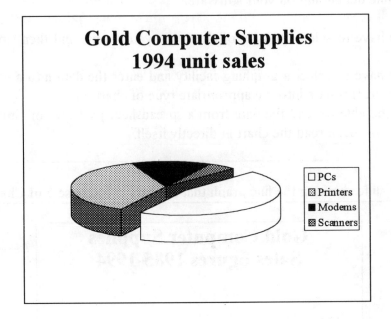

Exercise 12
Create a new slide showing the area chart that appears in Exercise 12 of Chapter 10.

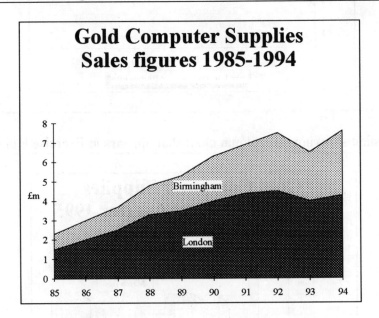

12. Organisation charts

You should find out if you are able to create organisation charts automatically in your software or whether you will have to use the drawing tools to build them yourself. This may mean creating and duplicating boxes, adding lines and adding text inside the boxes.

Exercise 13
Create a chart showing the organisation of Gold Computer Supplies as below. Format the text as shown below, i.e. use italics for the job titles.

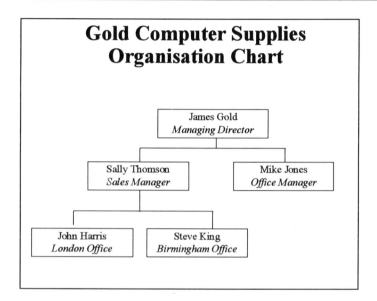

13. Using the slide sorter

You should find out how to use the *slide sorter* to view all the slides you have created, either as thumbnail sketches or as a list of filenames. You will then be able to move the slides into the order in which you wish to present them as well as delete any you do not wish to include.

Exercise 14
Make the following alterations to the presentation
(a) Move the slides into the following order:
Slide 1:   Slide created in Exercise 5 with the clipart;
Slide 2:   Title slide created in Exercise 7;
Slide 3:   Slide created in Exercise 13 showing the organisation of the company;
Slide 4:   Slide created in Exercises 1/2 showing the overview of the presentation;
Slide 5:   Slide created in Exercise 9 showing the line graph;
Slide 6:   Slide created in Exercise 3 showing the top selling PCs;
Slide 7:   Slide created in Exercise 11 showing the pie chart;
Slide 8:   Slide created in Exercise 8 showing the top selling software packages
Slide 9:   Slide created in Exercise 10 showing the 3-D column chart;
Slide 10: Slide created in Exercises 4/6 with the arrow.
(b) Delete the slide with the area chart created in Exercise 12.

14. Speaker notes

You should find out how to create notes for the speaker. The *notes* facility will normally display the slide on the top half of the page and allow you to type some notes underneath. You should investigate how to re-size the slide if you need more room.

Exercise 15
Add the following notes for Slide 2, i.e. the chart created in Exercise 7.

Welcome everyone
Special welcome to James Gold
Introduce myself and my colleagues
Remind colleagues of organisation's structure - see next chart

---

15. Productivity aids

You should investigate the use of the following:

- *spell checker*: if available, this will proof-read the whole presentation for both spelling and typographical errors.
- *find and replace facility*: this will allow you to find a word or phrase or even font and replace it with another word or phrase or font.
- *calculator*: if available, this will let you perform mathematical calculations, and use formulae and functions similar to a spreadsheet program.

Exercise 16
Spell check your presentation.

---

16. Printing

You should find out how to print:

- the *slides*: you should be able to select all or specified slides to print;
- the *outline;*
- the *audience handouts*: you may be able to choose the number of slides you want printed on one page, e.g. 1, 3 or 6; if you want to print only selected slides you may have to use the slide-sorter to move them into the required order.
- the *speakers notes.*

Your software will probably already have been set up to work with a particular printer, but there may be a number of further print options, for example, scaling the slides to fit the paper or converting the slides to black and white slides.

Exercise 17
Print the following:
(a) overheads (on paper or acetate);
(b) speakers notes for Slide No 2 (created in Exercise 15) as shown on page 207;
(c) audience handouts of slides 3, 5, 6, 7, 8 and 9 only, as shown on page 208.

Gold Computer Supplies

<u>Sales Presentation</u>

Your name

Welcome everyone

Special welcome to James Gold

Introduce myself and my colleagues

Remind colleagues of organisation's structure - see next chart

Organisation chart

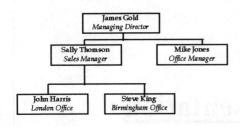

Gold Computer Supplies
Sales figures 1985-1994

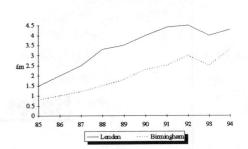

Top selling PCs

- Dell
- Compaq
- Olivetti
- IBM

Gold Computer Supplies
1994 unit sales

Top selling software packages

Word processing	Spreadsheets	Databases
Word for Windows	Excel	Access
WordPerfect for DOS	Lotus 123	dBASE IV
Ami Pro for Windows	SuperCalc	Approach

Gold Computer Supplies
Sales figures: first quarter 1995

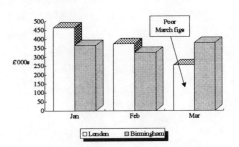

17. Creating a PC presentation

In order to create a PC presentation (also referred to as a *slide show* or *screen-show)* you will need to investigate how to:

- apply an appropriate *template* for display on a PC's video screen;
- use the *slide-sorter* to preview slides in the order of presentation;
- use the *rehearsal* or *demo* facility to view the presentation. The default presentation will probably be *manual advance* (i.e. you will need to press a key or click the mouse button to continue to the next screen);

Exercise 18
Using the presentation created in Exercises 1-17 above, apply an appropriate template for display on a PC screen and rehearse the default presentation.

- *build* slides: once the slide has been designed you should find out if you can select special effects to build up the (bulleted) items of the slide on-screen;

Exercise 19
If available in your software, use special effects to build the slide created in Exercise 3 showing the top selling PCs.

- use *transitions:* there may be a number of different transitions available to draw and erase the whole slide as well as a demo facility to try out each one;
- *automate* the presentation: you will need to specify the timings (usually in seconds) after which the screen is erased;
- *give* the presentation: you should investigate whether there is a separate *slide-viewer* to present the show. You should also find out whether you can use the mouse pointer on the screen and whether you can make annotations.
- *loop* the presentation: you should find out if you can display the presentation continuously until a particular key is pressed.

Exercise 20
Create transitions for each slide with appropriate timings. Rehearse the presentation and then display it through the slide viewer so that it loops continuously.

---

18. Customising the template

You should investigate the following ways in which you can create your own customised template. This is normally be done by making changes to the *master slide*:

- add *text* or a *logo*;
- include the *date, time* and *page/slide number*;
- *format* the text (as described in 9);
- change the shape of the *bullets*;
- add *lines* or *boxes* (using the drawing tools, as described in 7);
- change the *colour scheme* (or colour shading so that it is not all one colour);
- re-*size* (or *re-position*) the title or the body text.

Exercise 21
Make changes to the master slide, e.g. change text to a different font, add a logo, and change the bullet shape so that, for example the slide created in Exercises 1 and 2 might look as below:

19. Multimedia presentations

Provided you have the relevant hardware in place you should find out how to include:

- *sound*: this may either be stored in files on a **CD-ROM**, which can then be read in as clipart, or may have been recorded by the presenter;
- *motion video and animation*: this will probably be in the form of pre-recorded files which you can include in the same way as sound described above.

20. Integrating data

Using the information provided in **14:10**, you should find out how to:

- copy a table, worksheet, graph or chart into a presentation;
- copy an outline created in a word processed document into a presentation;
- copy an outline created into a presentation into a word processed document.

Integrated exercise
(This exercise uses material to be created in the Integrated Exercises in Chapters 9 and 10.)
You are the Finance Director of a small company. At the recent meeting of the Board of Directors you were asked to present a forecast of expenditure for the next year. Create a short presentation in which you produce:
(a) a text slide where you outline the reasons for the presentation;
(b) a slide in which you present the 1993 and 1994 sales figures (shown in the Integrated Exercise in Chapter 9);
(c) demonstrate the likely increase in figures for 1995 (by including the data from the worksheet set up in the Integrated Exercise in Chapter 9);
(d) demonstrate the breakdown of the 1995 costs (by including the bar chart set up in the Integrated Exercise in Chapter 10).

12
Database software

1. Getting started

Before beginning to use your database software package it is essential that you read Chapter 7 so that in particular:

- you are familiar with the use of both the keyboard and the mouse;
- you know how to start up the computer; and
- you have prepared your disks ready to hold your work.

2. Getting to know your database software package

You should refer to **7:14-15** to get advice on getting to know your database software package by finding out:

- how to load the database software;
- if there is an on-line tutorial;
- whether you will need to use the keyboard or the mouse or both;
- if there is on-line help and how to access it;
- what information is shown on the screen; and
- how to quit the package.

3. Creating a database

You should find out how to create a new database and how to design the structure of the data. For each field you will need to:

- *name the field*: You should find out if you have a limited number of characters to use for a fieldname, and whether you can use upper and lower case letters and spaces in the name;
- *specify the type of data to be held in the field*: You should find out how to specify the data type for text, numerical, logical, date, time and memo fields;
- *specify the size of the field*: For text data this will normally be the maximum characters you wish to hold in the field, for numerical data this may be specified in other ways. If the software has default options, it may be easier to use these for the time being.

You may also want to set a *primary key* or *index*.

Exercise 1
Create a database called GARAGES to hold details of used cars for sale at a group of garages owned by Larkins. Each record will hold the following data items: the make of the car; the year of manufacture; the registration letter; the price; and the garage at which the car is held. This last field will be coded to hold the first letter of the garage, i.e. M for Maidstone, T for Tonbridge and S for Sevenoaks. Use the design given below. (Note: you need not specify a primary key.)

Fieldname	Field type	Field size
Make	character	20
Year	character	2 (no calculations required)
Letter	character	1
Price	currency (or numeric)	5 (no decimal places)
Garage	character	1

4.   Entering data

You should find out how to enter data into the database. Depending on your software this will either be using a form or a table/datasheet. If you are using a datasheet in a Windows-based package you should be able to re-size the columns of the datasheet so that more data fits onto the screen.

If you are not sure if your software is *case-sensitive*, enter the data using CAPITALS. This way you should not experience difficulties later when retrieving data if you make data entry mistakes when using upper and lower case characters.

If you make any typing errors as you enter the data you should correct them by deleting and retyping the data.

You should also find out if there is an Undo facility which will *undo* any previous actions that you have carried out by mistake.

Exercise 2
Enter the following data into the GARAGES database, then save it.

MAKE	YEAR	LETTER	PRICE	GARAGE
Metro 1.4GS	93	L	7595	M
Rover 216S	89	G	4295	S
Metro 1.1L	93	K	7295	S
Rover 216SL	93	L	10995	T
Maestro Clubman	91	H	4995	S
Volvo 440GL	90	G	5995	M
Renault 19GTX	90	H	5995	S
Fiat Uno 45	92	K	4750	M
Montego 1.6LX	91	H	5495	S
Rover 220i Coupe	92	K	13995	T
Rover 620 GSi	93	L	18750	T

5. Amending data

You should find out how to view all the data (i.e. all the fields of all the records) on the screen. This will probably be the same way in which you entered it (i.e. either a form or a datasheet). As you view the data you should check each record for accuracy and make any necessary amendments. In particular you should find out how to:

- *edit* data in a record: this means inserting, deleting and overtyping data in a field with new data;
- *add* records to those already held: this is normally done at the end of the file;
- *delete* records: this does not mean "blanking" out the data from the fields since an empty record will still be retained in the database, but is usually a two-stage process of marking the record for deletion and then deleting it or confirming its deletion

---

Exercise 3

Using the GARAGES table make the following amendments:
(a) The price of the 89 G reg Rover 216s has been dropped to £3,995.
(b) The H reg Renault 19GTX has been moved to the Maidstone garage.
(c) A 1991 (J) registered Citroen XM 2.0i has just been acquired. Add its details to the database. It is to be sold at a price of £7,250 and will be held at the Sevenoaks garage
(d) The Montego 1.6LX has been sold. Delete its details from the database.

---

6. Printing data

You should find out how to print the data, i.e. all the fields of all the records that have been entered. Note: this might be known as "listing" the data.

Exercise 4

Using the GARAGES file, print all the records in the database. It should now look as below, although if you did not select currency type for the PRICE field the figures will not be displayed as below.

MAKE	YEAR	LETTER	PRICE	GARAGE
Metro 1.4GS	93	L	£7,595	M
Rover 216S	89	G	£3,995	S
Metro 1.1L	93	K	£7,295	S
Rover 216SL	93	L	£10,995	T
Maestro Clubman	91	H	£4,995	S
Volvo 440GL	90	G	£5,995	M
Renault 19GTX	90	H	£5,995	M
Fiat Uno 45	92	K	£4,750	M
Rover 220i Coupe	92	K	£13,995	T
Rover 620 GSi	93	L	£18,750	T
Citroen XM 2.0i	91	J	£7,250	S

You should also find out if you are able to print the structure of the database. This is possible in some software but not all. If not, you can display the database structure on the screen and then print the screen itself by pressing [**Shift**]+[**PrintScrn**]

7. Modifying the database

If you need to modify the structure of the database you should find out how to:

- *make changes* to the details of any existing fields, e.g. to the fieldnames, fieldtype or field size;
- *add* a new field;
- *delete* a field.

Exercise 5

(a) Using the GARAGES file add the following fields:

- a field called Acquired using the date type (to show the date of acquisition of each car);
- a field called Automatic using the logical type (to show whether the car is automatic or not);
- a field called Notes using the memo type (to give further details about the car, e.g. colour, service history, previous owners, etc.).

(b) Save the modified database and enter the extra data into the new fields as shown below. (The bold type shows existing data in the database which has been repeated in order to help identify the records.)

93(L) Metro 1.4GS; acquired 15/07/94; manual; Amethyst, one owner, 12,000 miles, good condition;

89(G) Rover 216S; acquired 22/08/94; manual; Quicksilver, two careful owners, very good condition, low mileage;

93(K) Metro 1.1L; acquired 29/09/94; manual; Nightfire red, 15,000 miles, superb condition;

93(L) Rover 216SL; acquired 03/10/94; manual; Pulsar silver, electric sunroof, electric windows, radio cassette, low mileage;

91(H) Maestro Clubman; acquired 10/10/94; manual; White, 1 owner, full service history, alarm, 36,000 miles;

90(G) Volvo 440GL; 12/10/94; automatic; White, electric windows, sunroof, air conditioning, full service history, only 22,000 miles;

90(H) Renault 19GTX; acquired 15/10/94; manual; Red, central locking, 2 owners, excellent condition, 56,000 miles, full service history;

92(K) Fiat Uno 45; acquired 22/10/94; manual; Black, sunroof, stereo, rear windscreen wiper, very good condition;

92(K) Rover 220i Coupe; acquired 03/11/94; manual; Stone grey, low mileage, stereo, 60,000 miles, two owners;

93(L) Rover 620 GSi; acquired 15/11/94; automatic; Caribbean blue, power assisted steering, central locking, radio/cassette, 5,000 miles

91(J) Citroen XM 2.0i; acquired 20/11/94; manual; Black, power assisted steering, central locking, one owner, 35,000 miles, full service history

(c) Save the file again and close it.

8. Querying the database

You should find out how to search the database using the QBE facility, if available:

- *specify the fields to be searched*: In DOS-based software you will have to type in the field names and search criteria or select them from menus, with Windows-based software you may be able to use the *drag and drop* facility to enter the field names from a list;
- *enter the search criteria*: It is important that you know how to use the correct notation for your software, e.g. to search for an exact match or a piece of text, number or date less than or before one specified;
- *specify the field or fields to be displayed in the search;*
- *view* the results of the queries;
- *save* the queries

Exercise 6

Using the GARAGES database, carry out the following searches, displaying on the screen only the specified fields. Save only those queries marked below. (Possible QBE queries and results are shown in Appendix 2.)

(a) All the cars manufactured in or after 1993, displaying Make, Year and Letter;

(b) All the cars that cost less than £5,000, displaying Make, Letter and Price;

(c) All the cars held at the Maidstone garage, displaying Make, Acquired and Garage;

(d) All the cars registered with a letter after and including J, displaying Make, Year, Letter - save this query as JREG;

(e) All the Rovers, displaying Make and Price - save this query as ROVER;

(f) All the automatic cars, displaying Make and Automatic;.

(g) All the cars acquired before 1 October 1994, displaying Make, Acquired and Garage - save this query as OCT94;

(h) All cars with power assisted steering, displaying, Make, Letter, Price and Notes.

You should also find out how to set up QBE queries using multiple search criteria on one or more fields:

- where two conditions must be met; and
- where either of two conditions must be met.

Exercise 7

Using the GARAGES file carry out the following searches. (Possible QBE queries and results are shown in Appendix 2.)

(a) All the Metros or Maestros, displaying Make, Year, Price and Garage;

(b) All the cars manufactured since 1991 and costing less than £7,000, displaying Make and Price.

You should find out how to:

- add *calculated fields* based on mathematical calculations or combinations of text fields; and
- *sort* the results of the query in a specified way.

Exercise 8
Using the GARAGES file, carry out the following searches: (Possible QBE queries and results are shown in Appendix 2.)
(a) Using the OCT94 query, add a new field to calculate a sale price representing 90% of the original price. Re-save this query.
(b) Using the ROVER query, add a new field to display the year and registration letter fields together in the format **Year(Letter)** Re-save this query.
(c) Using the JREG query, sort the results alphabetically, in descending order, by registration letter. Re-save this query.

9.   Designing forms: basic design

You should find out if there is a way of producing a quick form using the forms designer, and how to:

- select the table and/or the fields to be included:
- add a heading/title for the form;
- specify the type of layout and/or "look" of the form

Exercise 9
Use the forms designer to create a quick form for the GARAGES table:
(a) Include all the fields in the following order: Make, Price, Year, Letter, Automatic, Notes, Garage and Acquired.
(b) If possible, use the title: Larkins Garage
It should look something like the one below, which has been used to display the first record.

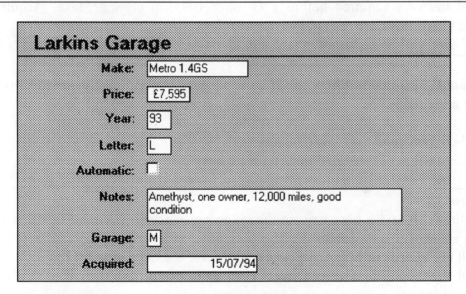

You should then find out how to use the forms designer in design mode. The design screen may be divided into a number of elements representing different parts of the form to be created: the title/header, the main body and the footer.

There may also be a ruler across the top of the screen and down the left hand side, or a coordinate system to mark the position of items on the screen.

You should find out how to:

- *replace labels:* this might be by overtyping or deleting and retyping;
- *add* extra text: this might mean adding text in a separate position on the form or increasing the size of the label in a text box to accommodate the extra text;
- change the *alignment* of text.

Exercise 10

Using the form created in Exercise 9:

(a) Replace the following field labels, making sure that all labels are left-aligned:

Make:	Make of car
Year:	Year of manufacture
Letter:	Registration letter
Garage:	Garage held
Acquired:	Date acquired

(b) Add the following explanatory text to two of the fields, in the most appropriate way:

Year of manufacture:	Garage held:
(last two digits)	(first letter)

The form should now look like the one below used to display an empty record:

Larkins Garage

Make of car:	
Price:	£0
Year of manufacture: (last two digits)	
Registration letter:	
Automatic:	
Notes:	
Garage held: (first letter)	
Date acquired:	

- *move* fields to new positions: data entry boxes and text labels can normally be moved together as well as separately The field labels and the field boxes can then be aligned either independently or together (whichever is the most appropriate), e.g. to the left, right, top or bottom with other fields;
- draw *lines and boxes* between and around data;

Exercise 11

Using the form created in Exercises 9 and 10:

(a) Centre the title.

(b) Move the fields into new positions, grouping them as shown below, making sure that the left and right margins are aligned.

(c) Use lines to separate the related data as shown below.

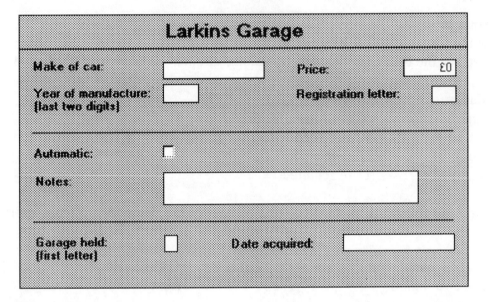

- *format* the data in fields, e.g. numeric and date values to be displayed in the most appropriate way.

Exercise 12

Using the form created in Exercises 9-11:

(a) Format the price to show currency values and no decimal places (if not already done so).

(b) Format the date to show the full, i.e. long date.

(c) Save the form and print a copy with the details of the last record in it. It should look something like the one below:

Larkins Garage

Make of car:	Citroen XM 2.0i	Price:	£7,250
Year of manufacture: [last two digits]	91	Registration letter:	J
Automatic:	☐		
Notes:	Black, power assisted steering, central locking, one owner, 35,000 milles, full service history		
Garage held: [first letter]	S	Date acquired:	20 November 1994

10. Designing forms: advanced design

Depending on your software and its capabilities you may be able to incorporate a number of advanced design features, although many will only be available in Windows-based software.

- Change the *font*, the font *size* and font *style*. (Note: you may have to "size to fit" the new text labels in their text boxes.)
- Change the *thickness* of lines and boxes.
- Give a *3-D*, e.g. sunken, raised or shadowed effect to labels and data-entry boxes;
- Use *colour* for text or lines.
- Create *list boxes, combo boxes, toggle buttons, check boxes* and *option buttons*.
- Create a new *tab order*.

Exercise 13
Using the form designed in Exercises 9-12, make the following enhancements:
(a) Change the font to Times Roman.
(b) Use a large font size for the heading (e.g. 15 or 16 point) and 10-12 point for the main text.
(c) Raise the field text labels and sink the field entry boxes, but leave the title as normal.
(d) Create a list box for the Garage field: using M, S and T as the only possible entries. Delete the explanatory text.
(e) Create a check box for the Automatic field (unless this has already been done by the software).
(f) Ensure the tab order is correct
The form should look something like the one below, used to display the 6th record.

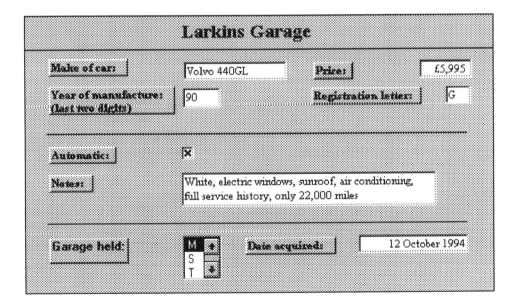

11. Data validation

You should find out how to write:

- data validation rules;
- data validation messages.

It will depend very much on your software where these rules and messages are entered and the notation that must be used.

Exercise 14

Set up the following data validation rules:

(a) For the Year field: only permit values from 85 onwards to be entered (since Larkins Garage does not acquire cars made before 1985); and set up the validation text message: "Garage only acquires cars manufactured after 1985."

(b) For the Acquired field: only permit a date earlier or including today's date to be entered; set up the validation text message: "Date must be today's date or earlier."

(c) If you have not been able to set up a list box for the Garage field, then set up a data validation rule to permit only the text "M", "S" or "T" to be entered; together with the supporting text message: "Only M for Maidstone, S for Sevenoaks and T for Tonbridge should be entered."

---

12. Designing reports: basic reports

You should find out if there is a way of producing a quick report using the reports designer, by specifying:

- the fields to be included;
- a heading/title for the report;
- the type of layout and/or the "look" of the report.
- the page orientation (portrait or landscape);
- the line spacing (single, one and half, double);

Exercise 15

Prepare a quick report to display the total car stock at Larkins Garage. (Note: if at any stage you are prompted whether you wish to group or sort the data, this is not necessary in this exercise.)

(a) Only include the following fields: Make, Letter, Automatic, Notes and Price.

(b) Use the title: Larkins Garage: Cars in Stock.

If the report looks something like the one on page 221, save it.

Larkins Garage: Cars in stock
today's date

Make	Letter	Automatic	Notes	Price
Metro 1.4GS	L	No	Amethyst, one owner, 12,000 miles, good condition	£7,595
Rover 216S	G	No	Quicksilver, two careful owners, very good condition, low mileage	£3,995
Metro 1.1L	K	No	Nightfire red, 15,000 miles, superb condition	£7,295
Rover 216SL	L	No	Pulsar silver, electric sunroof, electric windows, radio cassette, low mileage	£10,995
Maestro Clubman	H	No	White, 1 owner, full service history, alarm, 36,000 miles	£4,995
Volvo 440GL	G	Yes	White, electric windows, sunroof, air conditioning, full service history, only 22,000 miles	£5,995
Renault 19GTX	H	No	Red, central locking, 2 owners, excellent condition, 56,000 miles, full service history	£5,995
Fiat Uno 45	K	No	Black, sunroof, stereo, rear windscreen wiper, very good condition	£4,750
Rover 220i Coupe	K	No	Stone grey, low mileage, stereo, 60,000 miles, two owners	£13,995
Rover 620 GSi	L	Yes	Caribbean blue, power assisted steering, central locking, radio/cassette, 5,000 miles	£18,750
Citroen XM 2.0i	J	No	Black, power assisted steering, central locking, one owner, 35,000 miles, full service history	£7,250

£91,610

13. Designing reports: advanced design

You should find out how to use the design screen of the report designer: This may be divided into a number of elements, e.g. title/header, the detail of the body, and the footer.

There may also be a ruler across the top of the screen and down the left hand side, or a coordinate system to mark the position of items on the screen. You should now find out how to carry out the following:

- *move* columns of data to new positions: data and headings can normally be moved both together and separately;
- *increase and decrease the width of columns* in which the data is displayed;
- *add and delete* columns;
- *replace* text;
- *add extra text* on the report, e.g. a title or caption;
- *format* the *data* in fields, i.e. dates and numbers;
- draw *lines* above and below, and *boxes* around data;
- use *calculated fields* to perform calculations on numeric fields or combine text fields;
- *remove* any unnecessary totals;
- use *page headers* and *footers*.

Exercise 16

Modify the report begun in Exercise 15 to provide a more usable printout suitable to be given to customers:

(a) Move the columns of data, so that Letter is the first column, Make is the second, Automatic is the third and Price is the fourth.

(b) Amend the data in the Make column, so that it holds the combined text of the Make and Notes fields in the format: **Make: Notes** (Make sure there is enough space to display the longest details, but that the same amount of space is left between each row of data.)

(c) Decrease the width of the Letter column.

(d) Remove all the column headings, and give the first column the new heading: **Car details**, the third the heading: **Automatic transmission** (on two lines, right-aligned) and the fourth: **Price**

(c) Format the data in the price field to show currency (if this has not already been done) i.e. to display £ signs but no decimal places.

(d) Remove the price total and any totalling line.

(e) Add a page header showing the page number in the following format: **Page # of 1**
If the report looks as on page 223, save it again.

Page 1 of 1

Larkins Garage: Cars in stock
today's date

Car details	Automatic transmission	Price
L Metro 1.4GS: Amethyst, one owner, 12,000 miles, good condition	No	£7,595
G Rover 216S: Quicksilver, two careful owners, very good condition, low mileage	No	£3,995
K Metro 1.1L: Nightfire red, 15,000 miles, superb condition	No	£7,295
L Rover 216SL: Pulsar silver, electric sunroof, electric windows, radio cassette, low mileage	No	£10,995
H Maestro Clubman: White, 1 owner, full service history, alarm, 36,000 miles	No	£4,995
G Volvo 440GL: White, electric windows, sunroof, air conditioning, full service history, only 22,000 miles	Yes	£5,995
H Renault 19GTX: Red, central locking, 2 owners, excellent condition, 56,000 miles, full service history	No	£5,995
K Fiat Uno 45: Black, sunroof, stereo, rear windscreen wiper, very good condition	No	£4,750
K Rover 220i Coupe: Stone grey, low mileage, stereo, 60,000 miles, two owners	No	£13,995
L Rover 620 GSi: Caribbean blue, power assisted steering, central locking, radio/cassette, 5,000 miles	Yes	£18,750
J Citroen XM 2.0i: Black, power assisted steering, central locking, one owner, 35,000 miles, full service history	No	£7,250

You should also find out how to use the quick report facility or the full report designer to design reports that:

- *group data* together by a specified field; and
- *sort data* by one or more specified fields.

Exercise 17

Produce a report for management to show the cars held in each garage.

(a) Select the following fields: Garage, Year, Letter, Make, Acquired and Price.

(b) Group by Garage field and sort by Make field.

(c) Use the title: Larkins Garage: Garage Status Report.

(d) Either combine the Letter and Year fields in the format **Year (Letter)** or decrease the widths of Letter and Year fields so they appear close together

(e) Add a calculated field: **Sale price** to work out the price of each car if sold at 90% of price (e.g. **Price*0.9**) and set up sub- and grand totals for the prices and sale prices.

(f) Add short lines above the sub-and grand total prices, and explanatory text **Total value of cars:** for each group and **Total value of all cars:** at the end. Embolden the text.

(g) Format the Price and Sale price fields as well as the sub- and grand totals for Price and Sale price to display currency values (with no decimal places) and to be printed in bold.

The report should look something like the one below:

| | | Larkins Garage: Garage Status Report | | | |
		today's date			
Garage		**Make**	**Acquired**	**Price**	**Sale price**
M	92 (K)	Fiat Uno 45	25/10/94	£5,750	£4,275
	93 (L)	Metro 1.4GS	15/07/94	£7,595	£6,836
	90 (H)	Renault 19GTX	15/10/94	£5,995	£5,396
	90 (G)	Volvo 440GL	12/10/94	£5,995	£5,396
		Total value of cars:		**£24,335**	**£21,902**
S	91 (J)	Citroen XM 2.0i	20/11/94	£7,250	£6,525
	91 (H)	Maestro	10/10/94	£4,995	£4,496
	93 (K)	Metro 1.1L	29/09/94	£7,295	£6,566
	89 (G)	Rover 216S	22/08/94	£3,995	£3,596
		Total value of cars:		**£23,535**	**£21,182**
T	93(L)	Rover 216SL	03/10/94	£10,995	£9,896
	92(K)	Rover 220i Coupe	03/11/94	£13,995	£12,596
	93 (L)	Rover 620GSi	1/11/94	£18,750	£16,875
		Total value of cars:		**£43,740**	**£39,366**
		Total value of all cars:		**£91,610**	**£82,449**

14. Multimedia databases

Provided you have the relevant hardware in place you should investigate if your software is able to support the use of graphics, sound or video to create a multimedia database.

15. Relational databases: linking tables

You should find out if your software allows you to create a relational database and if so, how to:

- design the structure of each table of the database; and
- link or relate the tables.

Exercise 18

You work as a freelance conference organiser and are currently arranging a large three-day sales conference in Harrogate. In addition to the general sessions there are a number of seminars running throughout the conference, and conference delegates are invited to join one of these sessions. You want to set up a database to keep track of delegates at the conference and the seminar groups they join.

(a) Set up two tables: one called **Seminars** and one called **Delegates**, using the following field names, field data types and sizes:

SEMINARS

Fieldname	Field type	Field size	
Seminar ref	Character	3	primary key
Seminar name	Character	30	
From	Date	default	
To	Date	default	
Fee	Currency/numeric	5 (2 decimal places)	

DELEGATES

Delegate ref	Record no/counter/character	3	primary key
Delegate name	Character	30	
Company	Character	30	
Address 1	Character	30	
Address 2	Character	30	
Address 3	Character	30	
Telephone number	Character	12	
Seminar ref	Character	3	

(b) As each seminar will have many delegates but each delegate can only choose to attend one seminar, set up a one-to-many relationship between the seminars and the delegates field, linking the Seminar ref fields.

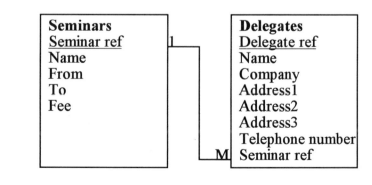

(c) Enter the following test data into the two tables:

SEMINARS

Ref Name	From	To	Fee
S01 Selling in the motor industry	25/07/95	26/07/95	£85.50
S02 Negotiating deals	26/07/95	26/07/95	£35.50
S03 Selling to Europe	26/07/95	27/07/95	£95.00
S04 Marketing and selling	27/07/95	27/07/95	£55.00

DELEGATES
Ref, Name, Company, Address, Telephone number, Seminar ref
1, Mr J Brown, Harlesdon Electronics, Station Road, Welwyn, WE6 9FR, 01438-478621, S03
2, Mrs L Smith, Arkwright Motors, Albany Park Road, Camberley, Surrey GU19 6GH, 01276-694321, S01
3, Miss M Victoria, Ambrose PLC, Dallow Road, Burnley, BB13 9BQ, 01282-979695, S02
4, Mr P M Jones, JK Components, 189 Farnborough Road, Fareham, Hants SL2 1HA, 01329-786543, S03
5, Mr F Lane, Blenheim Motors, Langley Business Park, Leigh, Lancs LA6 8JK, 01942-450976, S01
6, Mr J Phillips, Cooks Coaches, 30 Ash Grove, Glasgow, GU7 9JK, 0141-789012, S01
7, Mr S Scott, Martins Ltd, 25 Medway Road, Folkestone, DV9 4GH, 01303-642135, S01
8, Miss M Banks, Manley Motors, 3 Warren Road, Warren Park, Weston-super-Mare, 01934-567567, S02
9, Mr B Marsh, Rustling Garage, London Road, West Malling, Kent ME20 8GH, 01732-890432, S03
10, Mr P Reynolds, G Moores Ltd, Warnham Road, Industrial Park, York, 01904-235689, S04

16. Relational databases: querying

You should find out how to set up the tables that are to be queried ensuring that they are joined or related.

Exercise 19
Using both the Delegates and Seminars tables, related in the way described in Exercise 14, set up the following queries: (Possible QBE queries and the results are shown in Appendix 2.)
(a) Which delegates will be attending the S03: Selling to Europe seminar? Display the Seminar ref, Delegate Name, Company and Telephone fields.
(b) Who will be attending any seminar beginning 26/07/95? Display Seminar ref, Seminar name and Delegate Name.

17. Relational databases: designing forms

You should find out how to design a form that uses data from more than one table. It may be possible to design it in the normal way or you may have to create a main form and sub-form, or even use a saved query which incorporates data from both tables.

Exercise 20

Design a form to display the details of the Seminar at the top of the form (i.e. the main part of the form) and the delegates' details in a separate area underneath (in the sub-form) as described below:

(a) From the Seminars table, select: Seminar ref, Seminar name, From, To and Fee (for the main form or top part of the form).

(b) From the Delegates table, select Delegate ref, Delegate name and Company (for the sub-form or bottom part of the form).

(c) Include a title: Seminars

(d) Move the fields into the positions as shown below.

(e) Make any further enhancements you feel are appropriate.

(f) As this form is to display data, make sure it is "read only".

The form should look something like the one below that has been used to display the details of the Delegates attending Seminar ref: S01

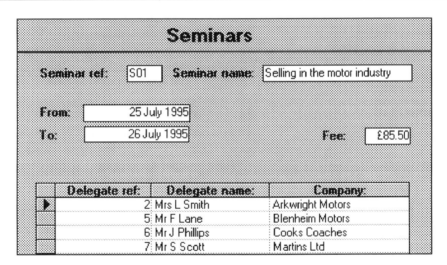

18. Relational databases: designing reports

You should find out how to design a report that uses data from more than one table. It may be possible to set this up in the normal way or via a saved query.

Exercise 21

Design a report to show the seminar groups and the delegates in each seminar.

(a) Using the Seminars table, select the following fields: Seminar ref, Seminar name and Fee.

(b) Using the Delegates table, select the following fields: Delegate name and Company.

(c) Group the data by Seminar ref and sort the data by Delegate name.

(d) Use the title: Conference delegates and fees.

(e) Display the Delegate name followed by a comma and then the Company name.

(f) Add a field to count the number of delegates for each seminar (e.g. =count([Delegate name]), and a field to calculate the total fees for each seminar (e.g. =(count(Delegate name])* [Fee]) Add explanatory text, as follows:

Total number of delegates for this seminar:

Total fees for this seminar:

(g) Add a field to calculate the total number of delegates at the conference, and a field to calculate the total fees for the conference. Add further explanatory text as follows:

TOTAL NUMBER OF DELEGATES AT CONFERENCE:

TOTAL SEMINAR FEES:

(h) Format the sub-total and grand total fees fields for currency (showing two decimal places), and the sub- and grand total fields that count the number of delegates to appear in bold.

The report should look something like the one below:

Conference delegates and fees
today's date

Seminar ref and name	Fee	Name and Company
S01 Selling in the motor industry	£85.50	Mrs L Smith, Arkwright Motors Mr F Lane, Blenheim Motors Mr J Philips, Cooks Coaches Mr S Scott, Martins Ltd
		Total number of delegates for this seminar: 4 **Total fees for this seminar: £342.00**
S02 Negotiating deals	£35.50	Miss M Victoria, Ambrose PLC Miss M Banks, Manley Motors
		Total number of delegates for this seminar: 2 **Total fees for this seminar: £70.00**
S03 Selling to Europe	£95.00	Mr J Brown, Harlesdon Electronics Mr P M Jones, JK Components Mr B Marsh, Rustling Garage
		Total number of delegates for this seminar: 3 **Total fees for this seminar: £285.00**
S04 Marketing and Selling	£55.00	
		Total number of delegates for this seminar: 1 **Total fees for this seminar: £55.00**

TOTAL NUMBER OF DELEGATES AT CONFERENCE: 10

TOTAL SEMINAR FEES: £753.00

19. Mailing labels

You should find out how to create mailing labels: you may be able to control the spacing, punctuation and lines on which the different items of the labels are to appear, as well as include extra text.

Exercise 22
(a) Using the Delegates table, create mailing labels. Select Name, Company, Address1, Address 2 and Address 3, and present them in the following format:
> For the attention of: Name
> Company
> Address 1
> Address 2
> Address 3

(b) Select 2 labels across the page, and print these on paper.
The mailing list should look as below. (Note: only the first two labels are shown here)

For the attention of Mr J Brown	For the attention of Mrs L Smith
Harlesdon Electronics	Arkwright Motors
Station Road	Albany Park Road
Welwyn	Camberley
WE6 9FR	Surrey GU19 6GH

20. Automating the database

You should find out how to automate your database, by using whichever method is most appropriate in your software:

- *the application generator*;

- *macros*: you should find out how to use the macro language to record and store macros. The normal and easiest way of creating macros consists of recording the macro as it is executed, then saving it and recalling it when required;

- *the programming language*.

Exercise 23
Automate the Conference database by setting up a menu system of the following nature (using either a numbering system or a button system).
(a) Option 1 should take the user to a data-entry form for entering Delegates details (yet to be created);
(b) Option 2 should take the user to the form created in Exercise 19 above;
(c) Option 3 should allow the user print labels;
(d) Option 4 should print the Summary report created in Exercise 20 above;
(e) Option 5 should exit the user from the database.

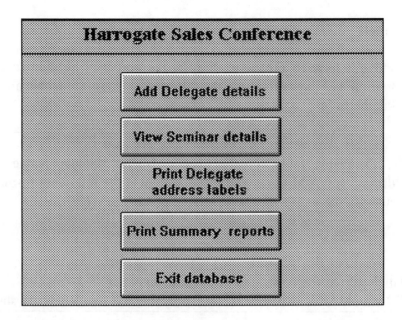

21. Integrating data

Using the information provided in **14:10** you should find out how to:

- import/attach databases created in other databases or spreadsheet programs;
- export databases to word processing software.

Integrated Exercise
(This exercise uses material to be created in the Integrated Exercises in Chapter 8.)
You are the Finance Director of a small company. At the recent meeting of the Board of Directors you were asked to present a forecast of expenditure for the next year.

(a) Create a small database of senior members of staff to be used as an internal mailing list with the following fields: Name, Position, Dept, Room No; there should be a number of further fields which hold details of the main committees these members of staff are on (i.e. Marketing, Health and Safety, Training) as well as whether they are members of the Board of Directors;
(a) Send the memo prepared in the Integrated Exercise in Chapter 8 to all members of the Board of Directors.
(b) Prepare labels for the members of the Board of Directors.

Part three

Reference section

13

Avoiding problems with PCs

1. Introduction

The previous two sections have demonstrated the potential benefits that can be had with PCs. However, the purpose of this chapter is to discuss how to avoid the difficulties that can arise with the use of PCs.

The intention of the chapter is not to be alarmist but to inform users of the very real problems that must be addressed to ensure the continuing effectiveness of their PCs, and additionally to provide some advice as to adequate and appropriate measures to safeguard themselves, their computer and the data stored on the computer.

This chapter therefore looks at systems management (2-6), security issues (7-13), software piracy (14), the protection of personal data (15-17) and health and safety issues (18-19). It concludes with a brief look at the way users can gain support from others through membership of user groups (20).

2. Systems management

If you are a networked-user it is likely that a number of systems management rules and procedures will already be in place to ensure that your computer system operates effectively. If you are a single-user, the onus will be upon you to establish your own.

In both cases, however, it is essential that users are disciplined in their use of PCs and that they obey all rules and carry out any procedures as frequently as required to ensure they remain effective in their work.

Systems management procedures include the following and these are discussed further below:

- general system rules
- general maintenance procedures
- disk management procedures
- backing up procedures

3.   Systems management: general system rules

There are a number of basic rules that should be observed by all users of PCs:

- *No smoking*: Smoking should not be allowed near PCs as smoke not only creates a dirty atmosphere but can damage the floppy disk drives.
- *No eating*: Food should not be consumed whilst using PCs as food particles can drop into the equipment, especially the keyboard and cause problems. Additionally, grease from fingers deposited on the keyboard or screen can attract dust and grime.
- *No drinking:* A user should not have drinks near the PC. Coffee, in particular, if spilt, can cause damage to both the hardware, e.g. the keys of the keyboard, and floppy disks.

4.   Systems management: general maintenance procedures

In order to ensure trouble-free performance of the PC itself, it is necessary to carry out:

- *regular cleaning*: there are a number of products on the market to clean screens, disk drives, keyboards, mice and printers and these should be used frequently to keep the PC clean and dust-free;
- *regular servicing*: adequate maintenance agreements should be in place so that if problems arise with hardware devices, e.g. printers or disk drives, they can be dealt with immediately.

5.   Systems management: disk management procedures

An important aspect of being an effective user is to ensure that disks are managed appropriately. One of the main features of computer systems is that they are able to store vast amounts of information and retrieve that information quickly and easily. However, in order to do so, the information stored on the disks needs to be organised optimally, and the disk space controlled, so that the operation of the computer system is not impaired.

Organising files on disks:

There are a number of aspects to this, in particular storing and naming files. Although a number of these points have already been discussed in Chapter 7, they are usefully repeated here as they are important and valid for this discussion.

- *Naming files*: With many different datafiles stored on a PC it is useful if the user adopts a logical approach to the naming of files so that they can be quickly retrieved when required. Although naming files sequentially, e.g. LETTER1, LETTER2, LETTER3, etc., seems logical, it is not useful if the user is unable to identify the contents of the files from their names.

- *Files on hard disks*: If files are to be kept on the hard disk, then related files should be grouped together in directories.

- *Files on floppy disks*: If, however, files are to be kept on floppy disks, then it is important that disks are labelled and dated. Disks should also be stored in fire-proof cabinets for safety.

Controlling the disk space

To ensure that the operation of the disk drives is not impaired, it is important that disks (both floppy and hard) should not be allowed to get more than about 90% full. This is essential because using a disk that is very full does not give much scope for editing documents. Old files should be deleted from the disk when no longer required, and from time to time the whole disk should be re-organised.

- *Deleting old files from disk*: Periodically, it is advisable to remove old files from the disk. They can either be deleted completely or copied onto floppy disks for archiving. If there are no printed copies, then archiving may be the best option, as there may come a time when the user has need of them (see **14:3** for the relevant DOS and Windows commands for deleting files and directories).

- *Reorganising the hard disk*: Every few months the user should *defragment* the hard disk. This effectively rearranges all the data held on the hard disk and ensures optimal performance (see **14:5**).

Floppy disk care

Although many manufacturers claim their disks are guaranteed for life, this should not be relied upon. After some time they may begin to develop faults and become unusable. If this happens and the PC is unable to read or write to the disk, a disk error message will appear (see **14:6**). The newer 3½" disks are not as vulnerable as 5¼" disks, since the former are protected by a plastic case and the magnetic areas are not exposed. Nevertheless there are still a number of basic rules to be obeyed when using floppy disks:

Disks should not be exposed to high temperatures, e.g. left in direct sunlight or on a radiator. They should not be allowed to come into contact with anything magnetic, e.g. a magnetised paperclip or a "ringing" telephone, as these can sometimes de-magnetise the disk. Finally, as mentioned above, coffee can be particularly destructive if spilt on disks.

5¼" disks need extra care: they should not be bent or folded and the exposed areas of the disk should not be touched. Additionally, the label for the disk should be written before it is attached to the disk so that the disk is not damaged.

Disks can be *write protected* to ensure that files are not accidentally overwritten or erased. This should be done, for example, to protect software master disks or disks that have archiving material stored on them. To write protect a 3½" disk, the small notch on the bottom right-hand corner on the back of the disk should be moved down to open the hole. To write-protect a 5¼" disk, the indentation on the side of the disk should be covered with tape.

6.   Systems management: backing-up procedures

Backing-up means copying files. The purpose of this is so that if anything happens to the original file, the back-up copy can be used. Backing-up of data is particularly important in businesses that rely on the use of up-to-date datafiles for their day-to-day operations, but is also necessary with any user who needs to be sure that they have a secure copy of any file. Although PC systems are generally reliable, things can and do go wrong for a number of reasons as will be shown in the next sections.

Most users do recognise the need for backing-up, but often because the task is viewed as boring and time-consuming it is frequently not done as it should be. The following are some guidelines for backing-up files.

At least two copies of every file should be kept on different disks. Some users believe that as some software creates a second back-up copy of their files on the disk they are protected. This is not so, because if the disk itself fails both copies of the file will be irretrievable. Therefore the minimum requirements are:

- if the original file is held on the hard disk, a back-up copy should be held on a floppy disk;
- if the original file is held on a floppy disk, a back-up copy should be held on a second floppy disk.

The relevant DOS and Window commands for copying files are provided in **14:2**.

Users of large hard disk systems often feel that backing-up onto floppy disk is far too time-consuming and takes up far too many disks. This is not a good enough reason to postpone backing-up the system, but rather to pursue the idea of installing a tape streamer so that backing-up takes place onto high-speed tape (see **15:10**).

Datafiles should be backed-up frequently. The definition of "frequently" depends on how often the data is edited.   Backing-up might need to take place daily or less often. A simple test to decide how often to back-up files is to work out at what point it would be no longer be viable to re-type any amendments.

Users often ask whether software program files should be backed up if a master copy of the software is already retained. This may not be necessary unless the program has been customised in such a way that it would take more time to re-install the software from the master copy and re-customise it rather than to back-up the hard disk and restore the back-up copies.

When using a network, users are responsible for the backing-up of their own data files held on their PC's hard disk as usually only the program files are stored on the "file server" and are backed-up by the network manager.

Back-up copies should be kept in a separate place from the original. In a business situation, back-up copies stored on floppy disk beside the PC will be of no use if there is a fire: they should therefore be kept in a separate room in a fire-proof cabinet.

7.   Security

In addition to general systems procedures, a number of other procedures need to be established to control the security of the system.   Security measures are necessary to ensure that both the hardware and the data held on the PC are kept safe at all times, and that if for any reason a problem occurs business can go on as usual.   There are a number of possible ways in which the security of a system can be breached, and these range from the common to the extreme.

Security has in the past been considered to be the responsibility of technical systems staff but all users must take responsibility for the security of their systems. All users need to carry out a *risk analysis* to assess the extent of the risk, and then put in place adequate security measures as well as formulate a *disaster recovery plan.*

8.   Security: risk analysis

How secure should your system be? In order to answer this question, a user should carry out a risk analysis. In simple terms this means assessing how much it would cost if a particular security problem occurred and how much it would cost to prevent it. If the cost of preventing a problem is more than the cost arising from that problem, then risk analysis would suggest that the implementation of measures to prevent that particular problem should not take place.

To assess risks the user must fully understand potential problems and preventative measures.   Therefore in the next few sections the most common problems are described and the most effective preventative measures outlined.

9.   Security: unauthorised access

Unauthorised access refers to the use of a computer by a person who has not been given permission to do so.   Anybody who gains unauthorised access to a computer system is known as a *hacker*. Most hackers who break into computer systems do so for the sheer challenge.   But there are others who have ulterior motives.   These can range from leaving "graffiti", i.e. messages around the system to let users know they have been in the system, to altering data or committing computer fraud.

The most common computer fraud, known as "input fraud", includes falsifying data held on the computer as well as transferring monies to fictitious accounts. It is interesting to note that most computer crime of this nature is in fact committed by employees of an organisation.

Unauthorised access to a computer for any of the reasons described above is an offence under the Computer Misuse Act 1990. If found guilty, the penalties range from up to six months' imprisonment and a £2,000 fine to five years' imprisonment and an unlimited fine.

However, organisations should not rely on using the law to deter people from unauthorised access to a computer system. Detection of the crime is not easy, and even when it is, organisations often do not want to report the matter to the police because of the embarrassment it would cause them.

It is therefore essential to control access to the system. The type of access control will depend very much on the type of the system and the number of potential people who could gain access to the system.

At the single-user level, access can usually be controlled at the applications level, e.g. it is fairly easy to make word processed documents files read-only or protect spreadsheet files with passwords.

However, in a multi-user system it will probably be necessary to control access at the system level. This will ensure firstly that only registered users can log onto the system, by entering their User ID, and then controlling access by a password.

Whereas user names are commonly known - they have to be so that users can e-mail one another - passwords should be carefully guarded and never revealed. If a user's password is discovered this means someone else can use it to gain access to the computer system. Normally, users are able to select their own password, so here are some simple guidelines on the choice of password:

- Passwords should not be easily "guessable", e.g. a relation's name.
- Passwords should not be too short (i.e. less than 4 letters) otherwise they can be easily decoded.
- Ideally, passwords should not be a real word, but simply a collection of alphanumeric characters, so that any de-coding program (and there are a number available) would find it difficult to "crack" the password. However, the user's car registration number, although it fits the bill, should not be used!
- Passwords should be changed frequently, e.g. every 6 weeks.
- Passwords should not be written down by users.

The password file on the system should be closely controlled by the system manager.

In some highly secure systems further means of preventing unauthorised access might be required, e.g. locks to rooms and machines, security staff, alarms, etc. It may also be necessary to *encrypt* data that is being passed from user to user: this is the scrambling of data so that it is unintelligible unless the user is able to decrypt it.

10. Security: viruses

A virus is a specially written program whose sole purpose is to infect computer systems and in most cases cause damage to the files on the disk. A virus can easily attach itself to a file or a floppy disk, and once activated in a PC can quickly infect the hard disk and any further floppy disks used in the system. It can also infect all the hard disks of the PCs attached to a network and in addition can be transmitted over the telephone line from one computer to another.

Some viruses are more destructive than others. A number simply display a message stating that the machine has been infected with a particular virus. The most serious delete or corrupt important and valuable data held on the disk   Some even wait for a particular date, e.g. Friday 13th, before being triggered. So in this latter case it may well be some time after infection that the virus is discovered.

In a similar way *worms*, which are programs that keep replicating themselves, and *Trojan horses*, which are destructive programs that pass themselves off as innocent programs, can wreak havoc in a computer system.

Viruses are now common-place and it is therefore quite likely that PC users who use files or floppy disks other than their own are vulnerable to an infection. Therefore all users, whether a large multi-user organisation or a single-user should adopt an anti-virus strategy.

The only effective way of preventing an infection is to ensure that all users are aware of the potential problem and are aware of how viruses are spread. They should be wary of all software, not only shareware and freeware, but even commercial software, and assume that all floppy disks are infected until proven otherwise.

Before files on a new floppy disk are used in a system the disk should be checked for viruses. There are now a large number of "anti-virus" software products that can detect as well as disinfect viruses from disks. The only real problem with such software is that they can only deal with known viruses, so as new ones are being written all the time, an upgrade policy is essential to remain fully protected. However, it has to be said that, in the main, it is the older and well-known viruses that remain the most significant. Examples include "Brain", "Stoned, "Tequila" and "Michelangelo".

Floppy disks should be write-protected wherever possible (as viruses can not penetrate this protection). For instance, when installing any new software the disks should first be checked for viruses, then write-protected and copies made of them. The software can then be installed from these copies. This will ensure that the originals are free of viruses.

If a virus is discovered, the following procedure should be followed: The PC should be switched off and not used for further work. It should then be started up using a write-protected virus-free DOS system disk. All the disks (both hard and floppy) should then be checked for infection, and any infected program files should either be deleted and re-installed from virus-free masters or should be disinfected using anti-virus software. Data files should not be restored from back-up disks unless or until they are proven to be virus-free.

As can be seen, if a virus infection is discovered, it can be a very time-consuming process as well as costly in terms of lost data and manpower hours to put it right, so prevention is better than cure. Although malicious insertion of a virus into a system is an offence under the Computer Misuse Act (1990), it is likely that the virus was introduced quite unwittingly by a user who failed to keep to the prevention procedures described above.

11. Security: power failure

Computers need electricity, so if there is no power supply they cannot be used. If a power cut is planned the user may be able to postpone use of the computer until the power supply is restored. However more problematic is the unexpected power cut which effectively switches the computer off without saving the work.

If this problem would cause significant disruption then the purchase of a UPS (uninterruptible power supply) is worth considering. This starts operating as soon as the power is interrupted and provides back-up power until the supply is resumed. Minor power fluctuations, e.g. "surges" and "spikes", can also cause damage to hardware and software but low-cost protection is available in the form of a surge plug.

12. Security: destruction of hardware

Although emphasis has been placed on the security of the software and data held on the system, in some extreme cases it may also be the hardware that is damaged as well. This could be due to a number of reasons, e.g. sabotage by users; or through fire, flood, or terrorist attack.

In the first case, fortunately, this is not a significant problem for most user-organisations, and in those where it is, video surveillance of the equipment may not be a viable solution, so education of users into feeling personally responsible for their own PCs is really the only way that this can be dealt with.

In the second case, there is unfortunately too much recent evidence to suggest that this is not an insignificant problem. Therefore in addition to providing adequate software back-up, some organisations might feel it necessary to have full back-up hardware facilities. Back-up sites are either secondary sites maintained elsewhere in the city or country that can be used at a moment's notice (and generally remain idle for most of the time) or are facilities belonging to other organisations with whom reciprocal arrangements have been made to use their hardware in an emergency situation.

13. Security: a disaster recovery plan

Every user, from the smallest single-user to the largest multi-user organisation, who relies on computing facilities for their business or other activities should develop a disaster recovery plan to ensure that they can continue work should a disaster (such as those outlined above) occur.

A disaster (or contingency) plan involves formulating the steps that need to be taken to restore computing facilities to a position where business can be resumed. These steps will include setting out:

- procedures to ensure there is adequate hardware and software provision;
- procedures to retrieve and update back-up datafiles.

In large organisations, the disaster recovery plan should be practised in a simulated emergency situation, at least once a year.

14. Software piracy

This is the illegal or unauthorised copying of software, whether perpetrated on a large scale by people for commercial gain or on a small scale by individual users. The *Copyright, Designs and Patents Act (1988)* provides protection from copying for all literary works, and this includes computer programs. However, the *Copyright (Computer Program) Regulations 1992* does allow for the making of copies for back-up use only.

It should be remembered that software is licensed, not sold, to the user, and the terms of the software licence usually do include the provision for a user to make one back-up copy of the software. However any further copying of the software usually infringes the terms of the licence.

Hence if an organisation requires more than one copy of a piece of software it must buy the number of copies it needs, although *site, multi-user* and *network* licences may be more appropriate. *Site* licences allow an organisation to make a specified number of copies for users at the site. *Multi-user* and *network* licences specify the number of users who can access the software at one time.

Illegal copying of software is an enormous problem and the Federation Against Software Theft (FAST) has been set up to deal with this problem. It has pressured the government to change the copyright laws and has also been responsible for instigating action against organisations with a large number of PC users who were suspected of using illegally-copied software.

It is therefore the responsibility of every organisation to ensure that only legal copies of software are used on its machines. It can do this by periodically carrying out a software audit to monitor the number and status of software in use.

15. Protection of personal data

Every PC user should be aware of the Data Protection Act, which since it was passed in 1984 requires that any organisation (or other user) that holds personal data of living individuals on a computer should register the fact with the Data Protection Registrar, unless they are exempt. It is a criminal offence not to register (if not exempt) and ignorance of the law is no defence. In fact there are frequent prosecutions under the Act for failing to register and fines imposed. Once registered, data users must comply with the eight principles of the Act and contravention of these principles will be dealt with by the Registrar.

The following sections briefly discuss the exemptions to the Act and the eight principles of the Act with which registered data users must comply. However, any organisation who believes they should register should get hold of a copy of the Act itself. Additionally a series of free Guidelines to the Act and a video information pack are available which provide useful clarification and explanation of the terms of the Act.

16. Data Protection Act: exemptions from the Act

There are a number of exemptions from registering under the Act. These include users who hold data for reasons of national security or if the information is required by law to be made available to the public.

However, users do not have to register if they hold personal data for "payroll, pensions and accounts purposes", for "domestic or recreational purposes", for "mailing lists", and if the data is held by an unincorporated members club, although there are some limitations.

Any organisation that is not exempt from the Act must register using a form available either from Head Post Offices or from the Data Protection Registrar. A registration fee is payable for registration for three years. The Register, which lists all entries, is available for viewing at the Office of the Data Protection Registrar in Wilmslow and at some large libraries.

17. Data Protection Act: The eight principles

Once registered the data user must comply with the following eight principles:

- *The information to be contained in personal data shall be obtained, and personal data should be processed fairly and lawfully.*

- *Personal data shall be held only for one or more specified and lawful purposes.*

- *Personal data held for any purpose or purposes shall not be used or disclosed in any manner incompatible with that purpose or purposes.*

  Users should note that there are a number of "non-disclosure exemptions", e.g. where data is held for the purpose of safeguarding national security, and for the prevention of crime and taxation purposes.

- *Personal data held for any purpose or purposes shall be adequate, relevant and not excessive in relation to that purpose or those purposes.*

- *Personal data shall be accurate, and where necessary, kept up to date.*

- *Personal data held for any purpose or purposes shall not be kept for longer than is necessary for that purpose or those purposes.*

- *An individual shall be entitled -*
    - *(a)   at reasonable intervals and without undue delay or expense -*
        - *(i)   to be informed by any data user whether he holds personal data of which that individual is the subject; and*
        - *(ii)   to access to any such data held by the data user; and*
    - *(b)   where appropriate, to have such data corrected or erased.*

This means that data subjects have the right to know that data is being held on them and to access that data. Any request for access must be in writing. The data user may charge a fee for dealing with such a request (up to a maximum specified) and must normally respond within 40 days. The data subject also has the right to have inaccuracies corrected or erased, and may have a possible claim for damage and distress due to, for example, loss or destruction of data, or inaccurate data, although data held before 11 May 1986 is not included.

However, there are exemptions to the rights of access by data subject users and these include where data is held for the following reasons: e.g. for the prevention of crime and for taxation purposes, statistical or research data or where personal data is held on computer for back-up purposes only.

- *Appropriate security measures shall be taken against unauthorised access to, or alteration, disclosure or destruction of personal data.*

If a registered user contravenes any of these principles, for example, it holds personal data other than that specified, or for a purpose other than that specified, the Registrar can enforce these principles by enforcement orders or even de-registration notices.

18. Health and safety: issues

Users of PCs should also be aware of possible health problems associated with the continual use of computers. The main problem areas are described below although the possibility of actually experiencing them depends on a number of factors which include the amount and length of time spent at the computer. These problems include those relating to musculo-skeletal problems, visual fatigue and stress:

Musculo-skeletal problems

These present themselves as pains in the neck, shoulders, back, arms or wrists. Although most symptoms disappear with rest, if they become persistent specialist advice should be sought. Most of the problems are due to poor posture at the computer possibly caused by poor workstation design. Some simple guidance on arrangement of the desk and chair includes the following:

- Chairs should be easily adjustable in height (whilst seated) and there should be adequate knee clearance between the chair and the desk. The chair back should also be adjustable and provide lumbar support. There should be enough space for users to move their legs and chair.
- Desks should have adequate work surface area so users are not cramped. Users should not have to adopt a strained or uncomfortable position.
- Document holders should be adjustable to cut down uncomfortable head and neck movements.
- Keyboards should be detachable from the system so that users can find a comfortable working position with enough space in front of the keyboard to provide support for the hands and arms of the user. The keyboard should be adjustable so that it provides a slope between 5° and 15° from the horizontal. Users should not have to bend their hands up at the wrists to use the keyboard.

Visual problems

These present themselves as sore or dry eyes, blurring, eye strain and headaches. Once again if problems persist specialist (i.e. ophthalmic) advice should be sought. To avoid these problems, however, the following should be observed:

- Characters on the screen should be well-defined and large enough to read without straining. The image should be stable, i.e. no flickering, and both the brightness and contrast should be controllable by the user.
- Glare (e.g. reflected light) should be cut down, for instance, by the use of an anti-glare filter, and lower levels of lighting in the room. Overhead lights, in particular, should not be too harsh and windows should be screened with movable blinds.

Stress

This can present itself as anxiety, headaches and stomach disorders. Stress can be caused by a number of factors, including pressure of work, difficulties with the computer system itself or be due to the working environment. The general working environment can be improved in a number of ways:

- Noise levels from equipment should be controlled, e.g. printers fitted with hoods.
- The temperature should not be uncomfortable, and there should be an adequate level of humidity and ventilation.
- Colour schemes should be natural, with light coloured ceilings and darker lower walls, and natural fibre furnishings to minimise build-up of static.

19. Health and safety: legislation

The *Health and Safety (Display Screen Equipment) Regulations 1992* sets out the minimum requirements that employers must implement for workers who use "display screen equipment" as a significant part of their work. These include:

- assessing the risk, by looking at the hardware and the working environment;
- ensuring workstations meet the minimum requirements;
- planning work breaks;
- arranging eyesight tests (as required); and
- providing information to users.

Employers have until the end of 1996 to improve existing equipment, although any new equipment that is purchased must comply with the regulations immediately. However, all users should take responsibility for their own health and safety.

20. User groups

If users feel they need further support and help, then joining a *user group* may be the answer. Although some user groups are allied to particular software or hardware manufacturers, others are independent. The basic function of a user group is to provide an opportunity for users with similar needs and problems to come together and support one another.

14

Further DOS and Windows

1. Introduction

This chapter contains important information that you will need in order to remain effective in your work. It explains how to carry out the essential file and disk management procedures described in Chapter 13 like copying, deleting and renaming files (2-4), it provides further information on DOS (5-7) and Windows (8-9), and also describes how inter-application sharing might take place (10) as well as how to install and customise applications software (11).

2. Copying files and disks

As has been explained in **13:6**, it is imperative that users keep a copy of their files on a second disk in case the originals become damaged or corrupted or if there is a disk failure. Although floppy disks are very durable, they have an annoying habit of developing problems just before a deadline for a piece of work. There are a number of different ways in which you may wish to copy files:

- copy the entire contents of one floppy disk to a second floppy disk;
- copy files from the hard disk to a floppy disk;
- copy files from the floppy disk to the hard disk;
- copy files from one directory of the hard disk to another;
- copy files from one floppy disk to a second floppy disk.

The different procedures for each of these types of file copying are given below. As with many procedures there are normally a number of ways of carrying them out, although only one way will be described here. Once again instructions for DOS users are shown on the left-hand side of the page and those for Windows-users on the right-hand side

Copying the entire contents of one floppy disk to another floppy disk

A quick and easy way of making back-up copies of a number of files on a floppy disk is to copy the entire contents of the floppy disk to a second disk. This can be done using the same floppy disk drive.

In the process described below, if the second disk is unformatted it will format it first, and if the second disk has files on it, these will be deleted:

DOS-users:	Windows-users:
Use the DISKCOPY command in the following way to make a copy of a disk in the A drive: Type: **DISKCOPY A: A:**	In the **File Manager**: Select the **[A]** disk icon; Select **Disk ...** Select **Copy disk**
A message will prompt the user when to insert the source disk (i.e. the first disk containing the files to be copied) and when to insert the destination disk (i.e. the second disk to hold the copied files).	

Copying one or more files from the hard disk to a floppy disk

DOS users:	Windows-users:
Working in the relevant hard disk directory: Use the COPY command in the following way to make a copy of a file with the same name: **COPY filename.ext drive:** Example: **COPY TEXT.DOC A:** Use the COPY command in the following way to make a copy of a file with a different name: **COPY name.ext drive:newname.ext** Example **COPY TEXT.DOC A:WPTEXT.DOC** To copy a group of files, make use of the wildcard * which will take the place of a number of characters, as in the following examples: **COPY *.DOC A:** to copy all the files with the file extension .DOC to the floppy disk **COPY *.* A:** to copy all the files in the current directory to the floppy disk, whatever their filename and whatever their extension.	In the **File Manager**, displaying the files in the relevant hard disk directory: To make a copy of a file with the same name: Select the relevant file and drag it over to the floppy disk drive icon (e.g. **[A]**) at the top of the left-hand side of the screen. The following message will appear: **Are you sure you want to copy the selected files or directories to A:?** Select **Yes.** To make a copy of a file with a different name: Select the relevant file; Select **File**; Select **Copy**; A dialogue box will appear showing, in the **From:** box, the name of the file to be copied; In the **To**: box, type in the drive, full name and extension of the new file e.g. **A:TEXT.DOC**. To copy a group of files that appear in sequence: Select the first file and holding down the [Shift] key select the last file in the group to be copied; Drag the files to the relevant drive icon. To copy a group of files that do not appear in sequence: Hold down the [Ctrl] key as you select each file you want to copy; Drag the files to the relevant drive icon.

Copying files from the floppy disk to the hard disk

DOS users:	Windows-users:
Working on the floppy disk: Use the COPY commands in the same way as shown above, except replace the drive name with C. Example: **COPY TEXT.DOC C:**	In the **File Manager**, displaying the files on the floppy disk: Select the relevant file or files in the same way as shown above and drag them over to the hard disk drive icon (i.e. **[C]**) at the top of the left-hand side of the screen.

Copying files from one hard disk directory to another

DOS users:	Windows-users:
Working in the relevant hard disk directory: Use the COPY command in the same way as shown above, except replace the drive name with \ followed by the directory name, i.e. **COPY filename.ext \directoryname** Example: **COPY TEXT.DOC \TEMP**	In the **File Manager**, displaying the files in the relevant hard disk directory: Select the relevant file or files in the same way as shown above and drag them over to the new directory displayed in the tree in the left-hand side of the screen.

Copying files from one floppy disk to a second floppy disk

This is a little more complex since it cannot be done using one floppy disk drive. It therefore involves a three-stage process:

- copying the file from the source (i.e. the first) floppy disk to a directory on the hard disk (e.g. a temporary directory called TEMP);
- copying the file from the hard disk to the destination (i.e. the second) floppy disk;
- deleting the file from the temporary directory (see **3** below).

3. Deleting files and directories

It may be necessary to delete files and directories, e.g. if you want to remove all the software program files for a software package no longer used, or to delete old datafiles to release precious disk space. However, in the latter case this should only be done after material that needs to be retained has been copied onto floppy disks.

Deleting files

DOS-users:	Windows-users:
Use the DEL command in the following way to delete a file : **DEL filename.ext** Example **DEL TEXT.DOC**	In the **File Manager**: To delete a file: Select the file; Press [Delete] or Select **File/Delete**

To delete a group of files make use of the wildcard * Examples: **DEL *.DOC** will delete all the files with the file extension DOC **DEL *.*** will delete all the files on the disk or directory, whatever their filename and whatever their extension. (This is a very powerful command so DOS will display a message asking you if you are sure you want to do this.) Note: you will not be able to remove the two files marked . and .. in a directory. These will only be deleted when and if the directory is deleted.	To delete a group of files that appear in sequence: Select the first file and holding down the [Shift] key, select the last file in the group; Press [Delete]. To delete a group of files not in sequence: Hold down the [Ctrl] key as you select each file; Press [Delete]. In all cases a message box will place the name of the file in a **Delete:** box and you will be asked to select either **OK** or **Cancel.** A second message box will ask you to confirm deletion of the files: **Yes to All** will confirm the deletion of all the files; **Yes** will require you to confirm each file individually.

Deleting directories

DOS-users:	Windows-users:
It is first necessary to delete all the files in the directory since it cannot be removed until it is empty. Note: you should be one level above the directory, then use the DEL command in the following way: **DEL directoryname** Use the RD command in the following way to remove the directory itself: **RD directoryname**, e.g. **RD TEMP** If the following message appears: **Invalid path, not directory or directory not empty** it is probably because there is a sub-directory in it, which will need to be deleted in the same way.	In the **File Manager**: To delete all the files in the directory and remove the directory itself: Select the directory; Press [Delete] A message box will appear for you to confirm the files to be deleted in the normal way.

4.   Renaming files

Occasionally it might be considered necessary to rename files, for instance to establish a group of related data files. This could be done in the following way:

DOS-users:	Windows-users:
Use the REN command in the following way to rename a file: **REN filename.ext newfilename.ext** Example: **REN TEXT.DOC WPTEXT.DOC**	In the **File Manager**: Select the file; Select **File**; Select **Rename...**; A dialogue box will appear showing in the **From:** box the name of the file to be copied; In the **To:** box, type in the new filename and extension, e.g. **WPTEXT.DOC**

5. Further DOS commands

MS-DOS consists of a number of internal and external commands. Internal commands are commands that are held in the COMMAND.COM file and are always resident in the computer's main memory. External commands are separate files stored on disk either as .COM or .EXE files, probably in the DOS directory.

The following are some common DOS commands you might find useful:

ATTRIB external	This command will let you display and change the attributes of a file, for instance. make it read-only, e.g. ATTRIB filename.ext +R (for read-only) or -R (to delete read-only).
BACKUP external	This command can be used to back up one or more files on the hard disk to floppy disk. These back-up files can only be restored using the RESTORE command.
CHDSK external	This command checks the status of a disk, and provides information on total disk space (in bytes), the number of bytes remaining and the number of bytes in any *bad sectors* (i.e. defective areas of the disk).
DATE internal	This command displays the system date and lets you change the date if required.
RESTORE external	This command is used to restore files backed-up used the BACKUP command.
TIME internal	This command displays the system time and lets you change the time if required.
TYPE internal	This command prints a copy of a text file on the screen. For example: TYPE AUTOEXEC.BAT will display a copy of the AUTOEXEC.BAT file. If you use the TYPE command with a .EXE file, however, the computer will only beep and display strange characters on the screen.
VER internal	This command displays the version number of DOS installed on the computer.
XCOPY external	This command lets you copy disks together with their directories, sub-directories and files.

The following external DOS commands are only available in later versions of DOS.

DEFRAG	This command is used to defragment the hard disk (i.e. re-arrange the data on it). It should be run occasionally, say every couple of months.
DOSSHELL	This command is used to load a graphical interface for DOS. However, this is only a halfway step towards Windows.
HELP	This command can be used to provide help on DOS commands. If used on its own it will display a reference list of DOS commands. If it precedes a specific DOS command it will provide the relevant syntax and examples.
MSAV	This command starts the anti-virus program that can scan both the hard and floppy disks for known viruses.
UNDELETE	This command can be used to undelete files deleted using the DEL command.
UNFORMAT	This command can be used to unformat floppy disks formatted using the FORMAT command.

There are a number of ways of correcting and re-using DOS commands after they have been typed in at the DOS prompt, the most useful of these are the following:

[Esc]	this key cancels the displayed DOS command
[F1]	this key displays the last DOS command one character at a time
[F3]	this key recalls the last DOS command in full

6. Further DOS messages

In addition to the DOS messages already mentioned in Chapter 7 and above, there are a number of other common messages. These are explained briefly below:

Data error reading drive A or General failure error reading A

This means the computer has difficulty reading the disk in drive A. This could signify a very serious problem but could also mean that the disk has simply not been formatted. If it has been formatted then the disk is probably unusable, although it may be possible to retrieve the files using disk utility software.

Abort, Retry, Fail?

This prompts the user to select an option when the error message displayed above appears. Type A to abort, R to retry, i.e. have another go, and F to fail (although in practice this actually means have another go too). If working on a floppy disk, the user will have to press F twice to escape from this message.

Non-system disk or disk error
Replace and strike any key when ready

This message normally appears if there is a floppy disk in the drive when the computer is booting up, and has unsuccessfully searched it for DOS. Just release the drive door and press any key, the computer will then move on to search the hard disk for DOS.

Insufficient disk space

This means the disk has not got enough spare space left on it to hold the file being saved. If the user wants to hold the file on the disk, then other files will have to be deleted to make room. Be careful about just inserting another disk, as this may corrupt the file since some of the work may already be saved on the first disk.

Insufficient memory

This error message means that there is not enough memory to perform the particular operation requested. It will be necessary to close some datafiles or applications to release some memory.

7. AUTOEXEC.BAT and CONFIG.SYS files

These two files have already been mentioned in Chapter 7. They are important files that run automatically when the computer is switched on, in order to set up the PC in a particular way. They are normally to be found in the root directory and can be viewed by using the TYPE command, e.g. TYPE AUTOEXEC.BAT

The **AUTOEXEC.BAT** file will probably include at least the following DOS commands:

@ECHO OFF	This command ensures that further DOS commands are not displayed on the screen.
PROMPT pg	This command is used to show the format of the prompt. In this case to show the drive letter and path ($p) and > sign ($g).
PATH C:\WINDOWS;C:\DOS	This command sets up the path to files, in this case to the files in the Windows and DOS directories.
WIN	This command loads Windows.

The **CONFIG.SYS** file sets up the configuration of your computer and will probably include some of the following items:

BREAK=ON	This command turns on the facility to stop the execution of the program by use of [Ctrl]+C
BUFFERS=20	This command sets up a number of buffers, here 20, to hold information being transferred to and from disks.
FILES=20	This command specifies the number of files that can be open at one time, here 20.
DEVICE=C;\DOS\HIMEM.SYS	This command loads device drivers, here the HIMEM used to manage extended memory.
COUNTRY=0.44,,C:\DOS\COUNTRY.SYS	This command tells DOS to use UK date, time and currency conventions.

It may be necessary to create or amend these files, e.g. if a new hardware component is added or if some new software is installed on the system. Before amending these files, a copy of the existing AUTOEXEC.BAT or CONFIG.SYS files should be saved (called, perhaps, AUTOEXEC.OLD and CONFIG.OLD), so that if anything goes wrong, the old versions can be reused. There are a number of ways of creating a file of this type, although it is advisable only to attempt this after some practice, the most convenient are:

- by using **EDIT**, a full-screen editor, included in DOS from version 5; or
- by using a word processing program: however, it is important that the file is saved as a text file, i.e. one that does not include any text formatting, otherwise it will not be readable by DOS.

8.   Further Windows

As has been demonstrated in **7:8** the **Program Manager** organises all the groups of programs within Windows.   This section takes a closer look at the most significant programs that are a part of the Windows software:

The **Main** group contains the Windows system applications programs. The Windows desktop shown in **7:8** displays the program icons in this group.   These include the following:

- **File Manager**: this lets the user view and organise files and directories, as well as set file attributes, e.g. read-only files. A file (together with the application in which it was created) can be opened simply by double-clicking on its name.
- **Control Panel**: this provides the user with the means for changing or customising the configuration of the system, e.g. to re-configure the mouse for left-handed people by swapping the functions of the left and right buttons; to change the colour scheme, the wallpaper, or set up a screensaver on the desktop; to alter the date and time; to change the country, language, date, time and currency formats; and to install and change printer settings.
- **Print Manager**: this provides the facility to install and configure printers as well as control the printing of files.
- **MS-DOS prompt**: this lets users leave Windows temporarily to work directly with DOS. A return to Windows is achieved by typing EXIT at the DOS prompt.

The **Accessories** group of programs provides Windows users with a number of useful applications, including

- **Write:** a basic word processing application;
- **Paintbrush:** a basic drawing application;
- **Terminal:** a program that connects the computer with another computer;
- **Calculator:** a standard and scientific calculator;
- **Calendar:** a monthly calendar and a daily appointments diary;
- **Cardfile:** a set of index cards that could be used for maintaining addresses, etc.;
- **Clock:** a digital and analogue clock.

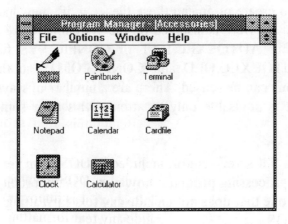

Windows applications can either be set up in their own group, e.g. a Word for Windows group, an Excel group, a Wordperfect for Windows group, and so on, or else a number of application files can be set up in one group, e.g. in a group called Applications.

It should be noted that one or more Windows applications can be open at any one time. By using the **[Alt]+[Tab]** keys, users can cycle through the open applications. Alternatively, pressing **[Ctrl]+[Esc]** will display the Task List.

Non-Windows applications can be set up in a non-Windows application group, or in their own individual application groups. When activating a non-Windows application from Windows, Windows is temporarily exited (although it still remains in memory) and is returned when the non-Windows application is left.

A **StartUp** group is created when Windows is installed on the system and users can add any program icon to this group to run immediately after Windows has loaded.

Windows users have the ability to customise their own desktop by arranging icons and windows as they wish to view them. There is no right and wrong way of setting up the desktop, but there is an optimum and most efficient way for each individual user. This may only be discovered after some experience and exploration of Windows.

9.   Windows for Workgroups

Windows for Workgroups is a further development of Windows that supports group working on a small network enabling the sharing of files and printers. It contains the same programs as Windows with the following additional group of **Network** programs:

- **Mail:** an electronic mail feature, enabling users to exchange files and messages;
- **Fax:** the facility to send and receive faxes;
- **Schedule+**: an appointments diary for all users in the workgroup;
- **Chat:**   the facility to allow members of the workgroup to communicate interactively by typing messages to one another;
- **WinPopup:** a means of sending messages to members of the workgroup.

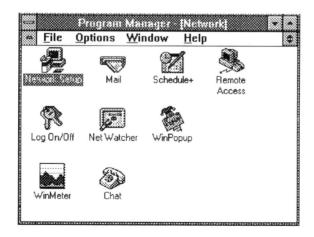

10. Inter-application sharing

Although most of a user's work will be prepared in one application software package, there may be times when material created in another application needs to be included, e.g. a chart or graph inserted in a word processed report. The way that this can be achieved will depend on the type of software that is being used.

Integrated software

Integrated software packages contain a number of different functions, notably a word processing function, a spreadsheet function, a database function as well as other supporting functions. Although each of these functions is probably not as sophisticated as stand-alone software packages, integrated software does offer a significant advantage in that data files are readable by each of the functions. Hence the word processing function would easily be able to read a file created in the spreadsheet function.

DOS-based software

Since most DOS-based software packages are not to a large extent compatible with one another, usually the only way to use data created in another DOS-based application is to convert datafiles into *text* files (i.e. files without any formatting) and then read them in. The applications software will normally support the production of a text file for data transfer purposes.

Windows-based software

Most Windows products support information sharing between applications through *OLE* which stands for *Object Linking and Embedding*. This requires further explanation:

An *object* is any piece of information created using a Windows application, e.g. a single cell or a whole worksheet created using spreadsheet software; one word or a whole document created using word processing software.

An object from one application can be *embedded* i.e. copied into another application. If the user wants to edit the object subsequently, it can be selected and the application in which it was created will open to edit it. It should be noted, however, that the original object is not amended.

An object from one application can be copied and *linked* to another application. This means that any changes made to the original object also update the copied object and also that if the user wants to edit the object, when it is selected, it is the original object that is edited.

There are a number of ways of embedding and linking objects. The procedure below describes one way in which an object, in this case a table of numerical data (created in a spreadsheet package), could be embedded in, or linked to, a word processed document.

With the relevant document open in the word processing application:

- open the worksheet: this can be done whilst the word processing application is open, by using **[Alt]+[Tab]** to return to the **Program Manager**, and then selecting the worksheet file from the **File Manager** in the **Main** group of programs;
- select the relevant data in the worksheet;
- select the **Edit** menu and then select **Copy**:
- return to the word processing application and document (using **[Alt]+[Tab]**);
- either embed the object by selecting the **Edit** menu then selecting **Paste**; or link the object by selecting the **Edit** menu and then selecting **Paste Special** (In the **Paste Special** box, select the relevant data type, and then select **Paste Link**).

Another possible way of embedding or linking objects, which obviates the need for commands, is to use the *drag and drop* facility, which in many Windows-based software packages is possible across applications.

As more and more users carry out tasks that require inter-application sharing, this particular feature will improve in future software packages.

11. Installing and customising applications

Installing software

It is very easy nowadays to install applications on a computer. A user simply runs the install program (normally INSTALL.EXE or SETUP.EXE) and follows the on-screen instructions. However, most applications software takes up a large amount of disk space, so if users are restricted in the amount of space available, then they should consider whether it is necessary to install all the tutorial, sample and other files that come with the software. Frequently, software installation programs allow users to choose the full installation, minimal installation (or laptop installation), or custom installation.

Customising software

Once the software is installed, it is possible to *customise* it to meet a user's individual needs. The most obvious way in which Windows-based software, in particular, can be customised is for the user to add *tools* or *buttons* to the toolbar to represent tasks that are commonly used but for which there is currently no tool available. For instance, if a user regularly needs to format text by capitalising it, then a "capitalisation" tool could be created.

15

Selecting a personal computer system

1. Introduction

This chapter is concerned with how to select a personal computer system to meet an individual's needs, be they professional, to run a small business, club or society, or for academic or research work. It therefore concentrates on selecting a single-user system although it does provide some guidance on selecting a system for a small number of users in the form of a network.

Because this chapter is intended for end-users, technical explanations are kept to a minimum and the aim is to provide a readable and understandable guide to the process of selecting a personal computer system, and in doing so introduce the terms that will allow a prospective purchaser to make sense of PC specifications and understand computer magazines. It also provides some guidance on selecting a supplier and budgeting for a system.

In the discussion of selecting a PC system, this chapter looks at not only the hardware and software components of the system but also the other start-up items like consumables. It specifically looks at the class of PCs termed IBM PCs and IBM-compatibles rather than the full range of microcomputers which includes other types like Apple Macintosh, etc., although what is said here is relevant to the selection of other microcomputers. The chapter concludes with a Case Study that describes the process of selecting a computer system for a small bookshop.

2. The process of selecting a personal computer system

Many people have a number of horror stories to tell about computers they have bought that they are unable to operate or use for any meaningful purpose. The reasons for dissatisfaction are generally due to the purchaser selecting a PC system simply by visiting a local computer store and buying whatever looks good on display, what they are told is "best" or "top-selling" by a salesman, or whatever they can afford.   Even those people who do some planning often only consider the hardware items and then are confused when they can not do anything useful with the computer they have bought.

To ensure that a usable and appropriate system is selected, it is necessary to carry out some pre-planning as would be done in any business or personal situation that involves large expenditure, and this involves three stages:

- Carrying out a needs analysis;
- Identifying the software that meets those needs; and
- Identifying the hardware that runs the software.

3.   Needs analysis

To carry out a needs analysis the following questions must be answered by the prospective user of the system:

What is to be computerised?

This question is to ascertain exactly what manual tasks the user wants to computerise if it is felt they can be more effectively carried out on a computer. Likely answers will be: to produce letters, to carry out financial analysis, etc. It should also take into account whether the user expects to expand on these requirements in the near future as it is important that a PC that is bought today is able to cope with tomorrow's demands.

Is there a need for integration of data or users?

Firstly, the user should consider whether the data in one application needs to be available for use in another application. For instance, if the user wants to maintain a record of customers to be used as a mailing list, or if the results of statistical or financial analysis need to be incorporated in reports.

Secondly, the user must specify whether data on the system needs to be accessible by other users on the same or another site since this might suggest that a single-user system may not be appropriate and a networked system should be considered.

What is the level of experience of the user?

The user needs to consider their level of expertise with PCs. Do they, for instance, class themselves as complete novices or do they have some knowledge of computer systems or particular software or are they expert users with considerable knowledge of a wide range of software. This will have an impact on the choice of software.

Is portability of a system a requirement?

The user should consider whether they will need to use the computer away from the normal operation site, e.g. at home or in another office.

Are there any special needs or requirements?

This is the opportunity for the user to specify any special requests they may have. For instance whether they anticipate maintaining a large volume of data or want to produce high quality printouts.

What is the purchaser's budget?

Finally, the user will need to indicate the maximum price they are prepared to pay for the whole working system.

4.   Applications software: identifying the type

Once the needs analysis has been completed the answers can be used to identify the *applications software* that will meet the user's requirements. Applications software is the software that is used to carry out specific tasks. It can be either *tailor-made* or *packaged*.

Tailor-made (or *bespoke*) software means that it is specially written for the organisation. This can take time, and can cost a lot but may be the only answer for specialised systems.

Packaged software is software that can be purchased "off-the-shelf" and is suitable for a variety of users. It is therefore ready to use and costs less, as obviously the development costs can be spread across many purchasers. (If packaged software does not exactly meet the requirements of the user, then it is possible to have it customised for users. This is a middle route, and one which is not as costly as having software tailor-made.) The term "package" refers to the fact the software is packaged together with all the related manuals and documentation.

In order to specify the software that is required, first of all the tasks to be computerised must be matched, in general terms, with the *type* of software that can be used to accomplish them.

Software falls into two main categories: *productivity tools* and *specialist software* and the software that falls within each of these categories is described below:

Productivity tools

This includes software that is useful for all types of users and their tasks, i.e. *word processing, spreadsheet, database* and *presentation graphics* software.

- *Word processing* software is used for the production of all kinds of business documents like correspondence, reports, etc., as well as some high quality documents like newspapers and brochures. (See Chapters 2 and 8.) Examples of major word processing packages include *Word, WordPerfect, Ami Pro* and *WordStar*.

- *Spreadsheet* software is used for numerical, financial and statistical analysis, as well as the creation of business graphics. (See Chapters 3, 4, 9 and 10.) Examples of major spreadsheet packages include *Excel, SuperCalc, Lotus 1-2-3* and *Quattro Pro*.

- *Database* software is used for the management of large amounts of related data, both textual and numeric, and also provides the facility to create customised data-entry screens and reports. (See Chapters 6 and 12.) Examples of file management packages include *Cardbox, FileMaker Pro* and *Q&A,* examples of relational database management packages include *Access, Approach, dBASE, DataEase* and *Paradox.*

- *Presentation graphics* software is used for the production of text and other charts or graphs on paper, acetate or 35mm slides, as well the development of PC presentations. (See Chapters 5 and 11.) Examples of major presentation graphics software packages include *Powerpoint, Harvard Graphics* and *Freelance Graphics.*

Productivity tools can be purchased as individual stand-alone packages, as a *suite* of packages, or as an *integrated software* package.

- *Suites* of software are made up of a number of major stand-alone software packages bundled together by the same supplier. Purchasing software produced by the same supplier usually means that copying of data across the packages is easy, and since similar commands are used. that learning time is cut down. The main drawback in purchasing a suite of packages, however, is that the user does not necessarily need all the different products.

    The three major software suites are *Microsoft Office Professional* (which includes *Word, Excel, Powerpoint* and *Access*), *Lotus SmartSuite* (which includes *Ami Pro, Lotus 123 for Windows, Freelance Graphics* and *Approach*) and *Borland WordPerfect Office* (which includes *WordPerfect, Quattro Pro* and *Paradox for Windows).*

- *Integrated software* packages contain the main functions: word processing, spreadsheets and databases, although they are generally not as sophisticated as stand-alone packages, or a suite of packages, e.g. they may have a substantially smaller size spreadsheet or the database may only be of the flat-file type. For the new user they probably provide most of the features required and therefore do not overwhelm them with functionality, experienced users on the other hand may find they do not provide them with all the features they expect.

    However, they often incorporate useful other accessories, like an address book, desk accessories or a time management function, and they are usually substantially cheaper than buying three or four stand-alone packages. Examples of integrated packages include *Microsoft Works, Claris Works, Lotus Works* and *WordPerfect Works.*

Specialist software

This includes the type of software that is used for specific tasks, e.g. *accounts, communications, drawing, painting, desk top publishing (DTP), project management, personal information management,* and *reference* software as well as *games* software.

- *Accounts* software is the most useful type of software in a business, since all businesses need to keep accounts. However, it is also the most complex and difficult to use. It is frequently module-based which allows a business to purchase modules separately, e.g. sales, purchasing and nominal ledger, to build up an accounts system gradually. (It should be noted however that if the user only wishes to produce the main accounting documents, like Balance Sheets and Profit and Loss accounts, then this can be more easily accomplished using spreadsheet software.) Examples of accounts packages include *Sage Sterling, Money Manager* and *Quicken.*

- *Communications* software lets the user communicate with another computer, for instance using e-mail software, e.g *Microsoft Mail* and *Lotus cc:Mail;* to access on-line information services, e.g. *DOSCIM or WinCIM* (see **1:10**) or to send fax messages, e.g. *Winfax.*

- *Drawing* and *painting* packages allow the user to create a variety of images, both 2-D and 3-D (e.g. *Adobe Illustrator, Micrografx Designer* and *CorelDRAW!)* whilst other packages provide image processing tools like morphing and warping (e.g. *PhotoShop). Computer-aided design (CAD)* packages are complex design tools for draughtsmen and engineers, e.g. *TurboCAD* and *AutoCAD.*

- *Desk top publishing* software uses text and graphics prepared in other packages and turns them into high quality publications. DTP packages go beyond what is possible in sophisticated word processing software. Examples include *PageMaker* and *Ventura.*

- *Project management* software supports managers who need to keep track of projects, by helping them to schedule tasks to optimise resources, and as the project progresses to re-allocate or re-schedule resources. Examples include *Microsoft Project* and *Schedule Express.*

- *Personal information managers (or PIMs)* software lets users maintain and control their personal information. This software generally includes a diary, address book, calculator and notepad, which can often be printed out to fit in the user's filofax®. Examples include *Lotus Agenda* and *Sidekick for Windows.*

- *Reference* software includes encyclopaedias, dictionaries, literature works, and these are mainly sold on CD-ROM (see **1:6**). Additionally there is a vast range of entertainment software, i.e. *games,* on the market and this includes arcade, adventure and sports games.

5. Applications software: identifying the particular packages

Once the type of software has been identified the next task is to identify the *particular* software packages that are required. This is not quite that easy since there are many different packages available in each category. In order to do this the following points should be considered: the functionality as well as the usability of the software, the quality of the accompanying documentation as well as the level of after-sales support, and of course the price. These are discussed in further detail below:

Functionality

Whereas most of the basic features of a software package within a given category are fundamentally the same, some packages will offer more functionality than others. It is therefore important to make a list of the essential features required in the software and then compare them with the features offered by the software itself. (This may mean looking at the specification of the software itself as provided by the supplier or in advertisements, or listed in "Buyers Guides" in computer magazines.) For the four main productivity tools and integrated software, the following tables suggest the main features that might need to be considered:

Word processing software	
size of spell checker	size of thesaurus
grammar/style checker facility	word count facility
templates	mail merge facility
newspaper columns facility	other DTP features

Spreadsheet software	
maximum size of worksheet	3-D worksheets
charting and graphing facility	spell checker facility
macro language	goal-seeking facility

Database software	
flat file or relational database package	calculate fields facility
forms designer	report designer
macros	programming language

Presentation graphics	
line, bar. pie, text, organisation charts	speaker notes facility
on-screen annotation facility	spell checker facility

Integrated software	
word processing function: spell checker, thesaurus, mailmerge, outliner	database function: flat file or relational, forms designer, report designer
spreadsheet function: maximum size of worksheet, graphing facility	dynamic sharing of data

Once the purchaser has identified a number of packages with features that match the lists that have been drawn up, reviews can be read in computer magazines to obtain more information about the software. It is important to remember, however, that as software is continually being updated, new versions of major software packages become available all the time, hence the magazines must be up-to-date to be of use.

Usability

This is a very important aspect as it will determine whether the product is actually used. It will largely be influenced by the environment in which the software operates, i.e. whether it is DOS-based or Windows-based. Although Windows-based software has become extremely popular, there are a large number of long-term PC users who still prefer the DOS environment. It is therefore essential to have a demonstration of the software to assess its usability.

When testing a piece of software for its usability, the purchaser should consider not only how easy it is for a new user to begin to work with the software but also how easy it would be to return to the software after a period of absence.

Although is not essential to select software packages that operate in the same environment, it is a good idea as it can assist with data sharing, and in the case of Windows-based software helps to cut down on the learning time.

Documentation

The quality of the accompanying documentation is an aspect that is frequently overlooked by prospective purchasers, but is an important factor especially if users are not going to receive any training in the use of the software, since they will have to rely heavily on the documentation.

User manuals have in the past had a bad name for their poor usability. This is because they were often written at the end of the development process by the programmers themselves who knew the software very well and found it difficult to write the documentation from a new user's point of view. Documentation often only consisted of a substantial manual full of technical detail describing the functionality of the system rather than how to use it.

Nowadays, however, more effort is spent in producing a usable set of documentation supporting varying levels of experience, e.g. a Getting Started manual for the complete novice, a User Manual for those with some experience of the type of software, as well as a Technical Manual.

On-line help also falls within the category of documentation. If available in the software, it should be context-sensitive (i.e. it should be able to detect what help the user wants from the task being carried out) and there should be a search facility. Some software producers now only provide documentation in this form.

On-line tutorials are also useful as they provide an interactive way of learning the software, and on-screen "advisors" or "tutors" provide additional guidance on how to carry out a task whilst the user is actually working on it.

The quality of both paper-based and on-line documentation is not always discussed by reviewers nor listed as a feature in Buyers Guides, so it is therefore a good idea to take a look at the manuals and the on-line help and bear in mind that the user will probably need them for two basic purposes: to teach the user how to use the software as well as to find answers to problems. It is therefore necessary to assess the documentation from both these perspectives.

After-sales support

Most software suppliers provide some form of after-sales support, but there are a number of factors to consider, and these include *time, cost, provider* and *availability* of support.

Time refers to the period that the supplier will support the software. It could be life-time support (as is generally the case with word processing, spreadsheet or database packages) or limited to the current version of the software, or even be for a stipulated period, e.g. 1 year or even 3 months.

Cost is concerned with whether the support is free or a charge will be made. Software support is never actually "free". Even if no charge is made, the cost will have been subsumed in the purchase price. There may be a charge made for a support contract, or there may be a "hidden charge", e.g. with some telephone support lines where the cost of the call is considerably higher than normal and a part of the charge goes directly to the support providor.   However, a few do operate free phone lines.

The user may also require some other support in the form of the purchase of other manuals or training guides. These are of course at the discretion of the user, but if it is anticipated that this will be necessary then the cost of such extra support will need to be taken into consideration.

The *provider* of the support may be either the company itself or some third party organisation. Whereas in the US support lines are generally open 365 days a year, in the UK this is generally limited to office hours from Monday to Friday, although this does appear to be changing.

Price

Finally, the question of the price of the software needs to be considered. In reality, of course, this may well be the first factor to be noted or at least borne heavily in mind when decisions are being made on functionality, usability, support, etc. It is probably difficult to separate the price from the other factors as there will be a need for some sort of trade-off.

When the price of software is being considered, the purchaser should note that Buyers Guides mainly show the retailers' recommended prices (RRP). However, it is usually possible to buy software much cheaper elsewhere since suppliers frequently offer special deals. Hence, Buyers Guides also often quote a lower so-called "street price". It should also be noted that some hardware manufacturers often sell their PCs with a "free" bundle of software.

There are a number of other ways of obtaining software, i.e. as *shareware* or *PD* (*public domain)* software. Shareware is software that is distributed free for users to try out. If they wish to keep it, they are asked to register with the author and they will then be entitled to upgrades to the next version together with a manual. Catalogues of shareware are easily available and software is substantially cheaper.

Public domain software is "freeware".   However, the software tends to be of a specialist nature, e.g. macros for spreadsheet and database packages, and there are usually a number of conditions attached to PD software, e.g. the user must not sell the program.

6.   PC operating systems

Having identified the particular software packages that are required, the next step is to ensure the relevant *operating system* is in place. For single-users of PCs this probably means a recent version of MS-DOS (or PC-DOS) and if a graphical interface is also required, MS-Windows too.

MS-DOS

Since DOS was originally developed in the early 1980s by Microsoft it has become the standard operating system for stand-alone PCs. But as PCs have developed over the years a number of versions of DOS have been developed to control the increasingly complex machines. The applications software will therefore specify the minimum version of DOS that is required to support the software. DOS is usually, but not always, pre-installed on the computer; however upgraded versions of DOS can also be purchased off the shelf.

Windows

Although Microsoft has made DOS versions 4, 5 and 6 more user-friendly, it has designed MS-Windows quite separately as an extension of DOS. This, too, has gone through a development process, and a number of versions of Windows are now in existence, and once again the applications software will specify the minimum version of Windows.

It should be noted that Windows is an extension of DOS so it cannot be used on its own, although in the future it will replace DOS completely. Windows is usually pre-installed on PCs nowadays but like DOS it can also be purchased separately. *Windows for Workgroups* although primarily intended for small networks is also sold for single-user PCs.

Other PC single-user operating systems

Although as stated above MS-DOS is the standard PC operating system, there are a number of other PC operating systems. Microsoft themselves have developed OS/2, which has not caught on quite as well as they anticipated. *DR-DOS* is a non-Microsoft operating system (which looks and feels like DOS) and there are PC versions of the popular mid-range operating system Unix, e.g. *Xenix*. Although these other operating systems can offer advantages over MS-DOS they are limiting in the amount of software they can support, although they do generally support DOS-based software.

Utility software

This type of systems software provides extra programs that can help to ensure an effective system, i.e. disk troubleshooting software (e.g. *PC-Tools, Norton Desktop, Xtree)*, disk compression software (e.g. *Stacker)* and anti-virus software (e.g. *Dr Solomon's Anti-Virus, Norton Anti-Virus)*.

7. Hardware requirements

Once the applications software has been selected, it will be necessary to note the minimum hardware specification required to run the software effectively. These details are usually shown in adverts, specifications and in Buyers Guides, and will include the following:

- the recommended processor
- the recommended size of main memory
- the disk space required to store the software
- any required input devices
- any recommended or supported output devices
- any communication hardware devices

The following sections will consider each of these aspects in turn so that a user can identify an appropriate PC to run the software. Although these sections will primarily consider *desktop* PCs, *portable* PCs are discussed separately in **14.**

8. Processors

Software programs generally state the minimum processor required to run the software optimally. The processor, also known as the CPU (Central Processing Unit), is where the processing of text, numeric data and graphics, etc., takes place. In a PC it is a microprocessor, that is a small silicon chip which has all the electronic circuitry etched onto it, which sits, together with all the other necessary electronic components, on the *motherboard* inside the system unit.

Intel designed the microprocessor that was used in the first IBM PC but now there are a number of other manufacturers. Microprocessors have developed over a number of years, and there is now a family of Intel chips which represent a development in the technology and hence performance of PCs. Processors are, in the main, identified by code numbers rather than names.

The first PC in 1983 and subsequently the PC-XT (the standard computer of its day) used the 8088 processor. There are still PCs around that use this chip but they are not capable of running today's software. In 1984, the 80286 processor was used in the first PC-AT machines. Later versions of the AT used the 80386DX processor or a "cut-down", and hence cheaper, version, the 80386SX processor. In 1989 the 80486 processor was used in PCs, first in its full-blown DX version and then in 1991 in its cut-down SX version. In 1993, the first machines based on a new generation of processors, the Pentium, were launched.

PCs are usually referred to by the processor they use, as in "an 80486-based machine" or by dropping the initial 80, as in "a 486-based machine". At the time of writing (September 1994), it is generally considered that an 80486-based machine is the standard business "entry-level" PC, and certainly essential to get the best out of the current sophisticated Windows-based software.

486DX2 and 486DX4 are further versions of the 80486 processor, which "run" faster. One factor that determines the processing power is the speed at which it operates. This is measured in Megahertz (MHz). Currently, standard speeds for 486-based machines are 25 MHz and 33 MHz, which means that PCs with the 486DX2 processor run twice as fast and with DX4 three-times as fast. Pentium-based machines can run at 60, 66, 90 or 100 MHz.

Computer specifications always show the processor on which the machine is based and the speed at which it runs, e.g. 80486DX 33 MHz CPU.

9.   Main memory

The second hardware requirement is the amount of main memory (or Random Access Memory) required to run the software. RAM, as it is known for short, is the temporary storage area in the computer that holds the software that is running and the data being processed. The contents of main memory are constantly changing as new data overwrites the old and new applications software is loaded. Main memory is also volatile, which means that when the computer is switched off everything in it is erased.

PCs come with a certain amount of memory fixed in place and this is measured in *bytes*. (Note: it takes one byte to hold the information for one character.) Nowadays the size of a computer's main memory is so great that it is actually measured in *kilobytes* or *K* (i.e. thousands of bytes) and *megabytes* or *Mb* (i.e. millions of bytes).

Basic Windows applications require at least 4 Mb of main memory. However, some require 8 Mb to run adequately, whereas high-performance graphics packages like DTP and CAD will require much more, and if a user wants to run more than one application at a time, then this may require more than 4 Mb.

Memory can be expanded using memory chips called *SIMMs (Single In-line Memory Modules)*, although there is a limit to how much extra memory can be fitted into a particular PC.

Cache memory is a small amount of high-speed memory which increases the speed at which data is accessed from main memory.

Computer specifications always show the amount of main memory installed and sometimes also the maximum amount that can be fitted, e.g. 4 Mb (32 Mb) RAM. They will also state the amount of cache memory, e.g. 256K cache RAM.

10.   Disk storage space

A further aspect to be considered is the size of disk space that is required to store the software. This is discussed in this section together with the general concept of storing data and programs permanently.

It has already been established that main memory only holds the essential parts of the software program and the data that the user is working with at the time. There is certainly not enough room to hold all the data and all the software that the user would ever require, notwithstanding the problem of the volatility of main memory - even if it were capable of holding all the user ever wanted, the computer could never be turned off! Hence, both data and programs have to be held externally from the computer's main memory and there a number of ways of doing this:

- on a hard disk;
- on floppy disks;
- on CD-ROMs; and
- on tape.

Hard disks

PCs are generally fitted with a hard disk (unless they are to be used as a disk-less workstation on a network). A hard disk is a sealed unit containing one or more rigid disks. The software and the data are held magnetically on the hard disk so that it does not require any power to maintain them. Hence when the computer is turned off the data remains on the disk and can be retrieved once the computer is turned back on.

A hard disk has an extremely large storage capacity which is usually measured in Megabytes although it is not uncommon to see disk capacities measured in *Gigabytes* (or *Gb*) (i.e. billions of bytes).

When deciding on the size of hard disk required, it is first necessary to find out how much disk space is required to hold the software. Note that current applications software programs, when fully installed, often require 20-30 Mb of disk space.

It is then necessary to estimate the space required to hold the data files. This is not so easy since it depends very much on the type of data held, e.g. text, graphics, etc., and the software within which they were created. As a rough guide, an A4 page of text could take up 10K, whilst a graphical image could take up 200K. If the disk is to hold a database, then the following calculation may be of use to estimate the amount of disk space required to hold the datafile: *record length (i.e. total number of characters) multiplied by number of records plus 10% for growth.*

It may therefore be easier to suggest that a purchaser should buy the largest hard disk they can afford. As a very rough guide a minimum usable size for a hard disk in a PC nowadays is probably about 150 Mb.

Because hard disks are fitted into the chassis of the computer and wired in to the computer, the software programs and data files can be accessed very quickly. Access times are measured in milliseconds (ms). When comparing hard disks, a faster access speed is indicated by a smaller number of milliseconds.

PC specifications generally show the hard disk size as well as the access time, e.g. 400 Mb (12 ms), and advertisements usually show the cost of upgrading to a larger hard disk.

Floppy disks

Floppy disks are another form of magnetic medium. They are a useful way of holding data externally from the system, and they can also be used on other compatible PCs, e.g. at home or at work.

Most software is sold on floppy disks, and such is the complexity of today's software that it is distributed on at least a dozen floppy disks. It therefore needs to be installed onto the hard disk in order to run it, and this is done via the floppy disk drive. PCs come with one floppy disk drive, sometimes two. There are two main sizes of floppy disk drives: the 5¼" (old style) drive and the 3½" (newer style) drive. Each can only read and write the comparable size of floppy disk.

The amount of data that can be held on the floppy disks themselves depends on the amount of data that can be packed onto the disk. Disks are generally known as being either double (or standard) density or high density disks. The following table shows the capacities of the two types of disk.

Size of disk	Double density disk	High density disk
5¼"	360 K	1.2 Mb
3½"	720 K	1.44 Mb

A computer specification will state the number and size of floppy disk drives that are supplied as standard, e.g. 3½" 1.44 Mb floppy drive or 1 x 1.44 Mb FD.

CD-ROMs

CD-ROM stands for Compact Disk-Read Only Memory. This type of disk uses optical storage technology to store data in much the same way as audio CDs. The storage capacities of CD-ROMs are very large: each CD can hold about 550 Mb of data, and in addition to text it makes it easier to hold graphics, sound, video and animation. Hence they are useful means of distributing software, especially multimedia software.

To read the data on a CD-ROM, a system needs to have a CD-ROM drive. These can be purchased separately and installed in one of the spare floppy disk drive slots. A PC with a CD-ROM drive and all the other necessary hardware to take advantage of the full range of sound, video and animation files, can be purchased as a complete system known as a *multimedia PC*.

In the future desktop systems that can write to optical storage will become more commonplace. The one disadvantage with CD-ROMs currently, as their name suggests, is that they are 'read-only", i.e. they are not erasable.

Tape streamers

These use tape cassettes or cartridges to save data very fast, for example at speeds of 2-4 Mb per minute and are useful for backing-up large quantities of data held on hard disks. Tape streamers are not normally included in a basic system but can easily be added as internal or external devices.

11. Input devices

There are a number of ways of interacting with the software and entering data and this section briefly describes a variety of input devices.

A *keyboard* is normally supplied with a PC. However the layout of the keyboard can vary. Older PCs came with an 84-key keyboard whereas the newer PCs come with an extended 102-key keyboard. For specialised applications, keyboards can be purchased that have fewer keys or specific layouts, e.g. separate numeric keypads.

Keyboards are an important component of a computer system and once a suitable PC has been identified, it is a good idea to try out the keyboard as there are definite differences in the "feel" as well as the size, shape and even the position of some of the keys. Users have been known to discard their systems simply because they were unable to get on with their keyboard.

Ergonomically designed keyboards are also available which split the keys on the keyboard, and are intended to help avoid some of the musculo-skeletal problems discussed in **13:18**.

An additional purchase might be a keyboard dustcover to protect the keyboard when not in use.

Some software, especially Windows-based software, requires a *pointing device* in order for the user to interact with it. Hence a *mouse* is usually included with a PC system especially if Windows is pre-installed on it, but if not, it can be purchased separately. A mouse pad is also useful for operating the mouse.

If there is a possibility that the cable joining the mouse to the PC will get tangled up with any work, a *cordless mouse* might be worth thinking about and if there might be a problem with limited space for using a mouse on the desktop, a *trackball* might be the answer. This is like an inverted mouse where the device remains stationary on the desk and the user moves the ball.

Scanners are input devices that "read" images into the computer. Some come with *OCR (Optical Character Recognition)* software which can interpret the images as text so that they can subsequently be edited in a word processing package. Scanners are usually of *flat-bed* (i.e. A4 size) or *hand-held* design.

Other input devices include

- *joysticks* or *yokes,* which are really only required with games software;
- *bar code readers*, which are especially useful in retailing;
- *touchscreens*, which only require the user to touch the screen to activate tasks;
- *pens* for use in systems that can be taught to recognise a user's handwriting;
- a *microphone* to record sound (although a *soundcard* will have to be installed in the system unit to provide the necessary electronic circuitry to process the sound).

12. Output devices

There are a number of output devices that are necessary to make a usable PC system: a screen, a printer, and for a multimedia PC system, speakers:

Screen

A screen (also referred to as a monitor or VDU (visual display unit)) will normally be supplied with a PC. Screens can be monochrome (either black and white, or green or amber and black) or colour. However, it is the resolution of the screen that dictates the clarity of the image. The screen is made up of a number of *pixels* (or picture elements) which are tiny points of light that are used to create the image. The greater the number of pixels on the screen the greater the resolution.

The two current standards for PC screens are VGA (which stands for Video Graphics Array) and SuperVGA. VGA resolution can display 16 colours using 640 x 480 pixels or 256 colours using 320 x 200 pixels. SuperVGA (or SVGA) can display 256 colours using 1024 x 768 pixels. The software will state the minimum standard of display that is required for the software. For example, certain high grade graphics packages can only run on SVGA screens.

Although the standard size of monitor is 14", a 15" monitor may be more suitable for Windows applications, a 17" monitor for DTP or graphical applications, and a 20" monitor for computer aided design work.

Computer specifications will generally show the monitor type that is supplied with the PC, e.g. 14" colour SVGA.

Printers

Printers are not normally sold as part of a PC system so must be purchased separately. There are a number of considerations when buying a printer in addition to ensuring that the printer is supported by the software. These include the quality of printout, the noise level, speed and price. The three main types of printer in use today are:

- dot matrix printers;
- inkjet printers; and
- laser printers

Dot-matrix printers use a number of pins to produce each character as the print head passes along the paper, e.g. a 9 pin dot matrix printer uses a matrix of 9 pins by 7 rows to create each letter. The output appears rather "dotty", but can be improved by using the NLQ (Near Letter Quality) facility which means that the printhead makes a double pass over the letters, slightly offset the second time and hence filling in the dots. However, 24 pin printers which use 2 sets of 12 pins can produce a better quality printout. The speed of dot matrix printers is measured in *cps* (characters per second) and they can achieve draft speeds of about 160 cps and NLQ speeds of about 50 cps. Although dot matrix printers are relatively noisy they are the cheapest type of printer.

Ink-jet printers spray tiny jets of ink onto the paper in the shape of each character using the same matrix principle as the dot matrix printer. As there are no moving parts they are silent, and the quality of printout is much better than a dot matrix printer. Inkjet printers can achieve print speeds of up to 300 cps although speeds of about 200 cps are more usual. The price of inkjet printers is not that much more than dot matrix printers and they therefore represent good value for money.

Laser printers work like photocopiers taking a copy of the image of the page, and hence the print quality is excellent. Print speeds are measured in *ppm* (pages per minute) and the resolution of the page in *dpi* (dots per inch). "Personal" or "desktop" lasers print at 4-6 ppm at 300 dpi. Although the price of laser printers is more than the other printers described above, prices are dropping. However, there are high maintenance and running costs and another disadvantage is that they can usually only cope with A4-size paper.

Accessories for dot matrix and inkjet printers include a *tractor feed* (for continuous stationery), a *cut-sheet feeder* (for single sheets), a *printer stand* (which saves desk space and protects continuous stationery), a *dustcover* (to protect the printer when not in use) and an *acoustic hood* (to reduce noise levels from dot-matrix printers). When purchasing a printer, a printer *cable* will also be required. It is necessary to mention this, as a cable is not usually supplied with the printer. If two or more single-user computers wish to share a printer, a *switch box* can be added, which will allow the users to switch the printer to the relevant computer.

Speakers

These are required to play back sound in a multimedia system. However, to ensure that others working in the same environment are not disturbed it may also be advisable to purchase a set of *headphones*.

13. Communication hardware devices

If a user wishes to link one computer to another computer via the telephone line, a *modem* will be required. One function of the modem is to convert the digital data from the computer into the type of data that can be fed down the telephone lines (known as analogue data) and back. In technical terminology, it *mo*dulates and *dem*odulates, hence its name.

Another function of the modem is to set up the computer to receive or transfer data at the same speed as the other computer. A speed of a modem is measured in bps (bits per second). This is often referred to as the baud rate, although it is not quite the same thing. If for example the computer is linked with CompuServe, this runs at a maximum of 9600 bps.

A modem can either be fixed internally into the system or be an external device, which will need to be linked to the PC by a cable and have its own power supply. *Fax modems* are an extension of the normal modem and allow the user to send and receive faxes via the computer rather than on an external fax machine, although the purchaser should beware as not all fax software works with all fax modems.

14. Portable PC systems

If mobile computing is required, then the user will need to consider a portable PC. This section covers some of the aspects applicable to selecting a portable system. Note that the term *portable PC* is used here to refer to any PC that is capable of being carried, i.e. *notebooks* (A4 size) or the smaller *pocketbooks, sub-notebooks, palmtops* or *PDAs (personal digital assistants)*.

Software

Applications and operating system software designed for desktop PCs are in most cases also appropriate for a portable PC. If a portable system is being purchased in addition to a desktop PC then it is essential to ensure that the portable runs the same software so that a document can be worked on in the same way. If the user only intends to use one of these machines at one time, it may only be necessary to buy one copy of the software rather than two. However, it is essential to check the position with the supplier to ensure that copyright is not infringed. *File transfer* software may be useful for transferring software between the portable and the desktop PC, e.g. *Traveling Software's LapLink.*

Batteries

Most portables have rechargeable batteries. These batteries are normally Nickel Metal Hydride (NimH) and battery life is normally about two or three hours. Some portables have processors which include the letters "SL", e.g. 80486SL, which are power-saving versions and have "power management" facilities that switch off the screen when not in use. Smaller portables, on the other hand, use AAA batteries.

Memory

Some portables use their batteries to maintain data in memory cards, known as PCMCIA (Personal Computer Memory Card International Association) cards. These cards are now also used for other devices like hard disks, network cards and other peripherals.   They are like thick credit cards, that can be moved in and out of slots. There are three types of slots: Type I slots, which are 3.3 mm thick, Type II, which are 5 mm thick and Type III, which is 10.5 mm thick and can hold either two Type I or two Type II cards. With some portables these cards can be added or removed without switching off, hence the term *plug and play*.

Input devices

As it is often difficult to use a mouse with a portable PC, some portables come equipped with a trackball, which is often incorporated into the keyboard or even the lid of the portable. Others are pen-based systems.

Screens

Although portable screens are classified in the same way as desktop PCs, because of the different technology involved in producing flat screens, a whole new set of terms can be found. Portable screens are of the LCD (*liquid crystal display*) type which are difficult to read when the light is not good. *Back-lit* or *side-lit* displays improve the readability but are more expensive and are an extra drain on the battery. Screens are either categorised as being *passive-matrix* or *active-matrix*. Mono LCDs use passive-matrix but the best colour screens use active-matrix.

Printers and modems

There are a number of dot matrix and ink jet printers on the market which are small enough to fit in a briefcase, and there are now combined notebook/printers available. If users wish to send their files back to the office using a modem, PCMCIA-based card modems or pocket modems (i.e. small portable modems) are useful.

15. Networked PC systems

During the needs analysis it may have been established that a number of PC users need to share information and resources (e.g. printers, modems, etc.) in an office. This means that single-user PC systems would not be appropriate as "sharing information" would mean passing floppy disks across the room from one PC to another. (Incidentally, sharing information in this way has been wittily termed "SneakerNet"!)

A local area network (LAN) is much more appropriate and also supports the concept of *workgroups*. Although selecting and installing a network requires considerable planning and more experience than is required to set up a single-user system, this section looks at some of the software and hardware considerations specific to networking PC systems.

One major consideration is the type of network. There are two main types: *peer-to-peer* networks, where each computer can have access to all the resources and hard disks of all the computers on the network (but is really only suitable for a small number of users); and *client-server* networks, where one computer, the file server, holds all the files, which are accessed by the other computers. In a client-server network the file server needs to be a high specification PC.

Peer-to-peer networking is cheaper and much easier to set up. There are a number of networking operating systems that support peer-to-peer networks, e.g. *Novell's NetWare Lite, Artisoft's Lantastic* and *Sage's MainLAN*. These provide starter packs for two users as well as add-on packs for further users, and usually include both the software and the hardware devices, e.g. the network cards to be fitted inside the PCs. *Microsoft's Windows for Workgroups* also supports peer-to-peer networks. Each PC can install DOS as normal but the network software is there to ensure that any calls to other devices can be sent across the network. Client-server networking is supported by an operating system like *Microsoft's LAN Manager* or *Novell's NetWare*, although *Windows for Workgroups* can also be used on a client-server network.

In addition to applications software that supports workgroups, *e-mail* or *voice-mail* software is useful as it provides an easy way for users to communicate with one another. Word processing software should then be *mail-enabled*, which means that electronic mail messages can be sent as easily as printing. As far as other applications software is concerned, single-user software will not always work on a network, especially if more than one user wants to access and update the same data, e.g. in accounts and database software. With peer-to-peer networks the operating system and applications software is usually licensed on a user basis, whereas with client-server networks users are licensed in blocks of 5 or 10.

16. Identifying a supplier

Once the required specification of PC and other hardware devices has been identified it is time to look around for a particular model and a supplier. It is also prudent to remember that some suppliers bundle software with their hardware, although it is vital to ensure that these are the latest versions.

One important consideration when selecting a supplier is the *warranty*. Although every PC system comes with a warranty, these can vary. Examples include a one year on-site warranty, a three year on-site warranty covering all parts and labour, and a free lifetime warranty. Additionally, a purchaser should consider the after-sales support, i.e. who will provide the technical support, and the response time (see **5**).

17. Consumables

A further expenditure which is often overlooked when budgeting for a PC, is the start-up and running costs of a computer system. Certain items have to be in place when the computer is purchased as well as replaced on a regular basis.

A good supply of floppy disks is required as these will be necessary for back-up and archive storage, therefore it is important to know what type of disk drive is installed in the PC so that the correct type of disks can be bought. Disk storage boxes will also be useful, and if a tape streamer is used, a supply of cartridges or cassettes will also be required.

Adequate supplies of the correct paper, be it continuous, single sheets or multi-part, as well as labels and envelopes, and acetates if used, will be needed. Some printers require special paper, however, for example, inkjet printers usually work better with clay-coated paper that stops the ink spreading after printing. Note also that laser printers, in general, cannot cope very well with glossy, embossed letter-headed paper. The recommended weight of paper for most printers is between 80 and 90 gm^2 (grammes per square metre). If recycled paper is to be used this should be smooth and dust-less.

As for labels, if they are to be used in laser printers they must be able to withstand the hot temperatures in the printing process; whereas if they are to be used in inkjet printers, labels must be of a similar quality to the paper to ensure no spreading of the ink.

Envelopes too should be of the same paper quality as the paper. If envelopes are too heavy or are damaged they can cause paper jams. Acetates are often unable to withstand the high temperatures and can often melt in laser printers.

Printers will also need to be maintained: dot matrix printers will need to have their ribbons changed from time to time; ink jet printers will require a regular supply of ink; and laser printers will need toner. Using the wrong ink or toner can seriously damage the printer, so only recommended products should be bought. Re-inking ribbons or re-filling toner cartridges is cost effective and can be done in-house.

It is also a good idea to keep a good stock of anti-static cleaning equipment to keep screens and keyboards clean.

18. Controlling the budget

When purchasing a PC it may be possible to use a spreadsheet program to keep control of the costs. The following is a template that could be used.

	A	B	C
1	PC purchase at:	=TODAY()	
2			
3	Budget	£0.00	
4			
5	Software		
6	Apps Package 1	£0.00	
7	Apps Package 2	£0.00	
8	Apps Package 3	£0.00	
9	Apps Package 4	£0.00	
10	Apps Package 5	£0.00	
11	DOS version	£0.00	
12	Windows version	£0.00	
13		*Software sub-total*	=SUM(B6:B12)
14	Hardware		
15	PC model:		
16	(processor, speed,		
17	memory size, disk drives,	£0.00	
18			
19	Upgrades		
20	extra memory	£0.00	
21	larger hard disk	£0.00	
22	mouse	£0.00	
23			
24	Printer model	£0.00	
25	Modem	£0.00	
26	Other devices	£0.00	
27		*Hardware sub-total*	=SUM(B17:B26)
28	Consumables		£0.00
29		*Total*	=C13+C27+C28
30	17.5	*% VAT*	=(A30*C29)/100
31		*GRAND TOTAL*	=C29+C30
32	Balance		=B3-C31

19. Case Study: Small bookshop

Background

John Wells runs a small antiquarian bookshop in a rural town in Kent. He would like to provide a better customer service enabling him to match books in stock with customer needs, and also provide more information on what becomes available in his shop.

Conducting the needs analysis

In response to the questions in the needs analysis, the following answers are elicited:

- The bookshop owner wants to hold his book stock (approx. 3,000 books) on computer, keep a record of his customers, prepare his main accounts (e.g. balance sheets, profit and loss account, but not his daily accounts) on computer, and also produce letters, price lists and mini posters. No major expansion of the bookshop is planned for the near future.
- At present there is no need for integration of data, and as there is to be only one PC no integration with other computers.
- The bookshop owner has some knowledge of using PCs and is prepared to take on the responsibility of learning the new system.
- He would like to produce high-quality posters and letters.
- The computer system will reside in the bookshop, portability is not required.
- The bookshop owner has earmarked approx. £2,000 for the purchase of the whole system.

Identifying the type of applications software

From the needs analysis, the following generic types of applications software can be identified:

- to maintain the keep stock of books: a database software package;
- to prepare the main accounts: spreadsheet software package *not* accounts software;
- to produce letters and mini-posters: a sophisticated word processing package is required *not* DTP software.

Identifying the specific applications software

The bookshop owner has drawn up a list of features that are essential for the application software identified:

- *word processing:* he is looking for a package with a good spell checker, thesaurus and grammar checker - after all he is in the "words" business; a mail merge facility and some basic DTP facilities;
- *spreadsheet:* no essential requirements beyond the basic features;

- *database*: although at the present stage only a flat-file will be created, in the future the bookshop owner would like to link information, therefore he would like a relational database, with both a forms and reports designer.

The bookshop owner checks these features with those shown in the Buyers Guide of a a computing magazine and comes up with a list of possible packages in each category. In order to refine his list he reads some reviews and identifies "best buys". He is therefore able to cut down his list to one or two packages in each category, but to make a final decision, he visits a local computer store to have a few demonstrations.

He eventually decides to opt for Microsoft Word for Windows as the word processing package, Excel for the spreadsheet package (although he realises he does not really need all the functionality it offers) and Access for the database (since he is tempted by the prospect of developing his database into a full-blown application).

He looks in computer magazines to find a supplier and finds some significant price savings on the RRPs of the products. However, he realises that he can purchase the Microsoft Office Pro suite of packages for practically the same price as the three individual packages, and although he presently has no need for the extra software at present, he decides to opt for the suite rather than the three individual packages.

Identifying the operating system

He now checks with the software that DOS (minimum version 3.3) and Windows (3.1) must be in place to ensure that the software runs optimally and he finds out the current price of both of these in the event they are not pre-installed on the PC he eventually purchases.

Identifying the hardware

The bookshop owner then lists the minimum hardware requirements of the Office Pro software: 80486 processor (DX or SX); 6 Mb RAM; 1 x 3½" 1.44 Mb floppy disk drive; keyboard and mouse; VGA monitor.

He also estimates the amount of disk space required: 82 Mb for Office Pro; 6 Mb for DOS, 10 Mb for Windows; the database datafile will take up approx 660K (200 characters x 3000 records = 600,000 bytes + 10% = 660K); and space will also be required to hold the word processed documents and spreadsheet worksheets - therefore a minimum of 150 Mb is probably acceptable.

He also feels he needs a printer of laser quality, and after consulting computing magazines, opts for the Hewlett Packard Laserjet 4L, with the following specification: 300 dpi and 4 ppm.

Identifying the supplier

He looks around and finds two manufacturers selling PCs with the required specification at the same price and with both DOS v6.2 and Windows 3.1 installed on the machine for £799 + VAT. However, when he looks at the warranty arrangements he decides that the manufacturer that is offering three year on-site warranty covering all parts and labour is better than the five year warranty arrangement which is equivalent to first year parts and labour return to base and subsequent years labour only. He is also able to identify a separate supplier for the HP Laserjet 4L at £460 + VAT.

Consumables

John Wells purchases a supply of 50 floppy disks and a disk storage box. He makes sure his headed letter paper supply is suitable for use with the laser printer and that he has an adequate supply of envelopes as well. He also buys some cleaning fluid for the keyboard and the screen.

Controlling his budget

He asks a friend to help him set up a worksheet to help him control his spending on the project, and give him some initial experience of using a spreadsheet program.

PC purchase at	31 September 1994	
Budget	£2,000.00	
Software		
Microsoft Office Pro 4.3:	£299.00	
(Word, Excel, Powerpoint and Access)		
DOS v 6.2 (installed on PC)		
Windows v 3.1 (installed on PC)		
	Software sub-total	£299.00
Hardware		
Packard Bell 486sx-33		
(486SX processor, 33 MHz, 4 Mb RAM		
250 Mb hard disk, 1 x 1.44 disk drive,	£799.00	
Upgrades		
RAM upgrade to 8 Mb	£150.00	
Printer model HP Laserjet 4L	£460.00	
Modem		
Other devices		
	Hardware sub-total	£1,409.00
Consumables		£50.00
	Total	£1,759.00
17.5	*% VAT*	£307.83
	GRAND TOTAL	£2056.83
Balance		-£56.83

Appendix 1
Selected further reading

This Appendix provides a number of selected references of up-to-date sources that might prove useful further reading on many of the aspects covered in the chapters.

Chapter 1: Information searching and retrieval

Anger, C P. (1994) *Information sources in grey literature.* Bowker-Saur.

Badley, Phil and Hanson, Terry. (1994) *Going on-line and CD ROM.* Aslib.

Clark, C. (1990) *Photocopying from books and journals: a guide to all users of copyright literary work.* British Copyright Council

Dern, Daniel. (1994) *The Internet guide for new users.* McGraw-Hill.

Flint, M. (1990) *A user's guide to copyright.* Butterworth.

Gardner, James. (1994) *A DOS user's guide to the Internet.* Prentice-Hall.

Hague, Paul N. (1993) *Questionnaire design.* Kogan Page.

Hartley, R J, Keen, E M, Tedd, L A. (1990) *On-line searching: principles and practice.* Bowker-Saur.

Haynes, David (ed). (1990) *Information sources in information technology.* Bowker-Saur.

Hills, Philip J. (1990) *Information management systems.* Ellis Horwood.

Internet world (magazine on subscription from Mecklermedia, Artillery House, Artillery Row, London SW1P 1RT)

Knight A V and Silk D J. (1990) *Managing information: information systems for today's general managers.* McGraw.

Mann, T. (1987) *A Guide to library research methods.* OUP.

Newby, Gregory B. (1994) *Directory of directories on the Internet: a guide to information sources.* Meckler.

Newlin, Barbara. (1985) *Answers on-line.* McGraw-Hill.

Que development Group. (1994) *Using CompuServe.* Que.

Sachs, David and Stair, Henry. (1994) *Hands-on Internet: a beginning guide for PC users,* Prentice-Hall.

Sanderson, David. (1993) *Smileys.* O'Reilly and Assocs.

Vernon, K D C. (1984) *Information sources in management and business.* Bowker-Saur.

Chapter 2 : Document production

Adamson, A. (1990) *A student's guide to assignments, projects and research.* Thamesman.

Bell, Judith. (1993) *Doing your research project: a guide for first-time users in education and social science.* OUP.

Benwie, Michael. (1991) *How to master business English.* HowTo Books.

Bivins, Thomas H. (1992) *Fundamentals of successful newsletters.* NTC Business Books.

Bowden, John. (1991) *How to write a report.* HowTo Books.

Economist. (1993) *Style guide.* Hamish Hamilton in association with The Economist books.

Goodworth, Clive. (1991) *Secrets of successful business report writing.* Butterworth/ Heinemann.

Gosling, Peter and Joanna, with Baskeyfield, Tony. (1991) *Easily into DTP.* Macmillan.

Inman, Colin. (1994) *Financial Times style guide.* Financial Times/Pitman.

Jay, Ros. (1994) *How to write reports that get results.* Institute of Management/ Pitman.

Murphy Elizabeth and Snell, Shelagh. (1991) *Effective writing: plain English at work.* Pitman.

Newson, Anna. (1991) *Business communication.* Chartered Insurance Institute.

Parker, Roger C. (1994) *One minute designer.* Que Computer Manuals.

Piotrowski, Maryan V. (1991) *Better business writing.* Piatkus.

Sassoon, R. (1993) *Computers and typography.* Intellect.

Searfoss, Glenn. (1992) *Computer font book: effective use of and design with typefaces.* Osborne/McGraw-Hill.

Sunday Times. (1993) *Wordpower guide.* Heinemann.

Sussams, John. (1991) *How to write effective reports.* Gower.

Chapter 3: Numerical data analysis

Amoroso, Donald. (1994) *Decision making using Lotus 123 for Windows: building quality applications.* McGraw-Hill.

Attwood, Gaynor. (1991) *Using spreadsheets effectively.* McGraw-Hill.

Bee, Roland and Frances. (1993) *Management information systems and statistics.* IPM.

Diacogianos, George. (1994) *Financial management: a modelling approach using spreadsheets.* McGraw-Hill.

Economist. (1993) *Numbers guide: the essentials of business numeracy.* Economist Business Books.

Gardiner, Everette. (1994) *The spreadsheet forecaster.* McGraw-Hill.

Gough, Leo. (1994) *The Financial Times guide to business numeracy.* Financial Times/Pitman.

Gregory, Derek. (1993) *Statistics for business.* McGraw-Hill.

Jackson, Mary. (1989) *Creative modelling with Lotus 123.* John Wiley.

Jackson, Mary. (1988) *Advanced spreadsheet modelling with Lotus 123.* John Wiley.

Johnson, John. (1990) *Case studies in finance using Excel*. McGraw-Hill.

Johnson, John. (1990) *Case studies in finance using Lotus*. McGraw-Hill.

Leeburg, Verlene and Purvis, Peggy. (1993) *Lotus 123 for Accounting: a beginners guide*. McGraw-Hill.

McCormack, V and Cassell, H. (1993) *Developing microcomputer models for cost analysis and decision making*. McGraw-Hill.

Secrett Malcolm (1989) *Mastering spreadsheet budgets and forecasts: a practical guide*. Institute of Management/Pitman

Whitehead, Geoffrey. (1992) *Statistics for business*. Pitman.

Chapter 4: Business graphics

Bowden, John. (1991) *How to write a report*. HowTo Books.

Economist. (1993) *Numbers guide*. Economist Business Books.

Manchester Open Learning. (1993) *Making effective presentations*. Kogan Page.

Chapter 5: Presentation graphics

Ehrenborg, Jons and Mattock, John. *(1993) Powerful presentations: 50 original ideas for making a real impact*. Kogan Page.

Forsyth, Patrick. (1994) *Ready-made activities for presentation skills*. Institute of Management/Pitman.

Howell, Parry. (1991) *Successful business presentations*. Croner.

Jay, Anthony. (1993) *Effective presentations*. Pitman.

Manchester Open Learning. (1993) *Making effective presentations*. Kogan Page.

Stevens, Michael. (1990) *Improving your presentation skills: a complete kit*. Kogan Page.

Chapter 6: Data Management

Date, C J. (1983) *Database: a primer*. Addison-Wesley.

Date, C J. (1990) *An introduction to database systems*. Addison-Wesley.

Desai, Bipin C. (1990) *An introduction to database systems*. West Publishing Co.

Eaglestone, Barry M. (1991) *Relational databases*. Thornes.

Harris, Wayne. (1994) *Databases for business users*. Pitman.

Jones, Edward. (1993) *Ready made Access applications*. McGraw-Hill.

Mannila, Heikki and Kari-Jouko, Raiha. (1992) *The design of relational databases*. Addison-Wesley.

Mortimer, Andrew. (1993) *Information structures for database design*. Butterworth/Heinemann.

Pascal, Fabian. (1993) *Understanding relational databases*. James Wiley.

Schocker, Schimon. (1992) *The art of business programming with dBASE III Plus and IV*. McGraw-Hill.

Wertz, Charles J. (1992) *Relational database design: a practitioner's guide*. Manning Pubs.

Chapter 7: Getting started with PCs; Chapter 8: Word processing software; Chapter 9: Spreadsheet software; Chapter 10: Business graphics software; Chapter 11: Presentation graphics software; Chapter 12: Database software; Chapter 14: Further DOS and Windows

Books

There are an enormous number of books covering the use of DOS, Windows and specific applications software. These range from the user manuals that come with the software, to other substantial reference manuals, training guides as well as quick reference guides. Examples include:

10 Minute Guide to ... (Alpha Books)	*PC Magazine Guide to ..* (Ziff Davis)
Using ... (Que Books)	*... for Dummies* (IDG Books)
... Instant Reference (Sybex)	*Quick reference guides* (DDC books)

Videos

There is also a range of videos training users in the use of specific software packages. Examples include:

Beginners Guide to ... and Advanced Guide to ... (Burgess Video Group)
Compututor Intro ... (Technology Productions)

Computer-based training (CBT)

There is a variety of disk- or CD-based computer-based training material, which ranges from teaching typing to the use of DOS, Windows and applications software. Examples include:

Typing Tutor (Que)	*Mavis Beacon Teaches Typing*
Teach Me/Teach Yourself ... (American Training Initiative)	

Chapter 13: Avoiding problems with computers

Computer Misuse Act (1990)
Copyright, Designs and Patents Act (1988)
Data Protection Act (1984)
Bainbridge, David. (1992) *Software Copyright Law.* Pitman.
Bainbridge, David. (1994) *Introduction to Computer Law.* Pitman.
Data Protection Registrar. (1989) *Guidelines* (free of charge from the Office of the
    Data Protection Registrar, Springfield House, Water Lane, Wilmslow,
    Cheshire, SK95AX.
Hearnden, Keith (Ed). (1990) *A Handbook of Computer Security.* Kogan Page.
HMSO. *Display Screen Equipmemt Work: The Health and Safety (Display Screen
    Equipment) Regulations 1992.*
HSE. *Display Screen Equipment.*

HSE. *Working with VDUs.*

Knight, Peter and Fitzsimons, James. (1990) *Legal Environment of computing.* Addison-Wesley.

Lloyd, Ian. (1993) *Information Technology Law.* Butterworth.

Savage, N and Edwards, C. (1988) *Guide to the Data Protection Act.* Blackstone.

Chapter 15:   Selecting a personal computer system

Computer magazines

There is a wide range of popular computing magazines that include useful articles and substantial advertisements. Examples include:

Byte	*CD-ROM today*	*Computer Shopper*
PC Direct	*PC Magazine*	*PC Plus*
What PC	*Which computer*	*Windows magazine*

Books

Babiel, H and R. (1994) *PC Buyers Survival Guide.* Sybex.

Edwards, J and Lewis Colin. (1994) *Business computing primer.* Pitman.

Clark, Alan. (1991) *Choosing the right computer.* Teach Yourself Books/Hodder and Stoughton.

Dvorak, John C. (1994) *PC Magazine Computer Buyers Guide.* Ziff Davis.

Jerome, M and Taylor, W. (Eds) (1992) *The streetwise guide to PCs.* Addison-Wesley.

Royall, David and Hughes, Michael. (1991) *Computerisation in business,* NatWest Business Handbooks/Pitman.

White, Ron. (1994) *How computers work.* Ziff Davis.

Appendix 2

Solutions to exercises

This Appendix provides solutions to many of the exercises in Part One as well as selected exercises from Part Two.

Chapter 1: Exercise 1

The answers below show one paper-based source where the information can be found:

(a) Stamp Act (*Encyclopaedia Brittanica*)

(b) Richard Whately, Archbishop of Dublin, 1787-1865 (*Oxford Dictionary of Quotations*)

(c) 7p (*Social Trends*)

(d) BS4623 (*BSI Standards Catalogue*)

(e) Database: Wastinfo; Host: Orbit (*On-line Manual*)

(f) NV Koninkliijke Nederlandsche Petroleum Miij, 1890 (*Europe's 15,000 largest companies*)

(g) Japanese (*CD-ROMs in print*)

(h) Reed Business Publishing Group, monthly, on first Friday of month *(Willings Press Guide)*

(i) 36,230 (*Whitaker's Almanac*)

Chapter 1: Exercise 2

"simulation of real world events and responses in a computer generated environment"
interfaces: gloves, handsets; design application: walkaround in virtual building
"Reality is harsh and virtual reality will be virtually harsh."
office application: planning display of merchandise in a supermarket
VR will give us a new 3-D spreadsheet type tool
VR will have serious impact and not all of it for the best

Source: Ciaran Redmond, (1993), Future technologies and their business impact, in Joe Peppard (Editor), IT strategy for business, Pitman.

Chapter 1: Exercise 3

Over the last 20 years (approx 1/3) decrease in numbers watching football in England, Wales and Scotland, whereas increase in spectators to rugby football league and union
Slightly larger decrease (approx 40%) in spectators to greyhound racing

Horse racing: decrease in first 10 years but resurgence in last 10 years
Spectators to county cricket and motorcycles sports has remained about the same (although no figures given for 1990-1991)
Basketball: significant increase over 20 years in spectators to English basketball, however in Scotland increase in first 10 years fell back to 1971 levels in 1991.

Source: Central Statistical Office, Social Trends, 1992.

Chapter 1: Exercise 4

(a) Details of relevant on-line databases, CD-ROMS and on-line services with access to same, through directories, product literature, newspaper articles, etc.
(b) Usability issues identified through interviews with people currently making use of relevant computer-based sources, e.g librarians, information officers, etc; either in person or by telephone with a structured list of questions.

Chapter 2: Exercise 1

(a) He lived *separately* from his wife. (*separate* and *separately* are common misspellings)
(b) She told him to *practise* the piece twice a day. (*practice* is the noun, *practise* the verb)
(c) *Their accommodation* was very basic. (*there*, *their* and *they're* are homonyms (i.e. they sound the same) so require care; *accommodation* is commonly misspelled)
(d) The *girl's* (or *girls'*) *embarrassment* was obvious.   (The apostrophe is missing: *girl's* is singular, *girls'* is plural; *embarrassment* is a common misspelling.)
(e) By doing this you will be able to improve your performance *continuously*. (*To continuously improve* is a split infinitive: these should be avoided if at all possible.)
(f) What did you do that for? (The use of prepositions should be avoided at the end of a sentence unless the sentence becomes too tortuous, e.g *For what did you do that?)*
(g) I should *have* asked his permission.   (Although pronounced *of*, it must be spelt correctly.)
(h) This new law will *affect* all of us. (*affect* is the verb; *effect* is the noun)
(i) *It's* (or *It is*) a pity he decided to carry on. (*It's* is a contraction, short for *it is*. In most instances it should be written in full.)
(j) I spoke to the man *whose* son had won the award. (*Whose* means *of whom*, *who's* is short for *who is.*)

Chapter 2: Exercise 2(a)

Passage A: (a) 25.25 words per sentence; (b) 23 words with 3 or more syllables; (c) (25.25+23) =48.25*0.4 = 19.3, therefore it is a very difficult passage
Passage B: (a) 18 words per sentence; (b) 7 words with 3 or more syllables; (c) (18+7) = 25*0.4 = 10, therefore it is easy reading

Chapter 2: Exercise 2(b)

Passage A: *The Times*, 18 October 1991;
Passage B: *Sun*, 31 October 1991

Chapter 2: Exercise 3

(a) View some of the in-house reports to get a feel for "good" and "bad" practice in terms of presentation, structure and style.

(b) Rules should be specified for the following areas, although they may well be linked:

Structure and implementation of structure: choose appropriate structure and its implementation, eg title page, table of contents, main body, references, appendices, use of headings and sub-headings; format of references.

Presentation: layout of title page, table of contents, body of report: typefaces to be used, type size and type style, etc. Define paragraph alignment and style, eg blocked and justified; page layout: e.g. style of headers, footers, page numbers

Style rules: advice on spellings of certain words, expressions to be avoided, and readability level required

(c) It would be useful to produce a printed example of a report in the correct format and style; and set up a template in the word processing software and make it available on the network and/or on disk.

Chapter 3: Exercise 1

(a) 10   (b) 14   (c) 16   (d) 7

Chapter 3: Exercise 2(a)

	A	B	C	D
1	Employees in employment: all industries			
2		1992 Q4	1993 Q4	Inc/dec
3		('000s)	('000s)	%
4	Agriculture	244	239	=(C4-B4)/B4*100
5	Production	4,653	4,583	↓
6	Construction	849	781	↓
7	Service	15,264	15,422	↓
8	Total	21,010	21,024	↓
9	Source: Monthly Digest of Statistics, CSO, August 1994			

Chapter 3: Exercise 2(b)

Employees in employment: all industries			
	1992 Q4 ('000s)	1993 Q4 ('000s)	Inc/dec %
Agriculture	244	239	-2.09
Production	4,653	4,583	-1.53
Construction	849	781	-8.71
Service	15,264	15,422	1.02
Total	**21,010**	**21,024**	**0.07**
Source: Monthly Digest of Statistics, CSO, August 1994			

Chapter 3: Exercise 2(c)

	A	B	C	D	E	F
1	Employees in employment: all industries					
2		1992 Q4	1993 Q4	Inc/dec (92-93)	1994 Q4	Inc/dec (93-94)
3		('000s)	('000s)	%	('000s)	
4	Agriculture	244	239	=(C4-B4)/B4*100		=(E4-C4)/C4*100
5	Production	4,653	4,583	↓		↓
6	Construction	849	781	↓		↓
7	Service	15,264	15,422	↓		↓
8	Total	21,010	21,024	↓		↓

Chapter 3: Exercise 3 (a)

	A	B	C	D	E	F
1	**EXECUTOYS: PROJECTED INCOME**					
2						
3	*Cost per unit:*			*Selling price per unit:*		=B3*1.2
4						
5		**Qtr 1**	**Qtr 2**	**Qtr 3**	**Qtr 4**	**Total**
6	Units sold		=1.1*B6	→	→	=SUM(B6:E6)
7						
8	Total sales	=$F$3*B6	→	→	→	↓
9	Total costs	=$B$3*B6	→	→	→	↓
10	**PROFIT**	=B8-B9	→	→	→	↓

Chapter 3: Exercise 3 (b)

- increase or decrease value in B3;

- modify formula in C6 to **=1.2*B6** and copy across to D6 and E6;

- EITHER modify formula in F3 to **=1.3*B3**

  OR if further changes in mark-up percentage are to be made, then this should be placed in a separate cell reference, e.g. as shown below:

	A	B	C	D	E	F
1	**EXECUTOYS: PROJECTED INCOME**					
2						
3	*Cost per unit:*		*Mark-up %*		*Selling price:*	=B3+(D3/100*B3)
4						

Chapter 3: Exercise 4

	A	B	C	D	E
1	**PETTY CASH BOOK**				
2	--------	-------------------------------------	------------------	--------------------	------------------------
3	*Date*	*Item*	*Out*	*In*	*Balance*
4	--------	-------------------------------------	------------------	--------------------	------------------------
5		Balance b/f			
6					=E5+D6-C6
7					↓
8					↓
9					↓
10					↓
11					↓
12		Balance c/f			=E11
13	--------	-------------------------------------	------------------	--------------------	------------------------
14		**Total**	=SUM(C6:C11)	=SUM(D6:D11)	
15	--------	-------------------------------------	------------------	--------------------	------------------------

Chapter 4: Exercise 1

(a) pie chart   (b) bar chart   (c) line chart

Chapter 4: Exercise 2

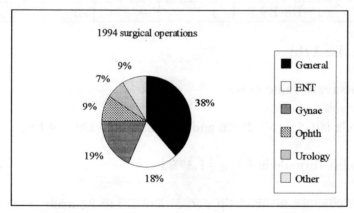

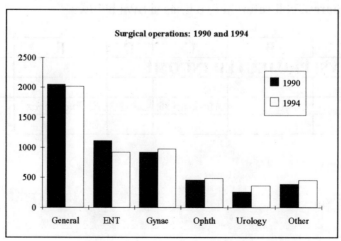

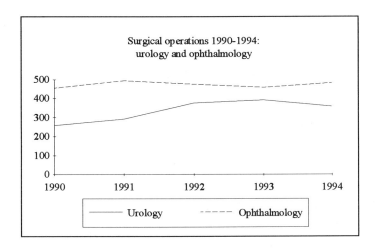

Chapter 6: Exercise 1

Fieldname	Data type	Size	Explanatory notes
Title	text	4	
Position	text	30	
Street	text	30	Address broken down into
Town	text	30	3 elements
Postcode	text	8	
Telephone number	text	12	5 digit code+dash+6 digit
Date of joining	date	default	
Education	memo	default	large amount of text required

Notes:
- County field not required, as this is the same in every case
- STD code required as they differ

Chapter 6: Exercise 2(a)

Title	Surname	Date of joining
		>=01/01/80

Chapter 6: Exercise 2(b)

Title	Surname	Education
		AL

Chapter 6: Exercise 2(c)

Title	Surname	Town
		="Leighton"

Note: if only one address field used and search for *Leighton* is made in Address field then those who live in Leighton Road would also be found.

Chapter 6: Exercise 3(a)

Title	Surname	Date of joining	Department
		>=01/01/80	="Acc"

Chapter 6: Exercise 3(b)

Title	Surname	Education
		GCSE OR *OL*

Chapter 6: Exercise 3(c)

Title	Surname	Date of joining
		="Mr" OR "Mrs" OR "Miss" OR "Ms"

Chapter 6: Exercise 4

Kings Fashions Ltd

Personal details

Title:	Mrs
First Name:	Susan
Surname:	Browne
Date of birth:	10 November 1967

Home address

Street:	25 Grange Road
Town:	Leighton
Postcode:	TH4 6GH
Telephone number:	01767-58745

Position:	Sales Assistant
Date of joining:	01 January 1984

Department:
Pac
Pur
Sal

Education: 3 OLs: English; Home Economics

Medical: ☐

Salary: £8,500

Chapter 6: Exercise 5

- only certain titles to be accepted, e.g. Mr, Mrs, Miss and Ms;
- only a date after organisation's start-up date to be accepted.

Chapter 6: Exercise 6

Staff details		
today's date		
Name	**Home address**	**Telephone number**
Miss Susan Browne	25 Grange Road	01767-587459
	Leighton	
	Sussex	
	TH4 6GH	

Notes:
"Sussex" added as an extra piece of text to be third line of address

Chapter 6: Exercise 7(a)

Fieldname	Data type	Size	Explanatory notes
Name	text	50	
Rating	text	5	to hold 1 to 5 *
Street	text	50	
Postcode	text	7	
Telephone number	text	6	STD code not required
Bedrooms	numeric/text	3	
Lift	logical	default	
Dogs allowed	logical	default	
No smoking areas	logical	default	
Child facilities	logical	default	
Conference facilities (max)	numeric/text	3	
Single room	currency	6	3 figures and 2 decimal prices
Double room	currency	6	3 figures and 2 decimal places

Chapter 6: Exercise 7(b)

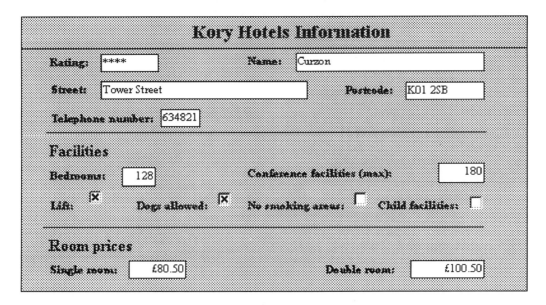

Chapter 6: Exercise 7(c)

	Kory Hotels Information *today's date*							
Rating	**Name**	**No of beds**	**Max conf**	**Lift**	**Dogs allowed**	**No smoking facilities**	**Child facilities areas**	**Room prices**
****	**Curzon** Tower Street KO1 2SB Tel: 634821	128	180	Yes	Yes	No	No	Single: £80.50 Double: £100.50

Notes:
"Tel:" added as extra explanatory text, as too "Single:" and "Double:"

Chapter 6: Exercise 8(a)

Database might consist of the following three linked tables (with primary keys underlined):

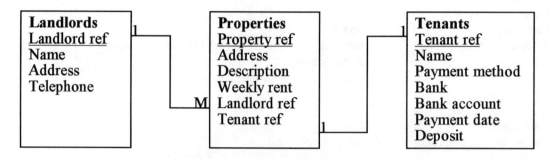

Landlords
Landlord ref
Name
Address
Telephone

Properties
Property ref
Address
Description
Weekly rent
Landlord ref
Tenant ref

Tenants
Tenant ref
Name
Payment method
Bank
Bank account
Payment date
Deposit

Chapter 6: Exercise 8(b)

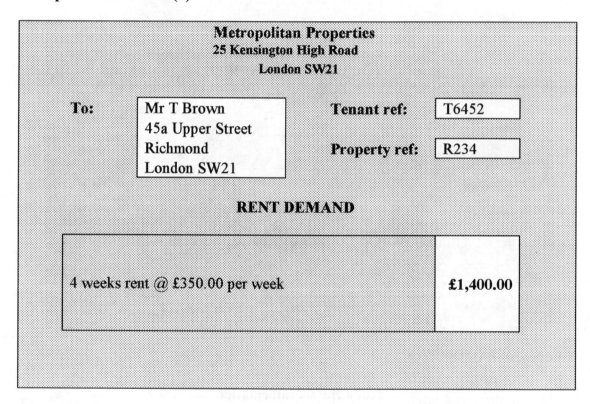

Metropolitan Properties
25 Kensington High Road
London SW21

To: | Mr T Brown | Tenant ref: | T6452
45a Upper Street
Richmond | Property ref: | R234
London SW21

RENT DEMAND

| 4 weeks rent @ £350.00 per week | £1,400.00 |

Chapter 6: Exercise 8(c)

Metropolitan Properties: unoccupied properties
today's date

| PROPERTY | | | LANDLORD | |
Ref	Description	Weekly rental	Ref	Name
R201	Small, 2-bed flat overlooking Hyde Park, 24-hour porterage	£600.00	T67	Lansdale PLC

Chapter 6: Exercise 9

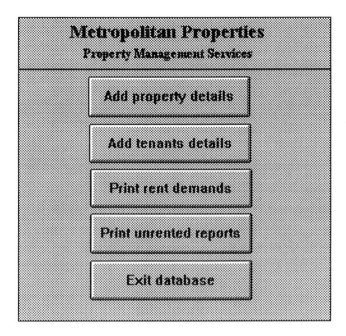

Chapter 8: Exercise 4(d)

207 words and 18.2 words per sentence; Flesch's Reading Ease: 60.5 and Grade Level: 9.0; Gunning Fog Index: 11.9

Chapter 9: Exercise 5

MATCH STATISTICS	
Total	460
Average	40
Max runs	103
Min runs	0

Chapter 9: Exercise 9

	A	B	C	D	E	F	G	H
1	FLEXI COMPANY LTD							
2	Pay rate:	4.25						
3	Name	Mon	Tues	Wed	Thu	Fri	Total	Gross
4							hours	pay
5	Amy	7	8	7	8	8	=SUM(B5:F5)	=$B$2*G5
6	Bob	6	5	6	7	6	=SUM(B6:F6)	=$B$2*G6
7	Claire	8	8	9	8	8	=SUM(B7:F7)	=$B$2*G7
8	David	6	6	7	6	7	=SUM(B8:F8)	=$B$2*G8
9	Total	=SUM (B5:B8)	=SUM (C5:C8)	=SUM (D5:D8)	=SUM (E5:E8)	=SUM (F5:F8)	=SUM(G5:G8)	=SUM(H5:H8)

Chapter 9: Exercise 13(m)
- In B3 enter 10000: worksheet appears on page 294
- Delete value in B3, and in B9 enter 1000: worksheet appears on page 295

CASH FLOW

	Apr-95	May-95	Jun-95	Jul-95	Aug-95	Sep-95	Oct-95	Nov-95	Dec-95	Jan-96	Feb-96	Mar-96
Loan	10,000											
Cash in bank	3,000	200	1,604	2,980	4,384	5,829	7,311	8,830	10,389	11,990	13,634	15,323
Total cash in bank	13,000	200	1,604	2,980	4,384	5,829	7,311	8,830	10,389	11,990	13,634	15,323
INCOME												
Training courses	4,000	4,000	4,000	4,000	4,000	4,000	4,000	4,000	4,000	4,000	4,000	4,000
Consultancy	500	525	551	579	608	638	670	704	739	776	814	855
Interest on cash in bank		54	0	0	12	18	24	30	37	43	50	57
TOTAL INCOME	4,500	4,579	4,551	4,579	4,620	4,656	4,694	4,734	4,776	4,819	4,864	4,912
OUTGOINGS												
Equipment	15,000											
Overheads	800	800	800	800	800	800	800	800	800	800	800	800
Salary	1,500	1,500	1,500	1,500	1,500	1,500	1,500	1,500	1,500	1,500	1,500	1,500
Loan repayments		875	875	875	875	875	875	875	875	875	875	875
Overdraft payments	0	0	0	0	0	0	0	0	0	0	0	0
TOTAL OUTGOINGS	17,300	3,175	3,175	3,175	3,175	3,175	3,175	3,175	3,175	3,175	3,175	3,175
To bank	200	1,604	2,980	4,384	5,829	7,311	8,830	10,389	11,990	13,634	15,323	17,060

CASH FLOW	Apr-95	May-95	Jun-95	Jul-95	Aug-95	Sep-95	Oct-95	Nov-95	Dec-95	Jan-96	Feb-96	Mar-96
Loan												
Cash in bank	3,000	-9,300	-6,538	-3,785	-977	1,888	4,814	7,855	10,982	14,192	17,489	20,877
Total cash in bank	3,000	-9,300	-6,538	-3,785	-977	1,888	4,814	7,855	10,982	14,192	17,489	20,877
INCOME												
Training courses	4,000	4,000	4,000	4,000	4,000	4,000	4,000	4,000	4,000	4,000	4,000	4,000
Consultancy	1,000	1,050	1,103	1,158	1,216	1,276	1,340	1,407	1,477	1,551	1,629	1,710
Interest on cash in bank		13	0	0	0	0	0	20	33	46	59	73
TOTAL INCOME	5,000	5,063	5,103	5,158	5,216	5,276	5,340	5,427	5,510	5,597	5,688	5,783
OUTGOINGS												
Equipment	15,000											
Overheads	800	800	800	800	800	800	800	800	800	800	800	800
Salary	1,500	1,500	1,500	1,500	1,500	1,500	1,500	1,500	1,500	1,500	1,500	1,500
Loan repayments		0	0	0	0	0	0	0	0	0	0	0
Overdraft payments		0	50	50	50	50	0	0	0	0	0	0
TOTAL OUTGOINGS	17,300	2,300	2,350	2,350	2,350	2,350	2,300	2,300	2,300	2,300	2,300	2,300
To bank	-9,300	-6,538	-3,785	-977	1,888	4,814	7,855	10,982	14,192	17,489	20,877	24,360

Chapter 9: Exercise 14(o)

SIMPSON'S TRAVEL						
Foreign Exchange: Buying						
Country	**Currency**	**Rate**	**Number bought**	**Amount to Customer**	**Less Commission**	**Total to Customer**
Germany	D Mark	2.43	600	£246.91	£4.94	£241.98

SIMPSON'S TRAVEL						
Foreign Exchange: Buying						
Country	**Currency**	**Rate**	**Number bought**	**Amount to Customer**	**Less Commission**	**Total to Customer**
Denmark	Krone	10.04	55	£5.48	£2.50	£2.98

SIMPSON'S TRAVEL						
Foreign Exchange: Buying						
Country	**Currency**	**Rate**	**Number bought**	**Amount to Customer**	**Less Commission**	**Total to Customer**
USA	US$	1.46	500	£342.47	£6.85	£335.62

Chapter 9: Exercise 18(d)

Loan repayment schedule				
Loan amount:	£25,000	Interest rate:	8.50%	Period in years:	10
Annual loan repayments:		£3,810	Monthly loan repayments:	£318

Loan repayment schedule				
Loan amount:	£12,000	Interest rate:	11.00%	Period in years:	3
Annual loan repayments:		£4,911	Monthly loan repayments:	£409

Chapter 9: Exercise 18(e)

25 year loan repayment schedule for £120,000 loan:

Loan repayment schedule				
Loan amount:	£120,000	Interest rate:	6.75%	Period in years:	25
Annual loan repayments:		£10,066	Monthly loan repayments:	£839

Year	Interest paid		Principal paid		Balance
1	£8,100		£1,966		£118,034
2	£7,967		£2,099		£115,934
3	£7,826		£2,241		£113,694
4	£7,674		£2,392		£111,301
5	£7,513		£2,554		£108,748
6	£7,340		£2,726		£106,022
7	£7,156		£2,910		£103,112
8	£6,960		£3,106		£100,006
9	£6,750		£3,316		£96,690
10	£6,527		£3,540		£93,150
11	£6,288		£3,779		£89,371
12	£6,033		£4,034		£85,337
13	£5,760		£4,306		£81,031
14	£5,470		£4,597		£76,434
15	£5,159		£4,907		£71,527
16	£4,828		£5,238		£66,288
17	£4,474		£5,592		£60,696
18	£4,097		£5,969		£54,727
19	£3,694		£6,372		£48,355
20	£3,264		£6,802		£41,552
21	£2,805		£7,262		£34,290
22	£2,315		£7,752		£26,539
23	£1,791		£8,275		£18,264
24	£1,233		£8,834		£9,430
25	£637		£9,430		£0

Chapter 12: Exercise 6(a)

Make	Year	Letter
	>="93"	

Make	Year	Letter
Metro 1.4GS	93	L
Metro 1.1.L	93	K
Rover 215SL	93	L
Rover 620 GSi	93	L

Chapter 12: Exercise 6(b)

Make	Letter	Price
		<5000

Make	Letter	Price
Rover 216S	G	£3,995
Maestro Clubman	H	£4,995
Fiat Uno 45	K	£4,750

Chapter 12: Exercise 6(c)

Make	Acquired	Garage
		="M"

Make	Acquired	Garage
Metro 1.4GS	15/07/94	M
Volvo 440GL	12/10/94	M
Renault 19GTX	15/10/94	M
Fiat Uno 45	22/10/94	M

Chapter 12: Exercise 6(d)

Make	Year	Letter
		>="J"

Make	Year	Letter
Metro 1.4GS	93	L
Metro 1.1.L	93	K
Rover 215SL	93	L
Fiat Uno 45	92	K
Rover 220i coupe	92	K
Rover 620 GSi	93	L
Citroen XM 2.0i	91	J

Chapter 12: Exercise 6(e)

Make	Price
Rover*	

Make	Price
Rover 216S	£3,995
Rover 215SL	£10,995
Rover 220i Coupe	£13,995
Rover 620 GSi	£18,750

Chapter 12: Exercise 6(f)

Make	Automatic
	=Yes

Make	Automatic
Volvo 440GL	Yes
Rover 620 GSi	Yes

Chapter 12: Exercise 6(g)

Make	Acquired	Garage
	<01/10/94	

Make	Acquired	Garage
Metro 1.4GS	15/07/94	M
Rover 216S	22/08/94	S
Metro 1.1L	29/09/94	S

Chapter 12: Exercise 6(h)

Make	Letter	Price	Notes
			power

Make	Letter	Price	Notes
Rover 620 GSi	L	£18,750	Caribbean blue, power assisted steering, central locking
Citroen XM 2.0i	J	£7,250	Black, power assisted steering, central locking, one owner, 35,000 miles, full service history

Chapter 10: Exercise 7(a)

Make	Year	Price	Garage
Metro* OR Maestro*			

Make	Year	Price	Garage
Metro 1.4GS	93	£7,595	M
Metro 1.1.L	93	£7,295	S
Maestro Clubman	91	£4,995	S

Chapter 12: Exercise 7(b)

Make	Year	Price
	>"91"	<7000

Make	Price
Fiat Uno 45	£4,750

Chapter 12: Exercise 8(a)

Make	Acquired	Garage	Sale price
	<01/10/94		[Price]*0.9

Make	Acquired	Garage	Sale price
Metro 1.4GS	15/07/94	M	£6,835.5
Rover 216S	22/08/94	S	£3,595.5
Metro 1.1L	29/09/94	S	£6,565.5

Chapter 12: Exercise 8(b)

Make	Price	Year
Rover*		[Year]&"("&[Letter]&")"

Make	Price	Year
Rover 216S	£3,995	89(G)
Rover 215SL	£10,995	93(L)
Rover 220i Coupe	£13,995	92(K)
Rover 620 GSi	£18,750	93(L)

Chapter 12: Exercise 8(c)

Make	Year	Letter
Metro 1.4GS	93	L
Rover 215SL	93	L
Rover 620 GSi	93	L
Metro 1.1.L	93	K
Fiat Uno 45	92	K
Rover 220i coupe	92	K
Citroen XM 2.0i	91	J

Chapter 12: Exercise 19(a)

Table:	Seminars	Delegates	Delegates	Delegates
Field:	Seminar ref	Delegate name	Company	Telephone number
	=SO3			

Seminars	Delegates	Delegates	Delegates
Seminar ref	Delegate name	Company	Telephone number
SO3	Mr P M Jones	JK Components	01931-786543
SO3	Mr J Brown	Harlesdon Electronics	01396-478621

Chapter 12: Exercise 19(b)

Table:	Seminars	Seminars	Seminars	Delegates
Field:	From	Seminar ref	Seminar name	Delegate name
	26/07/95			

Seminars	Seminars	Seminars	Delegates
From	Seminar ref	Seminar name	Delegate name
26/07/95	SO2	Negotiating deals	Miss M Victoria
26/07/95	SO3	Selling to Europe	Mr P M Jones
26/07/95	SO3	Selling to Europe	Mr J Brown

Appendix 3

Assignments

The assignments in this Appendix cover material from more than one chapter of this book, identified by the chapter numbers underneath the assignment number. In the main, these assignments have been kept fairly open-ended to allow for freedom of interpretation and expression.

Assignment 1: PCs as support tools
(Chapters 1, 2, 3 and 8)

You work for a small firm of builders that has yet to invest in IT. Prepare a short report (i.e. approx. 2,000 words) on how PCs could be used to support their general business activities.

Assignment 2: Commercial on-line services
(Chapters 1, 2, 3 and 8)

Investigate a commercial on-line service like CompuServe or CIX and write a short report (i.e. approx. 2,000 words) in favour of its adoption in your organisation, a firm of financial advisors, giving full details of how to get on-line.

Assignment 3: Viruses
(Chapters 1, 2, 8 and 13)

The firm of solicitors that you work for has recently experienced an outbreak of viruses on its PC network. Write a short report in which you formulate the steps of an anti-virus strategy.

Assignment 4: Marketing
(Chapters 1, 2 and 8)

You operate a small business that rents and sells plant displays for offices, showrooms, hotels, etc.

- Produce a 6-page brochure outlining the services that you offer;
- Using relevant business directories, draw up a list of 50 companies to whom you could send your brochure. Enter this data into a word processing data file and merge these details with a standard covering letter.

Assignment 5: Newsletter
(Chapters 2 and 8)

Produce a 2-page (A4) in-house newsletter for a firm of insurance brokers, in which you include news items, up and coming events, details of a social evening as well as job vacancies.

Assignment 6: Leaflet
(Chapters 2, 8 and 13)

You are responsible for the induction of new administrative staff in your organisation, a large retail outlet. Prepare a 4-page leaflet in which you provide a list of the systems rules and regulations to be observed by all PC users, together with any other advice on how to avoid problems and who to contact in case of difficulties.

Assignment 7: Displayed material
(Chapters 2 and 8)

You work in the office of a municipal leisure centre. During the summer holidays there is a full programme of sports and leisure events for children.

- Design a 4-page leaflet that provides full details of this programme;
- Design an A4 poster that highlights the main events and provides details of how to get hold of a copy of the programme.

Assignment 8: Data analysis and presentation
(Chapters 1, 3, 4, 9 and 10)

In order to prepare a marketing compaign for a new financial service for pensioners, you have been asked to collect data from published sources on the readership of the main daily newspapers and magazines. You are then required to analyse this data using spreadsheet software and present it in an appropriate graphical form in order to identify the most appropriate publications in which to advertise.

Assignment 9: Questionnaire design
(Chapters 1, 2, 3, 4, 8, 9 and 10)

You work for a tele-sales company. In order to assess any health and safety risks, you have been asked to draw up a questionnaire to be completed by your colleagues to ascertain if any are suffering from the results of continued use of their PCs.

Assignment 10: Cash flow analysis
(Chapters 2, 3, 8, 9 and 14)

You work in the administrative office of a private Sports and Leisure Club. The Club management would like to refurbish the Gym and want to know whether it will be financially possible for this work to be carried out in the next 6 months or whether they will have to raise extra income to do so.

In addition to cash in the bank, the Club's monthly source of income is through membership fees (adult, family and corporate) and ticket sales (junior and adult: leisure and swim) and their main items of expenditure are salaries and overheads.

- Set up a spreadsheet worksheet to calculate average monthly income
- Set up a second, linked, worksheet as a model for a cash-flow analysis over the next six months based on these average monthly figures.
- Demonstrate the effect if in two months time membership fees are increased by 10% (to the nearest £) and all tickets by 10p?
- Prepare a short memo to managers to outline your findings.

Assignment 11: Invoicing system
(Chapters 3 and 9)

You work for a small independent garage that undertakes servicing and mechanical repairs. You want to design a spreadsheet template to be used as an invoicing system for the garage. It should show the following information:

- name, address and telephone number of garage;
- name and address of client;
- invoice number and date;
- details of parts used and cost of each part and total cost of parts;
- number of hours of labour, price per hour and total labour hours;
- total cost of work, VAT rate, VAT charge on work, grand total of work.

Assignment 12: Car hire costings
(Chapters 3 and 9)

You work for a car and van rental firm that specialises in both short and long-term hire at very competitive daily rates and with free 500 mileage. You want to design a template that will calculate the cost of hire for prospective customers as well as act as an invoicing system. The template should show:

- details of model of car/van, daily rate and excess miles charge (extracted from a lookup table);
- dates of hire and return, and therefore number of days rental;
- cost of hire (i.e. daily rate by number of days rental);
- mileage when hired and mileage when returned, calculating mileage used;
- total cost of excess miles
- CWD (collision waiver damage) if taken
- total cost of hire of car/van

Assignment 13: PC presentation
(Chapters 5 and 11)

Design an automatic PC presentation for use at an office equipment exhibition in which you advertise your company's space planning and refurbishment service.

Assignment 14: Conference paper and speech
(Chapters 1, 2, 5, 8 and 11)

You have been asked to give a paper at a conference entitled: Computing: Visions of the Future, in which you are to speak on your ideas on the office of the future.

- Prepare the conference paper, using an appropriate academic format, and print a copy;
- Prepare the slides for the conference;
- Print the outline of the slides;
- Print audience handouts for selected slides.

Assignment 15: Employment agency database
(Chapters 6 and 12)

You work for a small employment agency that maintains a list of people who are available for emergency and temporary posts as secretaries, drivers, gardeners, domestics, bar and waiting staff, chefs, etc.

- Design a database to hold details of these temporary staff;
- Design a form to be used for on-screen data entry and also for new staff to complete showing their personal, educational, reference and other details.

Assignment 16: Garden centre database
(Chapters 6 and 12)

You work full-time at a garden centre. However, as most of the part-time staff who work there are not horticultural experts, you have decided to design a database that will hold plant information, e.g. colour, height, the type of soil required, any special planting or care instructions, etc., so that customers at the garden centre can use it to guide their purchasing.

- Design a test database;
- Design a report that could be printed for customers in response to queries they make of the database.

Assignment 17: Club membership database
(Chapters 6 and 12)

You are the membership secretary of a sports and social club. In the past no accurate records have been maintained on who has paid their subscription. You have therefore decided to hold membership details on your PC and in addition to personal details you also intend to keep details of payment of subscription fees, as well as provide a list of all current members.

- Design the structure of the database;
- Produce a report showing member details for distribution to all club members

Assignment 18: Choosing word processing software
(Chapters 2, 8 and 15)

Françoise Johnson is a French cookery expert. She writes a large number of articles for magazines and has written many books. For many years she has survived with an electric typewriter, but has now been convinced that it is time she opted for a word processing system.   She has turned to you for help.

As a first step, identify one or two suitable software packages you feel would meet her specific word processing requirements, and prepare a written proposal in which you explain the significant features of the software you have identified and how they will be able to help her with her work. You should then specify the hardware requirements needed to run the software optimally.

Assignment 19: Selecting a personal computer
(Chapters 2, 8 and 15)

Peter Henderson has recently set up in business on his own as a financial investment consultant after a number of years working for a large insurance company. He asks you for advice on buying a PC to help run his new business. Peter tells you that his main   activity will be financial analysis, i.e. working out complex investment arrangements for his clients, although he also wishes to keep extensive records of all his clients' details and their investments.

One particular request he has is that all documents he produces, including the inevitable letters, reports, etc. should be top quality. Peter also tells you that he has used PCs before in his previous job so he is not a complete beginner although he appreciates that the software that is recommended may not be the same. However, he reckons he is a quick learner and as this is still early days for his business he will have some time to get to grips with the PCs. He has budgeted around £3,000 but might be tempted to pay more if necessary. Prepare a written proposal for Peter Henderson together with a costings sheet.

Assignment 20: Ski-wear hire shop
(Chapters 1, 2, 3, 5, 6, 8, 9, 11 and 12)

You have just opened a ski-wear hire shop and intend specialising in the hire and sale of ski-wear to children on school ski trips. In addition you intend to provide an advice service for first-time skiers.

- Using appropriate business directories, identify the main schools and colleges in a 50 mile area and set up a database to hold this information;
- Prepare a personalised letter to the headteachers in which you introduce the new shop.
- Design a 6-page brochure which will give further details of your shop together with an informative PC presentation.
- Create an invoicing system that will calculate the cost of the hire and sale of ski-ware and also produce a form that could be used for ordering by post.

Index